P9-AQG-610

A Concise History of Bulgaria

Bulgaria is slated to become a member of the European Union in 2007, yet its history is amongst the least well-known in the rest of the continent. R. J. Crampton provides here a general introduction to this country at the crossroads of Christendom and Islam. The text and illustrations trace the rich and dramatic story from pre-history, through the days when Bulgaria was the centre of a powerful mediaeval empire and the five centuries of Ottoman rule, to the cultural renaissance of the nineteenth century and the political upheavals of the twentieth, upheavals which led Bulgaria into three wars. The new and updated edition covers the years from 1995 to 2004, a vital period in which Bulgaria endured financial meltdown, set itself seriously on the road to reform, elected its former king as prime minister, and finally secured membership of NATO and admission to the European Union.

R. J. CRAMPTON is Professor of East European History at the University of Oxford. He has written a number of books on modern East European history, including *Eastern Europe in the Twentieth Century – and After* (1996) and *The Balkans since the Second World War* (2002).

CAMBRIDGE CONCISE HISTORIES

This is a new series of illustrated 'concise histories' of selected individual countries, intended both as university and college text-books and as general historical introductions for general readers, travellers and members of the business community.

For a full list of titles in the series, please see the end of the book.

A Concise History
of Bulgaria

SECOND EDITION

R. J. CRAMPTON

CAMBRIDGE
UNIVERSITY PRESS

CAMBRIDGE
UNIVERSITY PRESS

University Printing House, Cambridge CB2 8BS, United Kingdom

Cambridge University Press is part of the University of Cambridge.

It furthers the University's mission by disseminating knowledge in the pursuit of education, learning and research at the highest international levels of excellence.

www.cambridge.org
Information on this title: www.cambridge.org/9780521616379

First published 1997
Reprinted 2000, 2003
Second edition 2005
Third printing 2008

A catalogue record for this publication is available from the British Library

Library of Congress Cataloguing in Publication data
Crampton, R. J.
A concise history of Bulgaria / by R. J. Crampton. – 2nd ed.
p. cm. – (Cambridge concise histories)
Includes bibliographical references and index.
ISBN 0 521 85085 1 (cloth) – ISBN 0 521 61637 9 (pbk.)
1. Bulgaria – History. I. Title. II. Series.
DR67.C72 2005
949.9 – dc22   2005045765

ISBN 978-0-521-85085-8 Hardback
ISBN 978-0-521-61637-9 Paperback

For my cousin

ROBERT GRAY

With affection and in
commemoration of our childhoods of
long, long ago

CONTENTS

List of illustrations   *page* xii
Preface   xv
Preface to the second edition   xviii
Note on transliteration   xxi

1 THE BULGARIAN LANDS FROM PREHISTORY TO THE ARRIVAL
  OF THE BULGARIANS   1

2 MEDIAEVAL BULGARIA, 681–1393   9
    Bulgaria under the Khans, 681–852   9
    The reign of Boris I (852–888) and the conversion to
      Christianity   11
    The reign of Simeon the great (893–927)   16
    The end of the first empire, 896–1018   17
    Bulgaria under Byzantine rule, 1018–1185   21
    The second Bulgarian empire, 1185–1393   22

3 OTTOMAN RULE IN THE BULGARIAN LANDS   29
    Ottoman society and administration   29
    The Bulgarian population under Ottoman rule   33
    The Bulgarian church under Ottoman rule   38
    Protest against Ottoman power   40
    The decline of the Ottoman empire   42

4 THE NATIONAL REVIVAL AND THE LIBERATION   45
    The Awakeners   45
    Economic, social and political change in the Ottoman empire   51
    The background to the Bulgarian cultural revival   56
    The cultural revival: education, literacy and literature   58

The struggle for a separate Bulgarian church   65
The struggle for political independence and the
   liberation of 1878   75

5   THE CONSOLIDATION OF THE BULGARIAN STATE,
   1878–1896   85
The Constituent Assembly and the Tûrnovo constitution   85
Constitutional conflicts, 1879–1883   89
The national question and union with Rumelia,
   1884–1885   93
The war with Serbia and the deposition of Alexander
   Battenberg, 1885–1886   99
The regency and the election of Prince Ferdinand,
   1886–1887   101
The *Stambolovshtina*, 1887–1894   103
The recognition of Prince Ferdinand   110
Ethnic and social change after the liberation   111

6   FERDINAND'S PERSONAL RULE, 1896–1918   117
Stoilov's programme for modernisation   117
The establishment of Ferdinand's personal rule   119
Social crisis and the emergence of the agrarian movement,
   1895–1908   121
The Macedonian crisis and the declaration of independence,
   1900–1908   126
Balkan diplomacy and the Balkan wars, 1908–1913   131
Bulgaria and the first world war   137

7   BULGARIA, 1918–1944   144
The peace settlement of 1919   144
Agrarian rule, 1919–1923   145
The Rule of the Democratic Alliance, 1923–1931   153
The rule of the *devetnaiseti*, May 1934–January 1935   158
The personal rule of King Boris, 1934–1941   160
Bulgaria and the second world war, 1941–1944   167

8   BULGARIA UNDER COMMUNIST RULE, 1944–1989   180
The communist takeover, 1944–1947   180
Destalinisation and the rise of Todor Zhivkov, 1953–1965   191
The *zhivkovshtina*, 1965–1981   193
The decline and fall of Todor Zhivkov, 1981–1989   201

Contents

9 POST-COMMUNIST BULGARIA   212
   Part I   Incomplete transition, 1989–1997   212
      Dismantling the apparatus of totalitarianism, November
         1989–December 1990   212
      Constructing the apparatus of democracy, December
         1990–October 1991   216
      The UDF government, October 1991–October 1992   219
      The Berov government, December 1992–September 1994   224
      The failure of economic reform, 1989–1994   225
      The Videnov government and the catastrophe of 1996   229
   Part II   Real transition, 1997–2004   236
      The Kostov government and the attainment of stability,
         April 1997–June 2001   236
      The government of 'the king'; the road to the EU and
         NATO   249

CONCLUSION   259

   Appendix 1   Bulgarian monarchs   270
   Appendix 2   Prime ministers of Bulgaria, 1879–2004   272
   Suggestions for further reading   274
   Index   278

ILLUSTRATIONS

PLATES

1.1 A Mother Goddess figure, sixth millennium BC   *page* 3
1.2 A one-handled vase from the Vratsa treasure   5
1.3 The Roman theatre in Plovdiv   8
2.1 Tsar Simeon defeating the Byzantines, Chronicles of Ivan
    Skilitsa, MS National Library of Spain, 12–13c.   18
2.2 Entrance to a hermit's cell   20
2.3 Detail from the frescoes at Boyana near Sofia, 1259   26
2.4 A page from the Ivan Alexander Gospels. Reproduced by
    permission of the British Library   27
3.1 Christian children taken under the *devshirme*. From an
    incunabulum. Reproduced by permission of the Austrian
    National Library, Vienna   32
3.2 Mediaeval Bulgarian peasants. Incunabulum. Reproduced by
    permission of the Austrian National Library, Vienna   36
3.3 Bulgarian church painting of the seventeenth century. Machiel
    Kiel, *Art and Society of Bulgaria in the Turkish Period*,
    Maastricht, Van Gorcum, 1985, p. xviii   41
4.1 A page of Paiisi's great history   49
4.2 Sofronii Vrachanski   50
4.3 National revival buildings: a clock tower in Zlatitsa   59
4.4 National revival buildings: the school in Karlovo   61
4.5 Ilarion Makariopolski   70
4.6 Vasil Levski   79
4.7 A wooden cannon used by Bulgarian insurgents   80
4.8 *Bashibazouks* at work   81

5.1 Alexander Battenberg   91
5.2 The sûbranie (parliament) building, Sofia   95
5.3 Volunteers in the 1885 war against Serbia   98
5.4 Prince Alexander's abdication, 1886   100
5.5 Stefan Stambolov   104
5.6 Stambolov's severed hands, 1895   109
6.1 Ferdinand of Saxe-Coburg-Gotha   120
6.2 Signing the armistice, November 1912   134
6.3 Bulgarian soldiers in the first world war   139
7.1 Aleksandûr Stamboliiski with his father   149
7.2 Sveta Nedelya cathedral, Sofia, 16 April 1925   155
7.3 Boris III, King of the Bulgarians, 1918–1943   163
7.4 Jews detained in Bulgaria, 1943–1944   172
7.5 King Boris's funeral, Sofia, September 1943   173
7.6 Sofia welcomes the Red Army in September 1944   178
8.1 Nikola Petkov on trial, August 1947   184
8.2 Typical communist propaganda   197
8.3 Liudmila Zhivkova as patron of the arts   201
8.4 The Imaret Mosque, Plovdiv, 1987   207
9.1 The fire in the Bulgarian Socialist Party (former Communist
     Party) headquarters, August 1990   216
9.2 Cartoon by Georgi Chaushov showing the loss of public
     respect for the Bulgarian Orthodox church   220
9.3 President Zheliu Zhelev   222
9.4 Nadezhda Mihailova   242
9.5 Simeon Saxecoburggotski casts his ballot, 17 June 2001 248
9.6 A female member of the US Air National Guard's 150th
     Fighter Wing   254

MAPS

The Bulgarian lands: main rivers and mountains   xxii
1.1 Ancient sites in present-day Bulgaria   2
1.2 The Roman empire in the Balkans   6–7
2.1 Bulgaria's borders during the first kingdom,
     681–1018   12
2.2 Bulgaria's borders during the second kingdom,
     1185–1393   23
3.1 The Bulgarian lands under Ottoman rule   31
4.1 The national revival   47
4.2 Bulgaria according to the treaties of San Stefano and Berlin 82

5.1   Bulgaria, 1878–1912   86
6.1   Territorial changes after the Balkan wars   136
6.2   The southern Balkan front during the first world war   141
7.1   Bulgaria's borders after the first and second world wars   146
7.2   Bulgaria and the second world war   170
8.1   Bulgaria in the 1980s   208

PREFACE

The crowded departure lounge at Gatwick airport on a busy summer Sunday morning may not seem the obvious place to encounter the effects of recent changes in Eastern Europe, but to see young British couples with their children queuing not to go on holiday but to go and work near the Black Sea coast assembling British cars for sale in the Balkans is something which would have been unthinkable ten years ago; it would have been even more of a fantasy in 1967 when I first went to Bulgaria. Bulgaria has opened itself to European and American culture and business.

This being so it is reasonable to assume that there is a growing need in the west for a concise history of a country which for the last fifty or so years has seldom attracted much attention. It is hoped the present volume will go some way to showing to western readers that Bulgaria has at least as much to offer in terms of historic interest as it does in financial reward.

All too often in the west we tend to blur the distinction between the nation and the state; when the Portuguese delegate suggested to the first meeting of the League of Nations that the organisation would be better called the League of States he was told that the difference was too insignificant to bother about. No-one who had any connection with the Balkans would make that mistake. And if this book is called A Concise History of Bulgaria it is also to some degree a concise history of the Bulgarians after they had arrived in the Balkans in the seventh century. For the most part the book concentrates on the various Bulgarian states but it cannot ignore the fate of the Bulgarians during the five hundred years when they were part of the Ottoman empire and there was no Bulgaria. Even when a Bulgarian state re-emerged in 1878 there still has to be a distinction between Bulgaria and the Bulgarians. Many who considered themselves to be Bulgarians lived outside Bulgaria; even more numerous were those outside Bulgaria whom the Bulgarians inside Bulgaria described as Bulgarian. Indeed, the difference between the territorial definitions of Bulgaria and the lands inhabited by the Bulgarians is one of the main themes of modern Bulgarian history.

It is on modern history that this book concentrates, though an attempt is made to illustrate how the Bulgarian nation and the Bulgarian state emerged in the second and third quarters of the nineteenth century. In that process the rebirth of Bulgarian literature and the revivifying of its culture played a vital part. In a general book limited to seventy thousand words it has not been possible to explore these phenomena to the extent which they deserve, but it is hoped that this short introduction to them will excite further interest and lead to further exploration of these fascinating processes.

For anyone writing on Balkan or East European history there are difficulties with nomenclature, dates and transliteration. In general, when English forms do not exist, I have used the modern Bulgarian name for towns or geographic features. There are however some exceptions. Istanbul seems inappropriate usage before the Ottomans took the city in 1453 and therefore I have preferred Byzantium or Constantinople; in the short chapter on the pre-Bulgarian period I have generally used classical rather than present-day names, though an obvious exception to this is 'Balkan' which is a post-classical term. Readers already familiar with Bulgaria might be surprised at the use of 'Tûrnovo' rather than 'Veliko Tûrnovo'; the adjective has been omitted for the sake of brevity and because no mention is made in the text of Malko Tûrnovo. I have, I hope, been more consistent with dates. I have used the Gregorian or western calendar rather than the Julian used by Orthodox Christians; the footnote on p. 130 gives more information on this point. For transliteration I have used the system set out on page xxi.

It would be impossible to thank directly all those, in Britain and Bulgaria, who have helped me formulate the ideas and amass the information presented in these pages. The librarians of the Bodleian Library in Oxford and the Kiril i Metodi Library in Sofia have made my life much easier, and Sasho and Daniella Shûrbanov and Andrei Pantev have always provided human companionship and endless hospitality when I have been in Bulgaria. In Britain teaching with Michael Hurst has been an enormously rewarding experience. I have also learnt much from my students, particularly Kyril Drezov, Ivan Krûstev, Marietta Stankova and Naoum Kaytchev; in addition to intellectual stimulation they have provided the dual satisfaction of seeing intelligent young Bulgarians making their way in a difficult world, and proving that Bulgarian scholarship is amongst the finest in that world. Aglika Markova and Ivan Stanciov transformed the official image of Bulgaria in Britain and for this I thank them, as well as for making it so easy to deal with Bulgaria. Vanya Stoyanova unearthed the gruesome photograph on page 109. Sheila Kane cast an expert and perceptive eye over the text and is responsible for many improvements in it. William Davies's gentle, civilised guidance made my task immeasurably easier; he is that rare and priceless phenomenon: the ideal editor. But above all I have to thank my wife for over thirty years of patience, understanding and unstinting support.

St Edmund Hall, Oxford
September 1995

PREFACE TO THE SECOND EDITION

Any observer of the contemporary world knows that much will change in a decade. This has been particularly true in the states of the former socialist bloc, and nowhere more so than in the Balkans. Bulgaria has naturally not been exempt from this process. Since the first edition of this book the country endured a serious social and political crisis after which it has rebuilt its economic foundations and made huge strides towards integration into the Euro-Atlantic structures. With entry into the EU the country also enters an entirely new chapter in its history, one in which it will be bound more tightly than ever in its past to the other states of Europe. How this monumental change affects the country and its people will be for future histories to relate.

Since the first appearance of this book friends, colleagues, and well-wishers previously unknown to me have helped me with constructive comments and suggestions for any future edition. I would like to thank them all but would also like to mention in particular Professor Martin Minchev of the University of Calgary, Canada. In the years between the publication of the original edition and now, other students have arrived in Oxford and enriched the university and my own life. In addition to those named in the original version I would like to express my thanks also to Teodora Parveva, Dimitûr Bechev, Patricia Curtis, Tressa Gipe, Ivana Gogova, Milena Grizo, Dimitrina Mihaylova, Yavor Siderov, and Matthew Tejada.

The hospitality and friendship of Sasho and Daniella Shûrbanov have contributed as much to this second edition as to the first.

Special mention must also be made of Aglika Markova without whom the illustrations for this book would have been much impoverished and the jacket design non-existent. Her generosity with her time, together with her indefatigable energy, have made me depend on her far more than I should have done; my gratitude to her is enormous.

I must also mention Isabelle Dambricourt who, in a remarkably short time, has acquired the expertise, the patience, and the good humour which go to make an excellent editor.

St Edmund Hall, Oxford
October 2004

A NOTE ON TRANSLITERATION

а	a	п	p
б	b	р	r
в	v	с	s
г	g (always hard)	т	t
д	d	у	u (long)
е	e (or é at the end of proper nouns)	ф	f
ж	zh (but дж has been transliterated 'dj')	х	h (but 'kh' in Russian and proto-Bulgarian words)
з	z	ц	ts
и	i	ч	ch
й	i	ш	sh
к	k	щ	sht (but 'shch' in Russian words)
л	l	ь	û
м	m	ю	iu
н	n	я	ya
о	o		

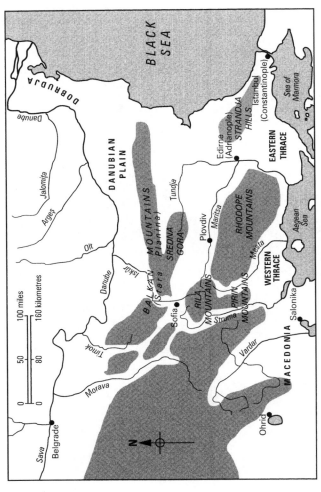

The Bulgarian lands: main rivers and mountains.

I

The Bulgarian lands from prehistory to the arrival of the Bulgarians

The lands which now constitute the state of Bulgaria were amongst the first in Europe to witness the emergence of organised, social life. Settlements existed in these lands as early as the middle palaeolithic period, from *c.* 100,000 to 40,000 BC. In neolithic times the population gradually forsook their caves for the plains where they began to work the land. By the third millennium BC they were cultivating non-food crops such as flax and had become adept at metal-working. In the sixth millennium BC an unknown people were producing objects of great originality and which experts consider to be the products of a spontaneously generated rather than an imported culture. This culture, in which the chief object of veneration appears to have been the mother goddess, reached its zenith in the fourth millennium BC.

By the end of the third millennium BC the lands to the east of the Morava–Vardar valleys were falling under the cultural influence of the Thracians. An Indo-European people, the Thracians lived in a loosely organised tribal society. They were masters of metal-working, particularly with silver and gold. Many spectacular hoards have been unearthed in present-day Bulgaria at sites such as Panagiurishte, Velchitrun and Vratsa, and many more remain to be excavated. In addition to a high level of proficiency in metal-working the Thracians were renowned for their horsemanship. Music too was an essential feature of Thracian culture for Orpheus himself was an early Thracian king who managed to unite the disparate tribes of Thrace and Macedonia for a short period. This

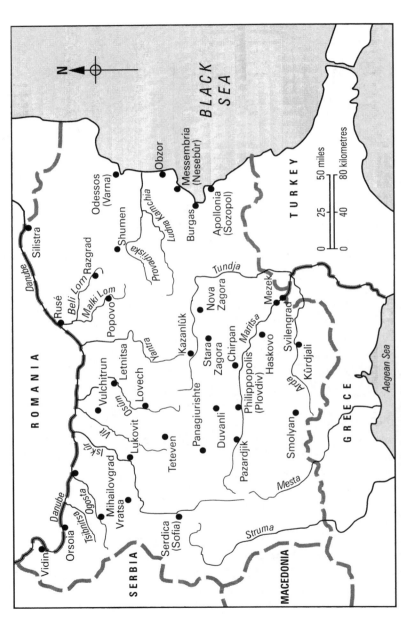

Map 1.1   Ancient sites in present-day Bulgaria.

Plate 1.1   A Mother Goddess figure produced by the unidentified people who thrived in the Bulgarian lands during the sixth millenium BC.

was a considerable feat in that the Thracians showed little disposition towards political cohesion and cooperation, Herodotus once noting that if the Thracians could only unite and subordinate themselves to one leader they would be invincible. As is so often the case in the Balkans, it was external pressures rather than internal inclinations which brought about political unity.

These pressures came from the Greeks who established mercantile centres and colonies along the Black Sea coast. The Greeks held the Thracians in low esteem, unjustifiably so because not only were the Thracians their equal in crafts and horsemanship, they also began minting coins at much the same time as their haughty southern neighbours. The Persian invasions of the Balkans in the sixth and fifth centuries BC were a much more serious threat than Greek cultural arrogance. This external danger brought about the Odryssian kingdom which united the Thracian tribes of the central Balkans.

The Persian storm was weathered but in the fourth century BC another threat appeared, this time from within the Balkan peninsula. The powerful new Macedonian state soon clashed with the Thracians. The latters' cultural achievements continued but they suffered chronic political weakness; they accepted Macedonian domination, and Thracian archers and horsemen formed a significant proportion of the army which Alexander the Great took to the frontiers of India. After the disappearance of the Macedonian danger came one much more ominous.

Landing first in the west of the Balkans to suppress pirates in the third century BC, the Romans spread inexorably inland. By the first century AD the entire peninsula south of the Danube was under their control. For a while they allowed a truncated Thracian kingdom to continue as a client state but eventually that too disappeared. The Thracian language survived in remote areas until the fifth century AD and their worship of the horse was continued by later inhabitants of the area; and some scholars still see the 'mummers' found in parts of the south-west of present-day Bulgaria as a relict of Thracian culture.

Roman rule was characteristically efficient and strict, giving the Balkan peninsula a unity and stability enjoyed neither before nor since. Under Roman law and the firm grip of the legions the provinces of Moesia, the area between the Balkan mountains and the Danube, and Thrace, from the Balkans to the Aegean, prospered. The new system of roads bound the Balkans together on both a north–south and an east–west axis. At the crossroad of important diagonal routes across the peninsula was to be found the city of Serdica, the site on which Sofia now stands. Other cities flourished, not least Trimontium, now Plovdiv, whose magnificent Roman theatre was discovered only in the 1970s when a new road was being built.

With Roman rule, eventually, came Christianity and when the empire was divided in 395 Moesia and Thrace became part of the

Plate 1.2   A one-handled vase from the Vratsa treasure, between 380 and 350 BC. The vase, 9 cm in height, illustrates the Thracian prowess in horsemanship.

eastern empire focused on Constantinople (Byzantium). For the next millennium and a half the city was to play a hugely important role in the history of the Bulgarian lands.

By the fourth century Roman power was weakening. Internal problems were compounded when tribes from the Asiatic steppes raided the north-east of the Balkans. In the following century ultimately fatal damage was inflicted on the Roman body politic by a series of such invaders who included the Alani, the Goths and the Huns, all of whom were enticed by the prospect of looting the fabled wealth of Byzantium. They failed in that aspiration and soon moved out of the Balkans in search of fresh plunder, but if these invaders were transient, the Slavs who also first appeared in the fifth century,

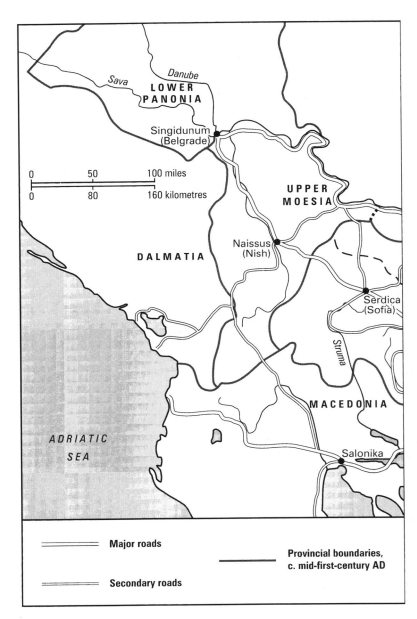

Major roads

Secondary roads

Provincial boundaries,
c. mid-first-century AD

Danube

Sava

LOWER
PANONIA

Singidunum
(Belgrade)

0   50   100 miles

0   80   160 kilometres

UPPER
MOESIA

DALMATIA

Naissus
(Nish)

Serdica
(Sofia)

Struma

MACEDONIA

ADRIATIC
SEA

Salonika

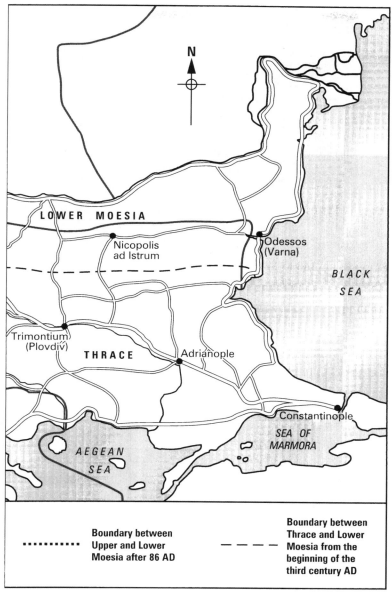

Map 1.2   The Roman empire in the Balkans.

Plate 1.3   The Roman theatre in Plovdiv which came to light only in the 1970s during the construction of a new inner city road.

were not. They were settlers. They colonised areas of the eastern Balkans and in the seventh century other Slav tribes combined with the Proto-Bulgars, a group of Turkic origin, to launch a fresh assault into the Balkans. The Proto-Bulgars originated in the area between the Urals and the Volga and were a pot-pourri of various ethnic elements, the word *Bulgar* being derived from a Turkic verb meaning 'to mix'. What differentiated the Proto-Bulgars from the Slavs was that they had, in addition to a formidable military reputation, a highly developed sense of political cohesion and organisation. In 680 their leader, Khan Asparukh, led an army across the Danube and in the following year established his capital at Pliska near what is now Shumen. A Bulgarian state had appeared in the Balkans.

2

Mediaeval Bulgaria, 681–1393

Two main problems confronted the new Bulgarian state at the end of the seventh century: the need to establish clearly defined and secure borders; and the need to weld together the two main human components of the state, the Proto-Bulgarian conquerors and the conquered Slavs. The second of these two problems was eventually to be resolved, but the first was seldom out of consideration for more than a few years; this problem was to be a persistent feature of Bulgarian states, modern as well as mediaeval.

The new state commanded a powerful position. From Pliska it could control the north–south routes through the eastern passes of the Balkan mountains and along the narrow lowland coastal strip. In the north, however, its extensive territories beyond the Danube inevitably led it into conflict with both the tribal groups milling around in the plains to the north-east, and with the succession of states which were established on the north-western borders. For the leaders of mediaeval Bulgaria, however, the most persistent and pressing problem was defining Bulgaria's relations with the great power to the south. The first mediaeval Bulgarian state was to be destroyed by Byzantium; the second was to fall to Byzantium's successor, the Ottoman empire.

BULGARIA UNDER THE KHANS, 681–852

After its foundation in 681 the new state enjoyed almost a century of growth. Initial tensions with Byzantium were contained and

9

regulated in a treaty of 716 which awarded northern Thrace to
Bulgaria and was unusual in the mediaeval era in that it contained
purely economic clauses. Immediately after the treaty the Bulgarian
state assisted Byzantium in the latter's conflict with the Arabs in
Asia Minor. By the middle of the eighth century part of the Morava
valley had been added to Bulgaria which then included much of
what is now southern Romania and parts of present-day Ukraine.

By this time the Black Sea was a virtual Byzantine lake, and in this
sector it went virtually unchallenged by Bulgaria because Bulgaria
never developed a sizeable sea-going force. Even if the strategic need
for a such a force had been recognised it is doubtful if anything
effective could have been done to act upon that need; the Bulgarian
state had a relatively low technological base and the degree of
planning and coordination needed to produce a navy would have
been difficult to achieve in an economy which did not even mint its
own coins, preferring instead to rely on Byzantine currency.

The lack of a navy ruled out expansion along the Black Sea coast
either to the north or the south, just as the chaos of the steppe area
made impossible any territorial gains to the north-east; the natural
direction of movement for the Bulgarian state was therefore to the
north-west and the south-west. In the north-west the collapse of the
Avar kingdom created a vacuum into which Bulgaria's rulers gladly
advanced, this taking their frontier up to the river Tisza;
Transylvania too became part of Bulgaria. Expansion to the south
and south-west was not so easy. Some of Macedonia had been taken
late in the eighth century but only at the cost of losing part of
Bulgaria's possessions in Thrace. Khan Krum (803–14) determined
to remedy this. In 811 he took the recently fortified Sredets (now
Sofia) from the Byzantines, went on to seize Nesebûr on the Black
Sea coast, and then marched as far as the walls of Byzantium itself.
This was a characteristically vicious war in which, in 811, the
Byzantine Emperor Nicephorus became the first of his rank for
almost five hundred years to lose his life on the battlefield; Krum
encrusted his deceased enemy's skull in silver and used it as a drink-
ing goblet.

In 814 his successor, Khan Omurtag (814–31), concluded a peace
which gave Bulgaria some territory in the Tundja valley, and later in
his reign he was able to add Belgrade (Singidunum) and its

surrounding district to his kingdom. In the second quarter of the ninth century Bulgaria, taking advantage of Byzantium's preoccupations with the iconoclast controversy and with threats to its power in Asia Minor, expanded into Macedonia, a predominantly Slav area which welcomed this alternative to Greek, Byzantine domination. By the middle of the century Ohrid and Prespa were incorporated into Bulgaria as was much of southern Albania; Byzantine power in Europe was now confined to western Albania, Greece, the southern Vardar valley and Thrace.

Omurtag, however, was not merely a warrior. He continued Krum's work in introducing a proper legal system into Bulgaria and he was an avid builder, his most notable achievement in this regard being the reconstruction of Pliska after the city had been burnt in 811. There are more extant inscriptions to Omurtag than to any other mediaeval Bulgarian ruler.

THE REIGN OF BORIS I (852–888) AND THE CONVERSION TO CHRISTIANITY

The celebration of Omurtag is perhaps surprising in view of the achievements of Boris I who in his three and a half decades of power was to impose huge and portentous changes on his realm and its inhabitants.

Boris was no less a warrior than his famous predecessors but his most important act was to impose Christianity upon Bulgaria. He did this in part to escape immediate military embarrassments and in particular to relieve pressure from the Byzantine armies, but there were also other long-standing causes, both domestic and external, for his decision.

In the first place, almost the entire civilised world was by now Christian, with only distant tribes such as the Letts and the Finns outside the Christian community; if Bulgaria were to be accepted as an equal amongst the powerful states of Europe, east and west, it would have to become part of their cultural and religious community. Even more importantly, conversion, it could reasonably be hoped, would help bridge the gap between the two main ethnic groups in Bulgaria, the Proto-Bulgarians and the Slavs. This gap still existed although the languages had merged

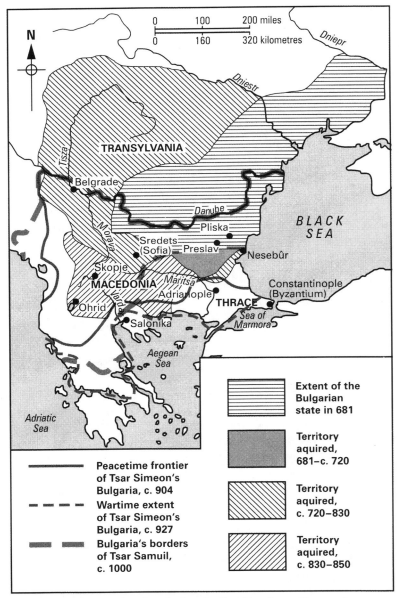

Map 2.1   Bulgaria's borders during the first kingdom, 681–1018.

into a Slavo-Bulgarian in which the Slav tongue of the conquered masses predominated.

Christianity had taken root in the Balkans during the later period of the Roman empire, and when they entered the area and colonised it the Slavs to a large degree adopted the Christian religion of those whom they had subdued. This was much less true of the Proto-Bulgarians, especially the nobility and the rulers, who for decades remained steadfastly pagan. It was not that its Christian Slav subjects had presented any threat to the Bulgarian state. On the contrary, they had provided the bulk of the armies which fought against Christian Byzantium, and they continued to guard the passes through the Balkan mountains, this being a vital service because if Byzantine forces had penetrated the Balkan range they could have strangled a Bulgarian state based on Pliska. The problem was potential rather than actual; the difference between Christian and pagan could provide a dividing line which might be exploited by an external enemy, and which might deepen dangerously in times of internal difficulty. This problem had been compounded by the wars of expansion waged during the eighth and ninth centuries. The acquisition of territory south of the Balkans and in Macedonia had greatly increased the number of Slavs and Christians within the state, thus making the Proto-Bulgarians quite obviously a minority. Also the wars, especially under Krum, had brought into Bulgaria thousands of prisoners of war, most of whom were Christians. Given the slavery and misery into which most of these unfortunates were plunged they had little alternative but to take refuge in whatever consolations their faith could offer them. This set an impressive example to many of their captors. Omurtag was not one of them; he continued to persecute the Christians, primarily in order to preserve the faith of his predecessors, but he was fighting a losing battle. Christianity continued to spread and reached even his own family, with one of his sons taking the new faith.

Omurtag had attempted to centralise the Bulgarian state, increasing the power of the ruler and diminishing that of the overwhelmingly Proto-Bulgarian boyars or nobility. Meanwhile, Byzantine Christianity was associated with a centralised, autocratic state. This truth was not lost on Boris and was one of the factors leading him to his decision in 864 to accept Christianity for himself and for all his subjects. A number of nobles reacted violently, stressing the decen-tralised traditions which were associated with paganism. Fifty-two of them were executed.

The conversion did not bring entirely satisfactory results for Boris. Bulgaria was made part of the Byzantine church and was denied the right to have its own, Bulgarian, patriarch or to appoint its own bishops. This strengthened existing fears in Bulgaria that, because in the empire the church was seen as an arm of the state, the church in Bulgaria would become an arm of the Byzantine state and would be used to interfere in the internal affairs of Bulgaria. Fears of potential subversion via the Byzantine church led Boris to ask if Byzantium's religious rival, Rome, would offer better terms. Emissaries were dispatched to enquire whether the pope would allow Boris to nomi-nate the Bulgarian bishops and appoint a Bulgarian patriarch. At the same time, Boris requested clarification of certain points of doctrine and religious regimen: could, he asked, the Bulgarian tradition of the ruler eating alone with his wife and followers relegated to separate, lower tables, continue? on what days was it permitted to hunt? and could sexual intercourse be allowed on Sundays? The answers to these specific questions, including the latter, were comfortingly indulgent, but on the critical political issue of the appointment of a patriarch and of subordinate bishops, they were not. Rome was as adamant as Byzantium in its refusal to allow the nomination of bishops by the secular power; nor would Rome permit the Bulgarians to have their own patriarch, though the pope did consent to their having an archbishop, who would, however, be nominated by the pope. These terms were no better than those offered by the emperor in Byzantium and Boris therefore remained with the devil he knew. In 870 a council regulated the organisation of the church in Bulgaria which was to be headed by an archbishop chosen by and dependent upon the patriarch in Constantinople.

The conversion caused other difficulties. The masses needed to be educated in their new faith, and though the Greeks sent missionaries to accomplish this task, they were too few in number. Furthermore, Slav and Proto-Bulgarian alike had been accustomed for the last two centuries to regard the Greeks as cunning but implacable enemies and therefore treated their new instructors with some suspicion. Nor did the indigenous population take kindly to the fact that the vast majority of the new clergy, especially its upper echelons, were Greek. With so many of the locals suspicious and/or ignorant of the new doctrines they were required to profess, it was hardly surprising that heresies rapidly gained a strong foothold in the Bulgarian lands. Some of them were to play a formative part in the later history of these lands. Nevertheless, despite these problems the conversion to Christianity was a watershed in the history of Bulgaria. Despite the many difficulties which it created it did facilitate the merging of the two constituent elements in the population. The Slavs could now more readily accept the state because it was Christian, and the Proto-Bulgarians had nothing to fear from Christianity because it was no longer divorced from the state and because it was no longer predominantly Slav or Greek. Thanks largely to the conversion, by the tenth century there were 'Bulgarians' as opposed to Slav and Proto-Bulgarian subjects of the Bulgarian state.

In a development which was parallel to the conversion in time and its equal in importance, an alphabet for use in the Slavonic languages emerged in the mid to late ninth century. The origin of this development is thought to be a request in 862 from the ruler of Moravia for an alphabet for use amongst his own people so that the influence of the Franks and Germans could be contained. Little is known of the origins of the Cyrillic alphabet, and what is known is extremely contentious, but its creation is generally acknowledged to be the work of two Salonika-born monks, Cyril and Methodius.

The introduction of the Cyrillic alphabet was of enormous importance. More than any other development it prevented the absorption of the Bulgarians by the Greeks to their south or the Franks to their west. It enabled the Bulgarians to create their own literature. And this they did with great rapidity. Kliment of Ohrid (Kliment Ohridski), who died in 896, and after whom Sofia university is named, established a thriving school of learning which embraced theological and many other studies and which attracted over three thousand students in its first seven years. The new alphabet also facilitated the production of important secular texts such as a legal code, *Zakon Sudnii Liudim*; and without an alphabet it is difficult to imagine how the Bulgarian state could have carried out administration in the Slavo-Bulgarian language. Above all, however, the new alphabet enabled the Bulgarian church to use Slavo-Bulgarian as the language of the liturgy, and had it not been able to do this it would have been impossible for the Bulgarian church to escape total Greek domination.

That Slavo-Bulgarian, or as we shall call it henceforth, Bulgarian, should become the language of the state and the Bulgarian church was decreed by an assembly of notables in 893.

THE REIGN OF SIMEON THE GREAT (893–927)

The assembly which decreed that Bulgarian should be the language of the state and the church, also accepted as ruler Simeon, who had come to power by a palace coup. In that he was not exceptional in the history of mediaeval Bulgaria, but he was the only monarch in those centuries to be accorded the epithet 'the Great'.

Simeon, who was brought up in Constantinople, originally intended to pursue a religious life and had been tipped as a prime candidate for the leadership of the church in Bulgaria. Despite his association with Constantinople Simeon spent much of the early part of his reign at war with the empire and with his other neighbours. He extended the boundaries of Bulgaria westwards to the Adriatic, south to the Aegean and north-westwards to incorporate most of modern Serbia and Montenegro. Twice he led his armies to the walls of Constantinople itself; on the second occasion he was forced to raise his siege only because of pressure from the Magyars in the north, where in fact Simeon witnessed the loss of almost all Bulgarian territory beyond the Danube. In 896 he concluded a peace with the empire which agreed to accept the independence of the Bulgarian church. Thirty years later, at the end of further wars, a second treaty confirmed this and recognised Simeon as *basileus*, that is, king or tsar; the only other monarch to whom Constantinople extended such recognition was the Holy Roman Emperor.

Simeon made a further significant change when he moved the Bulgarian capital from Pliska to the nearby Preslav. In the new capital the pagan tradition would be less strong. Preslav saw Bulgarian art and literature flower with unprecedented brilliance, Simeon having for long surrounded himself with men of letters such as the Monk Hrabr, John the Exarch and Konstantin of Preslav.

That flowering of literature was helped by the twenty years of peace and prosperity which followed the treaty of 896 with Constantinople. The prosperity of those golden years was based to a considerable degree on the close and healthy commercial relations with the empire, though trading links with Venetia and the west were also developing. The good times could not last, however, and the final years of Simeon's reign were again clouded by war, primarily against Constantinople.

THE END OF THE FIRST EMPIRE, 896–1018

Simeon died in 927 having nominated his second son, Petûr, as his successor. Petûr's reign was of exceptional duration – he remained king until 970 – but these were years of decline for Bulgaria. As usual, there were wars to be fought, though these were now defensive rather than expansionist, the chief threat being the Magyars in the north. There were also continuing clashes with the imperial power to the south. This almost constant warfare inevitably weakened the state.

There were also important internal explanations for the decline of Bulgarian power. Throughout the country there had been if not the expectation then at least the hope that the new reign would bring about a return to the golden days of peace. This illusion was shattered by the Magyar invasions. The disappointed nobility dreamed of a return to the old days, whilst the increasingly Byzantinified court harboured is own solutions. The church, meanwhile, fell to corruption and self-enrichment.

The latter development had a profound effect amongst the silent masses of the population. The tenth century saw a steady increase in the economic and social power of the landowner, partly because the central authority of the state was not as great as it had been under Boris and Simeon. One landowner whose property had been greatly extended was the church. Whilst the few grew rich, times became ever harder for the poor. Inevitably alienation set in.

Since the conversion to Christianity many Bulgarians had been left insufficiently educated in and therefore insecurely committed to their new church. It was no longer possible to revert to paganism, even if that had been desired, but this did not mean that unquestioning obedience had to be given to the official church: if

Plate 2.1   Tsar Simeon defeating the Byzantines, a miniature from the
Madrid manuscript of the Chronicles of Ivan Skilitsa, 12–13c., in the
National Library of Spain, Madrid.

the alienated could not revert to paganism they could at least escape
into heresy. Heresy had entered Bulgaria with Christianity itself.
First among the unofficial doctrines to arrive were those brought by
Syrians and Armenians, and very soon hermitism became popular
amongst the religiously committed; Bulgaria's national saint, Ivan
Rilski (John of Rila), was a hermit who was born between 876 and
880 and died in 947. Hermitism obviously indicated a willingness to
withdraw from the world and its problems, and this sense of 'internal migration' or dissociation from the temporal world was further
encouraged by the greatest and most lasting of the heresies to enter
Bulgaria: bogomilism.

The bogomils argued that the entire visible world, including man-
kind, was the creation of Satan; only the human soul was created by
God who sent his son, Christ, to show humanity the way to salvation.
The bogomils believed the gratification of all bodily pleasures to be an
expression of the diabolic side of creation, and therefore they
preached a formidable asceticism which enjoined poverty, celibacy,
temperance and vegetarianism. The few peripatetic 'Holy Ones' who
lived up to these exacting precepts were greatly respected by the
general body of the population, who were painfully aware of the

contrast between these 'Holy Ones' and the official clergy. The bogomils also questioned the social order by preaching that man should live in communities where property was shared and individual ownership unknown, and in which all men would be levelled by an equal participation in agricultural labour. The bogomils had no formal priesthood, though each district or area had a *dyado* or elder (literally a 'grandfather'), and there were loose links between different regions. The bogomils satisfied a spiritual hunger amongst the peasant masses. There was a need amongst the recently converted for an explanation of the increasingly harsh conditions in which they found themselves. The teachers and priests of the official church were neither as able nor as committed as the ones brought in by Boris and Simeon, and the many who felt abandoned by a clergy apparently more interested in self-enrichment than in the well-being of its flock naturally found more to respect in those who practised the exacting doctrine they preached. Because bogomilism was very much a reaction to mounting social pressures its popularity increased in times of hardship. This was understandable; in such times it was more easy than ever to believe that the temporal world was entirely the creation of the Evil One.

Bogomilism has been unfairly criticised for causing all or most of the misfortunes which befell mediaeval Bulgaria, but bogomilism, in declaring all institutions irredeemably evil, did implicitly condemn any effort to improve those institutions as in the long run irrelevant. For this reason bogomilism was essentially negative and did not give rise to any reformist movement or pressures, nor did it stimulate the creative intellectual revolution which the questioning of the Catholic church produced in the west.

The end of the tenth century saw the first Bulgarian kingdom decline rapidly to a tragic end. Wars continued with clashes with Kievan Rus in the north and, inevitably, resumed conflict with Constantinople in the south. In 971 Preslav was taken as the empire conquered much of eastern Bulgaria. The Bulgaria of Krum, Boris and Simeon was finished. The capital moved between a number of western centres before settling in Ohrid. Byzantine influence had always been less noticeable in the western section of the Bulgarian kingdom and by the mid-980s there was resurgence with the Bulgarians retaking much of the territory they had lost south of the Danube.

Plate 2.2   Hermitism was strong in mediaeval Bulgaria: the arrow indicates the entrance to the monastery church of Gospodev Dol near the village of Ivanovo in the Rusé district.

Under the leadership of Tsar Samuil (997–1014) Bulgaria expanded further into present-day Albania and Montenegro, but it was a false dawn. Bulgarian successes had come about primarily because Constantinople was again preoccupied with the Arab threat to its possessions in Asia Minor. A military victory in 1001 freed Constantinople of this concern and the emperor, Basil II, could turn his full attention to the Bulgarian problem; his efforts in this direction were to earn him the grim title, 'the Bulgar-slayer'.

The end for the first Bulgarian state came when the Bulgarian and imperial armies met in Macedonia in 1014. On the slopes of Mount Belassitsa fifteen thousand Bulgarian troops were captured. Legend has it that ninety-nine out of every hundred were blinded; the remainder were left with one eye to guide their comrades back to their leader who died three days after seeing his stricken soldiers. Many centuries later nationalist enthusiasms and passions were to be fired by this story. Whether it were true or false, there was no doubting the fact that four years after the battle the Bulgarian state collapsed and the country was incorporated into the Byzantine empire.

The first Bulgarian empire had achieved much. It had created a Bulgarian nation from the Proto-Bulgarians and the Slavs. As in the merging of the Normans and the Anglo-Saxons to produce the English, the process was neither easy nor rapid, yet by the beginning of the eleventh century there was a nation, a state, a language, a literature and a church, all of which were clearly Bulgarian. But the kingdom, despite the brilliance of a few of its rulers, also suffered grave weaknesses. The introduction of Christianity and the consolidation of boyar power which followed soon afterwards, required Bulgaria to undergo a fundamental reordering of its values and beliefs, and to adapt to far-reaching social changes. The Bulgarians were required to absorb in a few decades processes which in other lands lasted centuries, and inevitably the strains and fissures ran deep and far. The bogomils grew strong on such strains and fissures, and their dismissive attitude to the temporal world hardly encouraged full-scale commitment to the state in danger. The first Bulgarian state was also in some respects surprisingly backward. Not only did it fail to produce a navy but it failed to see the dangers of geography. Given its position in the Balkans the Bulgarian kingdom was exposed to threats from the south, the north-east and the north-west. There was perhaps *folie de grandeur* in the assumption that all these enemies could for ever be contained, and it was certainly a mistake, albeit an understandable one, to assume, as many Bulgarian leaders did, that danger could be circumvented by playing one enemy off against another. This *folie de grandeur* was all the greater when one takes into account that the kingdom was always heavily influenced by Byzantium and by Byzantine practices. The Bulgarian aristocracy aped that of its southern neighbour; the state and church administrations were similar to those of the empire, as was the tax system; the kingdom used mainly Byzantine currency; and even the vocabulary of administration, commerce and much of public life were derived from the empire.

BULGARIA UNDER BYZANTINE RULE, 1018–1185

In his treatment of the defeated Bulgaria Boris was as moderate in victory as he had been implacable in battle. Most importantly for the Bulgarians, the Bulgarian church was allowed to continue as a separate national institution. Headed by a patriarch in Ohrid the Bulgarian church included much of present day Bulgaria, Serbia, Albania and Macedonia. Basil's moderation, however, did not survive him. The Ohrid patriarchate increasingly fell under Greek influence, and the Bulgarian bishops were no longer allowed to elect their patriarch from amongst themselves. The tax system changed for the worse. Before, taxes had been levied mainly in kind but now, to feed the army, the government had to have recourse to forced purchases at fixed prices with taxes then being paid in cash not kind. A new form of land-holding was introduced: the *proniya*. The holders of this land had the right to its produce but could not pass it on by inheritance; they therefore worked it and its peasants for all they could get out of it in the time available; many of them were absentee landlords who used bailiffs who in turn took their share of the profits. In 1040 Petûr Delyan, a descendent of Samuil, collected an army and took the chief Bulgarian town, Skopje, and soon came to dominate Thrace, Epirus and Macedonia. His revolt was not a nationalist movement but a protest against worsening social conditions, and it was joined by some oppressed Greeks. In 1041 Delyan was betrayed by his allies, blinded, and later captured by Byzantine troops amongst whose ranks were Varangians under the command of Harald Hardrada, later prince of Norway and the founder of Oslo.

Bulgaria remained an integral part of the Byzantine imperium until the late twelfth century. There had been a few outbreaks of unrest, mainly social in origin, and it was clear that a sense of Bulgarian cultural identity and separateness survived. Ironically this was in part due to bogomil influence. Bogomil ideas tended to be absorbed more easily by the Slavs than the Greeks and this hindered the assimilation of the former by the latter. It also prevented any commitment to the ruling state or church.

THE SECOND BULGARIAN EMPIRE, 1185–1393

In the 1180s the Normans, who had already dislodged the Byzantines from Sicily, attacked imperial territory in Greece and along the Adriatic. In retaliation to this and other threats the imperial government was forced to increase taxation and conscription levels. It was more than many Bulgarians could bear. In 1185 two

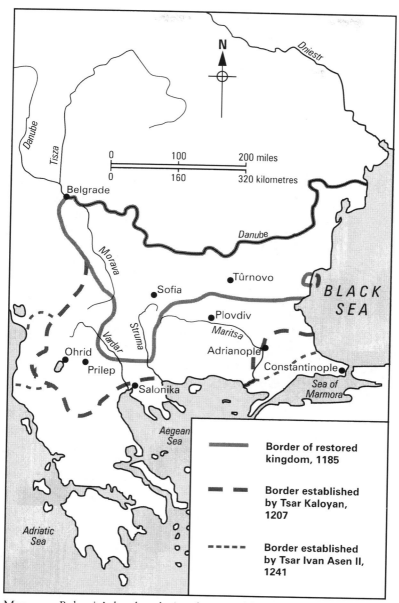

Map 2.2   Bulgaria's borders during the second kingdom, 1185–1393.

landowners from near Tûrnovo, Petûr and Asen, requested an alleviation of the new burdens along with concessions for themselves. Not only were they refused, one of them had his face slapped by a Byzantine courtier. News of this humiliation helped feed the already healthy fires of revolt and soon most of eastern Bulgaria had taken to arms and Petûr and then Asen had been proclaimed tsar in Tûrnovo.

The second Bulgarian kingdom, based on Tûrnovo, was to last for two centuries. Like its predecessor it fluctuated in size but it was seldom free either from external dangers or crippling internal divisions. It was stabilised by Tsar Kaloyan who ruled from 1197 to 1207. Much of his reign was spent in warfare. His first military achievement was to drive the Magyars out of northwest Bulgaria and in 1202 he concluded a much-needed peace with Constantinople. By now, however, a new factor had disturbed the delicate balance of power in the Balkans: the Crusaders. In 1204 they took Constantinople and proclaimed the Bulgarians their vassals. This effrontery Kaloyan demolished the following year in a fierce battle near Adrianople, the present-day Edirne. By 1207 Kaloyan had reconquered most of Macedonia but he was to be betrayed and murdered that year when laying siege to Salonika.

Unlike many Bulgarian rulers Kaloyan backed his military might with skilful diplomacy. That he was able to defeat the Crusaders was in no small measure due to an agreement he concluded in 1204 with the pope which did much to guarantee Bulgaria's western frontier. The essence of the agreement was that the Bulgarians would recognise the supreme authority of the bishop of Rome, though there was little actual papal interference in Bulgarian ecclesiastical affairs. Bulgaria, in fact, despite its endless political and territorial disputes with Constantinople, remained part of the Orthodox Christian east which had finally broken with the Catholic west in the schism of 1054.

In the disturbed years at the end of the twelfth century bogomilism had flourished and in 1211 a council in Tûrnovo, having heard the bogomil case, condemned the heresy and initiated severe persecution of it. This was relaxed when Bulgaria again found relative security and stability in the reign of Ivan Asen II (1218–41). Ivan

Asen II further reduced the Magyar threat to Bulgaria but his main achievement was to destroy the power of the despot of Epirus, Theodore Angelus Comnenus, who sought to drive the Crusaders from Constantinople. In 1230 at the battle of Klokotnitsa, near the present-day Haskovo, Theodore Angelus was captured and his extensive territories incorporated into Bulgaria which now spread from the Black Sea to the Aegean and the Adriatic.

Like Kaloyan, Ivan Asen II was an adept diplomat. In concluding a treaty with them against the Crusaders he was prepared to allow the Greeks the lion's share of any conquests that might be made, and in return he insisted upon only one condition: that the independence of the Bulgarian church and its patriarch be recognised by the Greeks. Having secured this, Ivan Asen successfully negotiated with Rome for the complete restoration of the independence of the Bulgarian church in 1235.

Ivan Asen II took the second Bulgarian kingdom to its greatest geographic extent and to the height of its power. He also did much to develop its capital, Tûrnovo. The kingdom went on to produce one of the masterpieces of mediaeval Balkan art: the frescoes in Boyana church near Sofia, begun in 1259, which are now a UNESCO protected monument and which deserve to be numbered amongst the greatest artistic attainments of the Slavonic world.

The political situation did not reflect the artistic world. In the early fourteenth century Bulgaria was forced for a while to acknowledge Tatar tutelage, and the Magyars were once again a danger, having taken Vidin in 1261, the year in which the Greeks finally drove the Crusaders out of Constantinople. Internally no strong monarch appeared and by the end of the thirteenth century the kingdom was on the point of disintegration, not least because of incessant feuding among its nobility. It was also beset by another debilitating heresy, hesychism, whose adherents called for the rejection of all social activity and for a life devoted to *hesychia*, or silent contemplation and prayer; this, its adherents argued, was the only condition in which God's true light could be perceived. Maybe it was; but it did little to help repel invaders.

In the fourteenth century two new invaders added to Bulgaria's difficulties: the Serbs from the west and the Ottomans from

Plate 2.3   The Christ child, detail from the frescoes at Boyana near Sofia which is now a UNESCO World Heritage site. The frescoes, which date from 1259, are remarkable for their sophistication and realism.

the south. There were flashes of recovery as when Tsar Mihail Shishman (1323–30) contained the Serbian threat for a while before losing his life on the battlefield near Kiustendil. The last monarch to achieve any form of stability was Ivan Alexander (1331–71). He recovered some lost territory whilst his lands enjoyed a welcome economic recovery caused in part because the landing of Ottoman forces on the Aegean coast had pushed trade routes northwards into the Bulgarian lands, and in part because he was able to improve relations with Serbia. It was during Ivan Alexander's reign that Bulgaria produced another of the great treasures of Slavonic art: the four

Plate 2.4   Tsar Ivan Alexander and his family from the Ivan Alexander
Gospels now in the British Museum. The tsar is holding the sceptre and is
surrounded by his sons, Ivan Shishman who reigned from 1371 to 1395, and
Ivan Stratsimir. The tsar's wife, the Tsaritsa Theodora, is described as the
'Newly Enlightened', a reference to her conversion to Christianity from
Judaism. The tsar is described as 'Autocrat of all Bulgarians and Greeks'. To
the tsaritsa's right are: Duke Constantine, the tsar's son-in-law; the tsar's
eldest daughter, Kera Thamara, the wife of Constantine; Keratsa, another
daughter of the tsar; and Desislava, the tsar's youngest daughter.

gospels which bear his name and are now in the British Museum.
Commissioned in 1355 the gospels, with their 367 miniatures, were
completed in the extraordinarily short period of one year.

Despite this, however, the costs of Ivan Alexander's wars were
high and taxes had to be raised. At the same time his preoccupation
with external affairs meant that the tsar could not check the seepage
of political power from the centre to the landowning aristocracy.
Once again the main victims were the peasantry.

After the death of Ivan Alexander, Bulgaria was no longer the
master of its own fate. This would be settled by the looming contest
between the two major Balkan powers: Serbia and the Ottoman
Turks. In the 1360s the latter had taken Adrianople, whence they

began to push up the Maritsa valley. In 1389 the issue was decided when the Serbs were broken in the battle of Kosovo Polje. Bulgaria's defeat came shortly afterwards. After a three-month siege, Tûrnovo capitulated in July 1393. The patriarch was shut up in a monastery, the dynasty deposed, the great aristocrats dispossessed and the state dissolved. Resistance continued in Vidin for three more years but it too was eclipsed in 1396. Bulgaria as a state was not to exist for almost half a millennium.

3

Ottoman rule in the Bulgarian lands

The vigorous but self-righteous Christians of the Victorian era created the impression that their co-religionists under Ottoman domination had suffered continual persecution for five hundred years. It
was not so. Ottoman history is certainly not free from terrible
incidents of hideous outrage, but in Europe these were occasional.
Many, if not most, followed acts of rebellion and if this does not
excuse the excess it perhaps goes some way to explain it. Other
outbursts were spontaneous, localised and random, the result
usually of a peculiar combination of personal, political, social or
economic factors. It would be unwise to imagine the Ottoman
empire as some form of lost, multi-cultural paradise, but on the
other hand it would also be wrong to deny that at some periods in
its history the empire assured for all its subjects, irrespective of
religion, stability, security and a reasonable degree of prosperity.

OTTOMAN SOCIETY AND ADMINISTRATION

If the Christians of the empire at times enjoyed the blessings of peace
and relative prosperity they were never given equality of status with
Muslims. The Ottoman empire was a theocracy. Its head of state,
the sultan, was also caliph, or the representative of God on earth and
the supreme Muslim religious authority; he was pope as well as
emperor. Non-Muslims were discriminated against in a variety of
ways: they paid higher taxes than Muslims; Christian churches
could not be as high as mosques; Christians could not wear the

sacred colour green; no attempt could be made to proselytise amongst Muslims; at times, Christians had to dismount from their horses when a Muslim passed the other way; Christians could not carry arms; they could not become tanners because that was Mohammed's trade; and, most importantly, Muslim law was always superior to any other.

Because temporal society and the state had, in the Muslim conception, so obvious a religious nature most of the imperial administration was placed on a religious basis. Under a system introduced in 1454, the year after Constantinople had fallen to the Ottomans, the population was divided according to creed. Each separate religious group, or *millet*, was allowed to regulate its internal affairs. This meant not merely the organisation of their own religious life but also such issues as education, property law and family law. The head of a *millet* was the head of the religious group in question and he represented that community before the sultan and the Sublime Porte, or Ottoman government. The head of a *millet* was held responsible by the latter for the good behaviour of his flock who would be expected to pay their taxes and, where necessary or appropriate, to provide troops for the army or navy. In larger settlements which included different religious communities the different *millets* continued to operate, so Ottoman rule therefore accepted separate jurisdictions within the same territorial unit. Originally there were four *millets*: the Muslim, the Orthodox, the Armenian Christian and the Jewish, the latter functioning from 1454 but not being officially recognised until 1839. Others were added later and to be awarded the status of a separate *millet* was a major achievement for any group. Although the non-Muslim *millets* enjoyed internal self-administration, they were subordinate to the Muslims; any legal dispute involving a Muslim had to be tried by Muslim law.

The *millet* system meant for the most part that Christian communities did not suffer pressures to convert to Islam, and although conversions, some of them involuntary, did take place, religious intolerance of the sort which plagued most of western and central Europe in the reformation and counter-reformation never became official policy in the Ottoman empire. Nor, at least in the early centuries of Ottoman rule in Europe, did official policy-makers recognise any concept of ethnicity. This created difficulties because

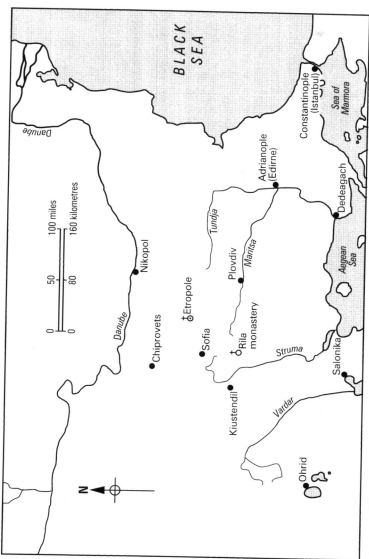

Map 3.1   The Bulgarian lands under Ottoman rule.

khriften kinder daraus man die
Janirfcharn macht

Plate 3.1   Christian children taken under the *devshirme* and turned into janissaries, from an incunabulum in the National Library, Vienna.

the administrators did not recognise that their system of categorising people by religion was not shared by others. They did not realise that all Orthodox Christians were not 'Greeks', that the Bulgarians and the Serbs had had their own national churches with a fully developed system of ecclesiastic administration and their own distinctive forms of liturgy and religious art. Because the Greeks for much of the period of Ottoman rule dominated the Orthodox church, the non-Greeks were in effect second-class citizens in a second-class *millet*.

In its heyday the military power of the empire was based on the *timar*. This was land held from the sultan in return for which the *spahi*, or tenant, was required in time of need to provide men for the imperial armies, the number of men varying directly with the amount of land held. The *spahi* also had various local government responsibilities. Land not held as *timars* could be in the hands of the sultan, his family or of a few influential members of the empire, and on this so-called *hass* land the tenants, Christian or Muslim, were free from most or sometimes all forms of taxation. Another crucially important category of land was the *vakûf*. *Vakûf* land was that whose income had by bequest been allotted to a charitable foundation. Initially this had been primarily to secure the upkeep of mosques or Islamic schools, but in later years Christian churches and monasteries could also hold *vakûf* land.

For those Christians not living in villages which enjoyed tax privileges the main levies were the poll tax and a tax levied in lieu of military service. There was also the *devshirme*. The *devshirme* was levied at intervals of between one and seven years, and it brought in not cash but Christian boys aged between seven and fourteen. The boys were chosen for their physical and mental ability and were taken from their families and villages to be converted to Islam and then given a rigorous education and military training, after which they entered the ranks of the janissary corps. For almost two centuries after the conquest of Constantinople the janissaries, forbidden to marry, formed the highly trained and totally disciplined élite of the Ottoman army. They also played an important part in the imperial administration; at times they remembered and favoured their home villages, and there are even records of villages requesting that the *devshirme* be levied on them in the hope that in future years such favours would be paid, but for the most part this tax in human kind was a dreaded feature of Ottoman rule until the late seventeenth century; the last full levy in the Bulgarian lands was in 1685.

THE BULGARIAN POPULATION UNDER OTTOMAN RULE

Shortly after the Ottoman conquest the Christian Bulgarians formed about a third of the total population of the empire in the Balkans, though precise figures are impossible to obtain because Christians living in privileged villages or on *hass* estates were not recorded because they did not pay taxes. By the beginning of the sixteenth century, Christian Bulgarians were only about 8 per cent of the total population. There were four main reasons for this relative decline. The first, and by far the most important, was that the empire expanded into the remainder of the Balkans and into Hungary thus greatly increasing the total population without adding many Bulgarians to its number. The second was persecution, especially following outbreaks of political or social unrest. The third was disease and pestilence. The fourth was the conversion of some Christian Bulgarians to Islam.

This has long been a contentious issue. There is no doubt that pressures for conversion were stronger amongst the Bulgarians than amongst other Balkan Christians because Bulgaria was more densely settled by Ottoman/Muslim elements than anywhere else; furthermore, the Bulgarians were at the very centre of the European section of the Ottoman empire, commanding the military and trade routes into central Europe and the defensive ring around Constantinople itself. Nor is there any doubt that some Bulgarian landowners accepted the faith of the conquerors in order to retain their property. The great aristocrats had been dispossessed immediately after the conquest but the lower nobility remained, merging gradually into the ranks of the *spahis*. Some Christian communities may also have been tempted into Islam by the prospect of easier tax burdens and the privileges which belonging to the dominant religion could offer. There were additional cases where Christian villages were enticed into Islam by being offered the freedom to loot and pillage local church or monastic property. Finally there were cases of enforced, violent conversion. There were a number of such instances in the third quarter of the seventeenth century in the Rhodope mountains. The motivation for this sudden outburst of militancy amongst the Muslims is unclear. This was a time when Islam seemed to be resurgent with the sultan's armies soon to press forward to Vienna, and the conversions could in part be explained by the exhilaration which this resurgence bred. A more sober explanation might be that the Ottoman military planners were anxious not to leave the passes through the Rhodopes in the hands of non-Muslims in view of the critical nature of the forthcoming campaigns; but this seems a risky strategy as the forcibly converted might be less reliable than Christians left in peace, besides which to forcibly convert relatively large areas to Islam would reduce the number of tax-payers, and this at a time when the imperial government was desperately short of revenue.

Of those who did convert, some, especially the landowners, were absorbed into the Muslim world and became entirely Islamicised and Turkified. Many converted villages, on the other hand, retained their Bulgarian language, folk traditions and costumes. The Bulgarian-speaking Muslims became known as Pomaks.

Most Bulgarians, Muslim or Christian, lived in villages. Most of these villages were small with between 150 and 200 inhabitants. Larger settlements were known, Kotel, for example, having over 2,500 in 1648, but these were rare. Villages were run by the family elders who chose from amongst themselves officials such as the local village headman, called in Bulgarian *kmet* (mayor) or sometimes even *knyaz* (prince), names which represented a continuum with the pre-conquest officials; by the nineteenth century many local *prominenti*, many of whom had recently acquired wealth and property, were known by the somewhat pejorative and Turkish-based, *chorbadjiya* (soup-provider). Ottoman officials seldom visited villages other than to collect taxes, including, of course, the *devshirme*. A number of communities, the so-called privileged villages, was granted freedom from taxation and left to order their own affairs in return for providing specified services to the sultan or his officials. A number of such villages were made responsible for guaranteeing safe passage for troops and traders through local mountain passes. Other tasks were more unusual. Some had to procure birds for the sultan's falconries and one, Dedovo, was required to provide two barrels of water per day from its spring for the nearby city of Plovdiv. The experience gained by these villages in self-administration were, centuries later, to be useful in organising the schools and other institutions which so helped the Bulgarian national revival.

In the seventeenth century only about one in fifty Christian Bulgarians lived in towns. This was in part because in the early and frequently violent days of the Ottoman occupation urban Bulgarians had fled or had been driven from their homes; villages, especially the

Plate 3.2   Bulgarian peasants from an incunabulum in the National
Library, Vienna.

remoter ones in the mountains, provided relative security and greater
opportunities to continue living a Christian, Bulgarian life. As
Ottoman society evolved its trade became dominated by the Greeks,
Jews and Armenians, though in the seventeenth century Bulgarian
traders were active as far afield as Transylvania, even if many of them
were described as or even called themselves 'Greek'.

The centres of Ottoman towns were generally occupied by administrative or military buildings, but in the surrounding areas were the *mahalla* or small urban districts. These were frequently based on ethnic identity, sometimes on occupation, and infrequently on both: in some larger towns, therefore, there would be a Christian shoe-makers' and a Muslim shoe-makers' district. In the *mahalla* the streets were narrow and the houses faced inwards onto courtyards rather than outwards onto the street.

In urban economic activity the *esnaf*, or guild, played a dominant role. The structure of the *esnaf*, with its ranking of apprentice, journeyman and master, and its ruling council elected by and from local masters, was similar to the structure of guilds in western Europe, and like those in the west they provided welfare for their members, but in the Ottoman empire the *esnaf* was subject to a great deal of interference from local officials of the central government; there was little of the fierce independence which frequently characterised western guilds. Many, but not all, *esnafs* had both Christian and Muslim members. After the initial decades of Ottoman rule Christian guilds encouraged the building or repair of many churches and other religious institutions, the church of Sveta Petka in Sofia, for example, being redecorated by the local saddle-makers' *esnaf*. Bulgarians were prominent in the textile guilds, those in Sofia being famous for dress-making and the production of hooded cloaks.

Although many Bulgarian guilds flourished under Ottoman rule the conquest had been a cultural as well as a political disaster for the Bulgarian nation. Not only did the state disappear and the church fall subject to the domination of Constantinople, Bulgarian language and literature seemed also to die. Bulgarian had once ranked with Greek, Latin and Arabic as the major tongues of the civilised European world, and it had produced a flourishing literature of secular as well as sacred works. But when, in the second half of the eighteenth century, Catherine the Great compiled her samples of 279 languages and dialects, included in which were some North American Indian tongues, Bulgarian was not mentioned, nor was Joseph Dobrovský, 'The Father of Slavicists', familiar with it, whilst the treatment of it in Šafařik's history of the Slavic languages and literature, published in 1826, is cursory and flawed.

Yet the language remained alive during the years of Ottoman rule and eventually its literature was to be reborn. The language survived primarily because most Bulgarians lived in their small, isolated and usually ethnically homogenous villages. In such communities there was no need to adopt Greek for everyday economic or commercial transactions, nor to use Turkish when dealing with government officials. The villages therefore preserved the Bulgarian language and with it Bulgarian names, Bulgarian folk tales and legends, Bulgarian forms of family organisation and Bulgarian festivals and holidays.

THE BULGARIAN CHURCH UNDER OTTOMAN RULE

The festivals and holidays which the small Bulgarian villages preserved were primarily religious and the church's role in keeping alive a separate sense of 'Bulgardom' was critical. In 1394, the year after the fall of Tûrnovo, the Bulgarian patriarchate was dissolved and the Bulgarian church subjected to the authority of the patriarch in Constantinople. The patriarchate of Ohrid, however, continued to be known as 'Bulgarian', although in fact most of its prelates were Greek and were nominated by the Greek patriarch in Constantinople. Despite the Ohrid patriarchate, therefore, the church in both eastern and western Bulgaria was subjected to Greek domination, more especially at its higher levels. At the parish level, however, many Bulgarian priests were still nominated and at least until the eighteenth century the liturgy was still usually held in Bulgarian if the congregation so desired. In many communities the parish priest provided guidance in every aspect of life as well as spiritual leadership, and it was significant that, particularly in the seventeenth century and afterwards, priests often came from the most affluent section of the local population; they were the only ones who could afford the increasingly stiff bribes required to secure a parish appointment. Had the church not played this role, however, the survival of the Bulgarian language would have been much more difficult.

In the early years after the conquest the Ottomans generally abided by the letter of their law forbidding the building or rebuilding of churches. Later this was relaxed but even then the process of building or rebuilding Christian places of worship was a slow one, and one greatly demanding of money, time and patience. Yet a long pocket and careful organisation on the part of the village council and the priest could secure the necessary permission and thus, as in Poland under the communists, church building and restoration assumed more than a mere spiritual significance: it became a contest with the dominant non-Christian authority and victory could bring a great sense of pride and achievement. It could also mean that Bulgarian iconographers and painters could go to work and thus keep alive Bulgarian traditions in religious art.

The Bulgarian monasteries too helped keep alive religious art. Immediately after the conquest they had fallen upon very hard times. By the middle of the fourteenth century many of them were destroyed or in a state of sad decline, but thereafter a slow regeneration began. Many were re-established far from the main routes used by the Ottoman armies, and some lucky ones were able to transform their properties into *vakûf* lands and thereby secure their income. The great foundation at Rila near where Ivan Rilski had spent his life as a hermit, was repopulated and rebuilt by three brothers from near Kiustendil and in 1469 it received an enormous boost when the remains of Ivan Rilski were brought back from Tûrnovo. Severe taxation was to threaten it once again in later years but the foundation survived, and with it its great library. Rila also helped to sponsor the flourishing school of religious painting to be found in the Sofia area in the seventeenth century and thereafter.

Monasteries also played a vital role in maintaining the rudiments of education. Mount Athos had provided refuge for a number of Bulgarian writers and other men of letters immediately after the fall of Tûrnovo, and when political conditions stabilised in the Bulgarian lands pilgrims were able to visit the holy mountain. Those monasteries on Athos, and others in the Bulgarian lands, which had retained their properties sent out monks to collect revenue and maintain contact with the inhabitants of those properties. The itinerant monks, or *taxidiots* as they were known, played an essential role in linking village and monastery. This was extremely important when monasteries began to develop 'cell schools' in which a small number of young men would be trained for service in the church or in monastic orders. In the fifteenth century, refugees from Tûrnovo founded a large Slav school in Zograf on Mount

Athos which later became a model for others throughout the Bulgarian lands, villages having encouraged the *taxidiots* to arrange for the establishment of such schools. These schools were relatively few in number and they did not produce either the questioning religious minds of the reformation and counter-reformation or anything resembling an intelligentsia, but they did keep literacy alive. They also facilitated the merging of the old Bulgarian language with more vernacular usages, a process which produced in the seventeenth century what philologists have called 'new Bulgarian'.

Some monks copied old hagiographies, one of which was that compiled by Patriarch Evtimii in Tûrnovo shortly before the conquest and which gave great prominence to Bulgarian saints and martyrs. However, one should not be tempted into making this process into anything approaching a modern national revival, or even a precursor of it: of the 261 extant Bulgarian manuscripts dating from the seventeenth century only 46 contain mention of specifically Bulgarian saints. What the monasteries and the scriptoria did was to preserve that basic sense of ethnic separateness without which a national revival would have been impossible.

PROTEST AGAINST OTTOMAN POWER

Protest against Ottoman rule was not a Christian monopoly. In 1416, for example, there was a rising by the Muslim Bedreddin order. In later centuries, however, political and social protest were predominantly Christian and when they came were usually based on the hope, always dashed, that Christian powers were about to inflict defeat upon the Ottoman empire. The 'long war' fought by the Habsburgs and their Transylvanian and Wallachian allies against the Turks at the turn of the sixteenth century created the belief that a campaign south of the Danube was imminent, the agents of Vienna and Rome using the Dubrovnik merchants who were so powerful in the Balkans to encourage such beliefs. The result was a rising in the Tûrnovo region in 1598. It was suppressed with the customary brutality, but further to the west, in the mountains near Sofia, there remained armed groups of so-called *haiduks* who were more than mere robbers, if less than the nationalist heroes depicted by some later historians.

Plate 3.3 Christ Sabaoth and Christ Pantocrator (below) from the church of Sveti Iliye, Boboshevo village, Struma district. Executed in 1678 these represent, in the words of the leading western scholar of the subject, 'one of the most complete and best preserved ensembles of Bulgarian painting from the Ottoman period'. Machiel Kiel, *Art and Society of Bulgaria in the Turkish Period*, Maastricht, Van Gorcum, 1985, p. xviii.

Almost a century later, in 1686, there was another rising around Tûrnovo, this time prompted by expectations of a Russian invasion. Two years later a larger outburst occurred around Chiprovets in the north-west of the Bulgarian lands. The Chiprovets area was unusual. It was rich in mines which had originally been worked by Serbs imported in the thirteenth century and then by Saxons whom the Ottomans settled there. The Orthodox Serbs were rapidly assimilated into the local Bulgarian population but the Saxons, though they became Bulgarian-speaking, retained their Catholicism. When it was learned that Habsburg armies were approaching from the north a rebellion was organised and the flag raised when it was believed the Christian forces were but a day's march away. Some rebel units managed to fight their way through to join the Habsburg soldiers but the latter gave no assistance to the rising which was crushed with exceptional severity. The town of Chiprovets was destroyed and some estimates put local fatalities at two-thirds of the population. Many of those who survived fled to the Banat of Temesvar, now in Romania, where their descendants still live as one of Eastern Europe's lesser known minority groups.

THE DECLINE OF THE OTTOMAN EMPIRE

The Habsburg advance into the Balkans in the 1680s had followed the failure of the Ottomans to take Vienna in 1683. By this date the sultan's empire was in obvious decline. The *timar* system no longer functioned adequately. Too many properties had been allowed to convert to *vakûf* status with their inhabitants naming their descendants as the testamentary beneficiaries. This had a number of results. In the first place it made easier the emergence of estates which were worked purely for revenue rather than to equip the sultan's forces, and on the new properties the peasants were subjected to much greater exploitation. The decline of the *timars* also meant that too few soldiers were recruited from the *timar* lands thus forcing the government to rely more upon the janissaries as the mainstay of the army. But the janissaries were not the force they had once been. They were no longer as exclusive, as élitist, or as disciplined as in the first days of Ottoman power in Europe. They had long since been allowed to marry, then they had been allowed to admit their own children to their ranks, and finally other Muslim children had also been allowed to become janissaries.

Another effect of the decline of the *timar* system was the disappearance of the *beglerbeg*, the official who had once been the commander in chief of the *spahis* in his area and at the same time entrusted with the civil governance of that area. He was replaced by the *vali*. The *vali*'s main task was the collection of tax revenue in his allotted district and there were few restrictions on the way he could go about achieving this objective. The appearance of the *vali* was in part a consequence of the intensifying financial crisis which faced the Ottoman empire in the sixteenth and seventeenth centuries. The burden was in large measure the consequence of the almost constant state of war in which the empire found itself, but this burden was made less easy to bear because as the European–Asian trade routes shifted from land to sea the empire lost revenue levied on goods in transit. Nor did it benefit from the opening of western Europe's links with the Americas, not least because it suffered greatly from the inflation which followed. Increased military expenditure without a concomitant increase in revenue merely compounded the inflationary problem. The government naturally did all it could to maximise revenues and the tax burden which in the beginning of the seventeenth century had been approximately a third of the average value of family property in the Bulgarian lands was by the end of the century over four-fifths of that value.

A minor but useful source of revenue for the Sublime Porte was that derived from the bribes which those appointed to important offices were expected to donate to the government. The highest religious dignitaries were state appointees and they paid handsomely to assume their posts, no-one more so than the head of the Orthodox church, the patriarch of Constantinople. In the financial crisis of the seventeenth century the Porte would use any excuse to remove a patriarch and thus raise another bribe from his successor. By the end of the century only the wealthiest Greek families could afford high office; most of these Greeks were resident in the Phanar district of Constantinople, then, much in contrast to the present day, one of the wealthiest districts in the city. The 'Phanariots' thus came to dominate the patriarchate. Because ecclesiastic appointments in the provinces also required financial sweeteners, the policy whereby wealthy locals, again usually Greeks, came to dominate the church was repeated. Each cleric expected to recoup his expenses from those below him and this process percolated down until the burden fell eventually upon the ordinary villager and town-dweller. So onerous were church taxes in the seventeenth century that Orthodox bishops frequently used Ottoman troops to help collect them.

The sale of office and therefore the concentration of high posts in the hands of the financially capable also affected the civil administration. Here again it was the Greeks of the Phanar who could pay the most and it was they in the eighteenth century who came to dominate the Ottoman administrative system as well as the Orthodox church. But not even the undoubted ability of the Phanariots could save the Ottoman empire from decline. The pace of that decline accelerated during the eighteenth century and from it eventually emerged the seeds of the Bulgarian national revival.

4

The national revival
and the liberation

The *vûzrazhdane*, or national revival, is a phenomenon in which the Bulgarians take considerable and justifiable pride. As a historic process the revival was long and complicated with economic, social, cultural and psychological factors interweaving in intriguing and complex patterns. The first calls for a cultural revival were made by a small number of 'awakeners' in the eighteenth and very early nineteenth centuries, but though they saw the need for a revival they had no concept of what form it might take. The cultural revival, when it did take place, was made possible by the profound economic, social and political changes which overcame the Ottoman empire in the eighteenth and early nineteenth centuries. The manner in which the cultural revival was transformed into a national revival with its own institutions, first ecclesiastical and then political, was the work of the activists who emerged from the economic recovery and the cultural revival.

THE AWAKENERS

The seminal work of the Bulgarian national revival was that of Paiisi, a monk in the monastery of Hilendar on Mount Athos. Paiisi Hilendarski was born in the town of Bansko in 1722. In 1745 he entered Hilendar where after a few years he became a *taxidiot* and as such travelled around the Bulgarian lands on monastery business. His travels left a deep impression of the tribulations of the ordinary people and of the inferior status of the Bulgarians *vis-à-vis* the

45

Greeks. As a natural scholar Paiisi seems to have become almost obsessed with the contrast between the present low standing of Bulgarian culture and its glorious past, a past with which he had become familiar through his avid reading of history; Paiisi is known to have travelled in 1761 as far as Sremski Karlovac in the Habsburg monarchy where he consulted copies of Russian manuscripts. In 1762, exhausted and ill, he moved from Hilendar to the nearby monastery of Zograf, where he consulted an earlier history of the Bulgarians. All this experience and learning he poured into his own great work, *A Slavonic-Bulgarian History of the Peoples, Tsars, Saints, and of all their Deeds and of the Bulgarian Way of Life*. Written in Old Church Slavonic but with the enlivening addition of some contemporary spoken forms, the book recalled the lost and great days of the mediaeval Bulgarian state and church. The work looked both backwards and forwards because together with his evocation of past greatness Paiisi warned of the dangers for the future posed by the Bulgarians' capitulation to hellenisation and he called upon his contemporary co-nationals to change their attitudes, to stand firm against Greek influences, and to 'keep close to your heart your race and your Bulgarian homeland'. He pointed out why there was reason to be proud of that homeland:

of all the Slav peoples the must glorious were the Bulgarians; they were the first who called themselves tsars, the first to have a patriarch, the first to adopt the Christian faith, and they it was who conquered the largest amount of territory. Thus, of all the Slav peoples they were the strongest and the most honoured, and the first Slav saints cast their radiance from amongst the Bulgarian people and through the Bulgarian language.

Given this glorious past, said Paiisi, the Bulgarians need not feel inferior to the Greeks, quite the contrary:

But, they say, the Greeks are wiser and more cultured, while the Bulgarians are simple and foolish and have no refined words. That is why, they say, we had better join the Greeks. But ... There are many peoples wiser and more glorious than the Greeks. Is any Greek foolish enough to abandon his language and his teaching and his people as you abandon yours ...? Bulgarian, do not deceive yourself, know your own nation and language and study in your own tongue.

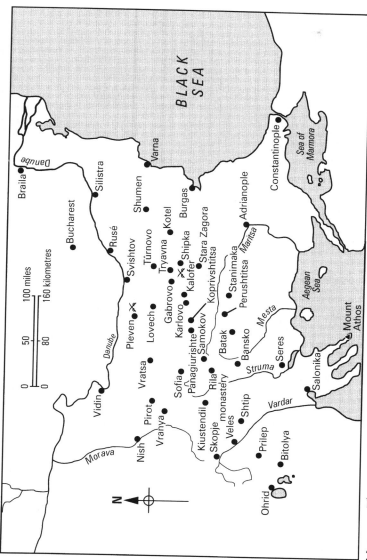

Map 4.1 The national revival.

In the mid-1760s Paiisi took to the roads again, this time primarily to propagandise his manuscript which had been, he said, written 'for the ordinary Bulgarian' and for 'the benefit of the whole Bulgarian nation'. In 1765 in Kotel he met Sofronii Vrachanski (of Vratsa) who was so impressed with the *History* that he had it copied and placed in his church. Paiisi's work was much copied in subsequent decades and at least fifty copies are now extant, but knowledge of its author faded. When a printed version of the great text appeared in 1844 in Budapest, it was as an anonymous work; not until 1871 did Marin Drinov, Bulgaria's first modern, professional historian, reidentify Paiisi as the author.

Until Drinov's identification of Paiisi the most notable of the awakeners was Yuri Venelin, a Habsburg subject and pioneer Slavicist who did much to rediscover the Bulgarian language and bring it to the notice of foreign scholars. Born in 1802 in Ruthenia, Venelin had been schooled in theology in Hungary but this he abandoned for history which he read at the University of Lemberg (Lvov). In 1829 he published *The Ancient and Present-Day Bulgarians in their Political, Ethnographic and Religious Relationship to the Russians. Historical-Critical Researches*. The main purpose of the book was to argue that the Bulgarians were of Slavic rather than Turkic origin. This argument gained as few supporters as his call for Bulgarian to be made into a virtual dialect of Russian.

The importance of Paiisi and his fellow awakeners lay not so much in their roles as creators of the national revival as in the fact that they provided *post facto* explanations for it. By the time Paiisi was widely read, let alone reidentified as the author of the *History*, the cultural revival was well under way. What prompted Bulgarians to call for more recognition of their cultural identity was not so much a consciousness of the past gained from reading Paiisi or one of the other awakeners, but contact with the world outside the Bulgarian lands, a contact gained through commerce, through education abroad, through the seepage of modern ideas into the Balkans during and after the French Revolution, and through participation in or knowledge of the Serbian and Greek revolts against rule from Constantinople. And few if any of these developments would have taken place without the upheavals experienced in the Ottoman

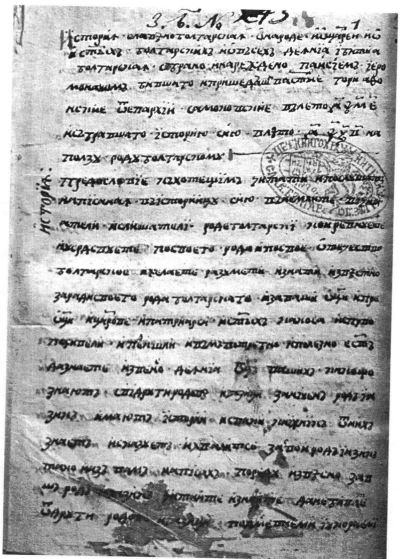

Plate 4.1   A page of Paiisi's great history. The original of the manuscript was returned to Bulgaria after the revolution of 1989, since when mystery surrounds its whereabouts.

Plate 4.2   Sofronii Vrachanski, a self portrait.

empire in the late eighteenth and early nineteenth centuries, upheavals which both delayed the spread of the awakeners' ideas and yet brought about the profound economic, social and political changes without which those ideas could not have been translated into action.

ECONOMIC, SOCIAL AND POLITICAL CHANGE IN THE OTTOMAN EMPIRE

As the Ottoman empire contracted it became more open to trade with the rest of Europe. The treaty of Passarowitz allowed Habsburg subjects to use the Danube for commercial purposes and in the 1740s Britain and France were given trading concessions. By the third quarter of the eighteenth century Russia was becoming an increasingly important factor in Balkan affairs. The treaty of Kutchuk Kainardji of July 1774 gave Russia control of the northern Black Sea littoral, but more importantly it allowed Russian trading vessels to operate in the Black Sea and to pass through the Straits into the Mediterranean. The treaty also sanctioned the opening up of the Danube to Russian traders.

Even more important than its commercial provisions were those clauses of the treaty of Kutchuk Kainardji which gave permission for the construction of a Russian Orthodox church in Constantinople and which extended to the ruler of Russia vaguely defined rights to protect Orthodox Christians in the Ottoman empire. The 'Eastern Question' which so plagued nineteenth-century European diplomacy had been born; in it the emergence of a new Bulgarian nation and eventually of a new Bulgarian state was to play an integral part.

The Ottoman empire's reduced international power was inextricably linked with a deterioration in its internal cohesion. Throughout the century the quality of Ottoman administration was in decline. Tax farming spread to the detriment of the peasant; the janissaries became less and less disciplined as their numbers increased; and in some areas commercial agriculture appeared with the production of cash crops such as cotton, and in these areas the exploitation of the peasants increased considerably. The most serious problem, particularly in the second half of the century, was the failure of the central government to control the *ayans*. The *ayans* were overmighty subjects. In origin they could be local officials who had simply turned their area of responsibility into a personal fiefdom – the pasha of Salonika, for example, collected the sum of 360,000 groschen in one year from his territory; they could be janissaries who had done much the same; they might be local figures who had accumulated sufficient wealth through agriculture, usury or trade to establish political as well as economic domination in an area; or they might be members of a traditionally influential clan or family. The most famous amongst them were Ali Pasha of Yanina, who ruled over southern Albania and northern Greece, and Osman Pasvantoglu, who controlled over two hundred villages in the Vidin region, but there were many others such Ismail Trestenikioglu in Rusé and Ikilikioglu in Silistra. The rise of the *ayans* led to a virtual breakdown in central government in the Balkans, a period known in Bulgarian as the *kûrdjaliistvo*. Its effects on the villagers of Vilitsa in southern Macedonia in the 1780s were described by the English traveller E. D. Clarke:

They are at present in a most wretched condition, owing to the extortions of *Ali Pasha*, or of those who have plundered in his name. In the short space of six months, they had paid to his tax-gatherers, as they told us, eighty purses, a sum equivalent to forty thousand piastres. Poverty is very apparent in their dwellings ... Nor can it be otherwise, where the wretched inhabitants are so oppressed by their lords. The whole of the earnings of the peasant is here taken from him; he is scarcely allowed any means of subsistence. Add to this the frequent calamities of sickness and fire, and 'plague, pestilence and famine' will be found to have done their work. This village has been twice burned within one year by *banditti* ...

The beginnings of the *kûrdjaliistvo* can be seen in the 1770s but it reached its culmination in the 1790s and 1800s. In 1791 Sultan Selim III attempted to introduce a reform programme which would re-establish central authority but the *ayans* proved too strong for him, and his failure merely intensified the process he had endeavoured to check. In 1792 there were large numbers of inadequately controlled Ottoman soldiers milling around in the Balkans at the conclusion of the war of 1787–92 against Russia; and in 1793 a rebellion took place in the Rhodope area under the leadership of Mehmed Sinap. In 1804 it was the conduct of local *ayans* which precipitated the revolt by various clan and village elders in Serbia, a revolt which was to lead to an autonomous and eventually an independent Serbia. In subsequent years the disorders were more noticeable to the north of the Balkan mountains but they were still disturbing much of Thrace in the 1800s whilst most of the Plovdiv district was under the sway of Kara Mustafa in 1810–12; even as late as 1816 much of the Adrianople area was beyond the reach of the central government and around Burgas the only effective authority was a band of brigands some three hundred strong.

The upheavals of the late eighteenth and early nineteenth centuries, and especially the wars, had a profound effect on the demographic composition of the Bulgarian lands, and on the distribution of the Bulgarian peoples.

The eighteenth century had seen an increase in the Bulgarian population in the towns. Some scholars in the past have attributed this to declining levels of health amongst the Turks, and one traveller believed that abortion, a widespread practice amongst Muslims in the seventeenth century, was a major reason for the enfeeblement of the Turks. In fact, there is little hard evidence that the absolute as opposed to the relative number of Turks in the towns did fall. More Bulgarians came into the towns because trade and manufacturing were expanding and, in some cases, because life in the countryside was beginning to become insecure. The *kûrdjaliistvo* speeded up this process but it did so selectively. The *kûrdjaliistvo* affected mainly the plains – the word derives from a Turkish one meaning fields or plains – and those threatened by it therefore sought refuge in the small mountain towns which were less likely to receive the unwelcome attention of the *ayans* and their hangers-on. This was an important development because the mountain towns were predominantly Bulgarian whereas those in the lowlands were much more likely to be subject to strong Greek cultural pressures. The flight to the mountains therefore tended to save Bulgarians not only from the unruly Muslim *ayans* but also from the hellenising forces which had been operating in many towns in the eighteenth century. At the same time, the insecurity of the lowland settlements increased the economic potential of those towns which remained less affected by the disorders, i.e. the Bulgarian mountain towns. They were to become of great importance when peace and security returned after the 1820s.

Some Bulgarians, however, fled much further afield than the mountain towns. As in the past, the end of a war produced a wave of emigration, not least because past experience had taught that the Ottoman authorities were likely to take revenge on any area which had showed sympathy with the sultan's enemies. After each major conflict huge numbers of Bulgarians emigrated, usually joining departing Russian troops. Precise figures are impossible to give, but after the treaty of Kutchuk Kainardji an estimated 160,000 Bulgarians left and after the wars of 1806 to 1812 the number was in the region of 100,000. After the Russo-Turkish war of 1828–9 there was emigration on a massive scale from eastern Bulgaria south of the Balkans, with some estimates putting the numbers of those who left as high as a quarter of a million. This seems to be a huge figure but many travellers in subsequent years attest to the depopulated state of this area.

The departing Bulgarians settled in what is now Romania, southern Ukraine and Russia. The communities they formed were to play an important part in the later development of Bulgarian culture, none more so than that in Braila, Romania, whose first Bulgarian *émigrés* had been those fleeing after the abortive Tûrnovo rising of 1598. The Bulgarians of Bucharest were also to become powerful and influential in later years, whilst the many thousands who settled further north are still a distinct ethnic group in the republic of Moldova.

The upheavals which beset the Ottoman empire in Europe between the 1770s and the 1820s cut short what had been promising economic growth for the Bulgarians. By the third quarter of the eighteenth century trade was noticeably better than it had been fifty or twenty-five years previously. There were Bulgarian trading concerns with links to Buda, Vienna, Venice, Livorno, Marseilles, Leipzig, Braşov and Odessa, and in most of these cities there were small Bulgarian colonies. In the Vardar valley cotton was being produced for sale in distant markets such as Leipzig, Dresden and Vienna and resident cotton merchants from these and other central European cities were to be found in a number of Balkan towns. Some of this cotton was shipped out through the Mediterranean but most of it went all the way to central Europe by pack horse or was taken thus to Danubian ports such as Vidin or Svishtov. With tobacco, cotton formed the most important export commodity produced in the Bulgarian lands in the eighteenth century, though wax was also exported to western Europe as was some of the rice grown in the Maritsa valley. A commodity with a more limited market appeal was *aba*, a coarse-grained cloth produced by many Bulgarian guilds in towns such as Stara Zagora, Kalofer, Karlovo, Plovdiv, Sliven and others. Another lucrative occupation was animal husbandry. Centres such as Constantinople and Adrianople with their large Muslim populations consumed considerable quantities of meat, particularly mutton, and the Bulgarian sheep raisers who supplied them became wealthy; many inhabitants of Kotel in the Balkan mountains spent their time rearing sheep in the Dobrudja plains and then driving them to market in the cities to the south of the Balkan range. The profits from animal husbandry greatly outstripped those from arable farming in part because the government exercised a monopoly over the grain trade, buying in the domestic market at low prices and strenuously forbidding exports. The *kûrdjaliistvo* interrupted but did not destroy their established trade which recovered rapidly as soon as order had been restored. It was upon the wealth thus created that the Bulgarian cultural revival was built.

The *kûrdjaliistvo* had a much more lasting impact on the efficiency of the Ottoman war machine as had become apparent during the war of 1806–12 against Russia. When the war was concluded the Porte could not yet turn its full attention to the reform of the army because first it had to deal with the Serbian rebellion. In doing so it greatly strengthened central authority in the empire. By 1814 the original Serbian leader had been defeated and in the following two years an arrangement was finally made by which a small area around Belgrade was left free to administer its own affairs. The appearance of the Serbian danger, however, had sobered the local *ayans* who had made the *kûrdjaliistvo*, as did the military expedition sent into Vidin to subdue Pasvantoglu's successor. The Bulgarian lands were the first to benefit from this move back towards order and stability because they were those nearest to Constantinople. By 1820 in the Balkans the only warlords outwith the control of the Porte were the Albanian rulers of Yanina and Scutari.

Just as operations to subdue these remnants of the *kûrdjaliistvo* were beginning the Greek revolt broke out in Wallachia and the

Peloponnese in 1821. The revolt once more threw the Ottoman empire and the Balkans into turmoil but once again the result was an ultimate strengthening rather than a weakening of central power, even if that power extended to a smaller area, and even before the small Greek kingdom emerged in 1830 the Ottoman empire had embarked upon a thoroughgoing process of reform.

One cause of the *kûrdjaliistvo* had been the rebelliousness of the janissaries. They had continued to proliferate in the eighteenth century and their discipline seemed to be in inverse proportion to their numbers. By the end of the century they had become a vast force which, like any debased praetorian guard, had become a byword for intrigue and corruption. They also fiercely resisted any attempt to reform the machinery of the army and government, knowing that any attempt at the restoration of central power and the return to anything approaching honest government must involve an attack upon their powers and their privileges. The war of 1806–12 had shown that the janissaries were also now woefully inadequate and hopelessly outdated as a military force. In June 1826 Sultan Mahmud II, taking advantage of a respite from international pressure on the Greek question, at last seized the janissary nettle. In a swift and bloody operation he liquidated the corps. Thousands were sent to exile in Asia Minor but between five and six thousand were slaughtered in Constantinople itself. It was the first step towards the radical reform which the Ottoman empire clearly needed.

THE BACKGROUND TO THE BULGARIAN CULTURAL REVIVAL

The destruction of the janissaries had two results which in the long run greatly affected the Bulgarians. First, to replace the janissaries the sultan and his ministers decided to create a regular army on the European model. Such an army had to be fed and clothed. And it was primarily to the rearers of sheep and the producers of cloth in the Bulgarian lands that the Porte looked for its sources of supply. The sheep-rearers rapidly grew more wealthy, as did the manufacturers of *aba* and those of *gaitan*, the decorative lace used to adorn uniforms, primarily those of the officers. The large-scale purchase of *aba* and *gaitan* began in the late 1820s and in 1848 the Porte concluded a commercial agreement with the *aba* guilds. The need for *aba* was so great that in order to meet it the Ottoman government in the late 1830s built a factory, its first, at Sliven, whilst in the following decade a private mill began operating near Plovdiv.

The second effect of the dissolution of the janissary corps and the setting up of the regular army was to increase pressure for a fundamental reform of the landowning system in the empire. This was still, in theory at least, tied to the need to produce *spahis* for the sultan's forces, a need obviated by the creation of the regular army. The usefulness of the *spahi* as a military factor had been in decline throughout the eighteenth century but the profits to be gained from the land he held had increased, and did so even more rapidly after the foundation of the army had multiplied the returns on sheep-rearing. Thus as the military reasons for a *spahi* holding lands disappeared the economic incentives for him to retain it strengthened. The *spahi* had originally collected a tithe from his tenants in order to furnish troops for the sultan but now that this function had been discontinued it was the state which had to collect the rent from the *spahi* lands. In fact there was no longer any justification for the continuation of the *spahi* system, and during the 1830s it was gradually dismantled. New tenancy agreements were drawn up and though the Ottoman officials generally attempted to carry out this task with fairness and efficiency tensions were sometimes created, especially in the north- and south-west of the Bulgarian lands where tenancies were particularly complicated. At the same time the judicial powers once exercised by the *spahi* were transferred to state officials, whilst the remaining *spahis* were given a pension and sent into retirement. The *spahis'* pensions were to be funded by a yearly sum paid by each peasant. This occasioned much resentment which, together with the suspicions created by the introduction of the revised tenancy arrangements, added another social factor to the evolution of the Bulgarian national revival. However, agrarian unrest, though it was present, especially in the western regions, was never a dominant feature of the *vûzrazhdane* and in later years the political programmes produced by the nationalists made little or no mention of it.

Whilst the peasantry in the north- and south-west still encountered difficulties many merchants and manufacturers grew ever more wealthy. Their new prosperity was reflected in the increasingly opulent houses they built. The splendid vernacular architecture of Kotel, Plovdiv, Koprivshtitsa and other towns which the modern tourist can enjoy was almost always the product of the economic revival of the second and third quarters of the nineteenth century.

Wealth was accumulated not merely by individuals. In the successful manufacturing and trading ventures economic activity remained predominantly under the control of the *esnafs* or guilds. By the 1830s they were beginning to have their own disposable surpluses and these they tended to spend on what may be broadly defined as 'public works'. Under the strict rules of the early Ottoman empire Christian villages were not allowed to erect buildings for public use and thus in most communities even the churches were small and insignificant. With greater political and social freedom, and with the necessary funds, guilds in the 1830s and thereafter frequently invested in new church buildings, the old, single-aisle edifice usually being replaced by a much larger, three-aisle structure. Monasteries, whose incomes were often already rising as returns from their lands increased, also benefited from the generosity of the guilds, and one of the great symbols of the Bulgarian cultural renaissance was the rebuilding of Rila monastery after a disastrous fire in 1833. In addition to religious foundations local civic institutions were also beneficiaries of the economic boom. Covered markets replaced the old open-air stalls; fountains were installed, and, most typically, a clock tower was erected in the centre of the community; it gave the time according to the Christian as opposed to the Muslim clock and was therefore a symbol of cultural self-assertion and modernity as well as a material attestation of recent attainments.

THE CULTURAL REVIVAL: EDUCATION, LITERACY
AND LITERATURE

A further outlet for charitable investment was in education, be it in the form of school buildings or public reading-rooms, in equipment such as books, or, in later years, in scholarships for gifted children to study away from home, frequently in Europe; in 1867 the city of Plovdiv was financing five students in Paris, four in Vienna, seven in Russia, two in Britain, and forty in Constantinople.

Plate 4.3   National revival buildings: a clock tower in Zlatitsa. Wealth accumulated by merchants was frequently expended on buildings such as these; a clock tower bore national significance in that it relayed time according to the Christian rather than the Muslim system.

Without the educational movement the Bulgarian national revival would have been impossible. The cell schools which had appeared in monasteries and then spread to some villages had not entirely disappeared but by the 1820s they were widely recognised as inadequate for a nineteenth-century community. Consciousness of the need to expand and reshape education came from a variety of sources. A number of Bulgarians had already received education abroad, most of them in Russia, but a few had graduated from Prague and other Slavic centres in central Europe. The French Revolution and the Napoleonic wars had also brought the concept of secular education into the Balkans. Some revolutionary literature had spread to Wallachia, Moldavia and elsewhere, and for a while the French had even occupied parts of Dalmatia and the Ionian islands; and the latter after 1815 were to remain under British trusteeship until 1864. Some adventurous Bulgarians had taken part in the Greek war of independence and here again they had come into contact with new, western ideas, all of which depended on popular education if they were to be spread amongst the Balkan peoples. After the Greeks achieved independence a number of Bulgarian students went to schools or universities in Greece; such experiences only underlined the need for more education for the Bulgarians.

In 1824, Neofit Bozveli, a monk and a former pupil of Sofronii Vrachanski, had introduced some Slav liturgical training into the seminary at Svishtov but for many younger Bulgarians the desire was now that education in their own language should be secular as well as religious. However, it was not until a decade later, in 1834 in Gabrovo, that the first lay school teaching in Bulgarian was established. The Gabrovo school had been set up by Vasil Aprilov and taught on the Bell-Lancaster system in which older children taught the younger ones. Thereafter the number of schools increased gradually until 1840, when thirteen had been established, but after 1840 the pace of growth accelerated and by 1850 most Bulgarian communities of any size had a school teaching in the vernacular. In 1840 in Pleven the first school for girls was opened and others followed rapidly. Although most schools could provide no more than primary education there were also a number of specialist schools for older pupils, including a commercial school at Svishtov, pedagogic schools in Prilep and Shtip, and theological schools in Samokov and at the

Plate 4.4 National revival buildings: the school in Karlovo first built in 1848 with funds provided by the local community. The photograph shows the building after restoration.

Petropavlovsk monastery near Lyaskovets. By the liberation in 1878 there were an estimated two thousand schools in Bulgaria. Almost all of them were financed either by local guilds or by the village council or its urban equivalent.

This pedagogic achievement is all the more remarkable in view of the low level from which the educational movement began. In the 1820s there were no teaching materials. In 1824 in Braşov Petûr Beron had published his *Riben Bukvar* (Fish ABC), so-called because of the motif on its back cover. Like the Greek books on which it was modelled the *Riben Bukvar* was a compendium of grammatical instruction and general information and it was not ideally suited to classroom use. Others followed, again most of them based on Greek models, but the production of standard teaching manuals was almost impossible when there was no standard orthography or grammar. The early monastic writers had not been consistent even within the confines of a single text, and when the nature of 'correct' Bulgarian grammar was first discussed there were widespread dis-agreements over such issues as whether the written language should retain the case endings which were disappearing as a feature of spoken Bulgarian, and whether the post-substantive definite article, universally used in the spoken form, should be a feature of the literary language. Venelin argued that the post-substantive article should be jettisoned to make Bulgarian more akin to other Slavonic languages, especially Russian. His arguments were fiercely rejected by later educational activists such as Ivan Bogorov who was ever vigilant against Russian gaining too much influence over his native tongue. In 1844 a grammar published by Bogorov did find widespread acceptance. When, in the 1870s, agreement was finally reached on a standard literary form, one which was based on the Gabrovo dialect with a few west-Bulgarian additions, it was a victory for the Bogorov tendency rather than the small Venelin school. By then elementary literacy was widespread amongst the younger generation of Bulgarians.

In addition to schools the spread of literacy and education was aided by the *chitalishta*. The English translation of this word is usually 'Reading Rooms' but it is inadequate. The German 'Kulturheime' and the cumbersome English 'Community Centres' come nearer to capturing the essence of this particularly Balkan institution. The *chitalishta* provided books and newspapers as well as places in which to read them, but they were also used to stage plays, to conduct meetings, and to present lectures. In many of them adults were taught the rudiments of reading and writing and in later years they were convenient venues for secret, conspiratorial gatherings. The first *chitalishta* had been established in Serbia and the first to appear in the Bulgarian lands was that in Svishtov in 1856. They spread rapidly and by 1878 there were 186 of them. Ivan Vazov, Bulgaria's leading nineteenth-century literary figure, described the *chitalishta* as 'Bulgaria's ministry of national education'.

By the time the Svishtov *chitalishte* was established the publication of books, newspapers and journals was expanding rapidly. But such expansion had initially been slow and spasmodic. The first book published in Bulgarian is now generally agreed to be Sofronii Vrachanski's collection of sermons, *Nedelnik* (from the word for Sunday) which appeared in Bucharest in 1806. Between that year and 1834 an average of less than one book per year was published with the largest number in any single year being three.

Again, however, the pace of growth intensified with the economic recovery of the 1820s and thereafter, with 9 books being published between 1821 and 1830, 42 between 1831 and 1840, 143 between 1841 and 1850, 291 between 1851 and 1860, and 709 between 1861 and 1870.

Many of these books, particularly in the earlier years, were published outside the Ottoman empire and were mainly teaching manuals and textbooks, but other literature became more common as printing facilities multiplied. The first Bulgarian printing press in the Ottoman empire did not appear until 1840 and then it was in Smyrna (Izmir) in Asia Minor; it was owned by a Greek who had imported Slav type from the United States at the request of the British and Foreign Bible Society. In the same year a Bulgarian press was established in European Turkey; located in Salonika it was again primarily religious in function, mass producing for the first time vernacular Bulgarian bibles and other religious items. The Smyrna press was also used for secular purposes. In 1844 Konstantin Fotinov used it when he began printing *Liuboslovie* (Love of Words). This was the first Bulgarian periodical, though it was to last no more than two years, failing partly because it was written in an archaic form of Bulgarian. The first periodical in Bulgarian to have anything more than an ephemeral existence was *Tsarigradski Vestnik* (Constantinople Gazette) which was edited by Ivan Bogorov and produced in the imperial capital on printing presses acquired by the city's Bulgarian community. It first appeared in 1848 and ran until 1861. Such longevity was exceptional and before the liberation few periodicals or newspapers had anything more than a short existence. Of the ninety such items which appeared between 1844 and 1878 thirty-three lasted for less than a year and only ten survived for over five years. Of those ninety items, fifty-six were newspapers and thirty-four periodicals; thirty-four of the ninety were published in the Ottoman empire and fifty-six by Bulgarian communities in other countries. Of the latter forty-three (77 per cent) were published in Romania, twenty-one of them in Bucharest and thirteen in Braila.

A significant role in the sponsoring of education and the cultural revival which followed it was played by a number of learned societies. As early as 1823, in Braşov, Vasil Nenovich had founded the

Philological Society to promote the use of Bulgarian as a literary medium and to stimulate the publication of books in Bulgarian, but clearly with no agreement on a standard literary form and with no available presses he was destined to disappointment. A much better timed and more successful venture was the Society for Bulgarian Literature founded in Constantinople in 1856; between 1857 and 1862 it published the bi-weekly journal *Bûlgarski Knizhitsi* (Bulgarian Papers), which at the height of its popularity had as many as 600 subscribers. The most important and successful of such societies, however, was the Bulgarian Literary Society founded in Braila in 1869 from which was to emerge the Bulgarian Academy of Sciences.

The spread of education and literacy meant the creation of a new element in Bulgarian society: the intelligentsia. Composed of priests and professional groups, above all teachers, the intelligentsia maintained strong links with the peasantry from which it mostly came. The sturdy alliance of intelligentsia and peasantry was the basis of the successes which the Bulgarian nation was to achieve in the second half of the nineteenth century.

The cultural revival went further than education and the spread of literacy. In the 1840s there was the first attempt to produce a modern Bulgarian literature, especially in poetry, where the early efforts of Dobri Chintulov pointed to the glories that were to follow in subsequent years. By the 1870s Hristo Botev, soon to lose his life in the political struggle, was also writing poetry of real worth. In the 1840s Bulgarian art began to break away from the formalism which had characterised most of it in the last century or more; new colours and previously neglected folk motifs enlivened even religious art, whilst secular painting at last found a figure of real stature in Zahari Zograf. Folk motifs also enhanced the output of the typically Bulgarian craft of wood-carving. In church music an identifiable Bulgarian form had emerged by the end of the eighteenth century and by the 1840s the first musical ensembles had been formed.

In the Bulgarian lands almost all forms of cultural and artistic activity were transformed in the years 1840 to 1860, but it was in the endeavour to establish a national church that these various forms of educational and cultural activity combined to precipitate the formation of the modern Bulgarian nation.

THE STRUGGLE FOR A SEPARATE BULGARIAN CHURCH

In the early eighteenth century most branches of civil administration in the Ottoman empire were dominated by the Phanariot Greeks. Nowhere was this more true than in the Orthodox church. The growing power and influence of the Greeks which had distressed and enraged Paiisi continued throughout the century. In 1766 the Serbian patriarchate at Peć was dissolved and in the following year the same fate befell the Bulgarian patriarchate in Ohrid. Church appointments at the higher levels had long been a virtual Greek monopoly but in the later eighteenth century there were numerous cases of Greek-speaking priests being nominated even for Bulgarian parishes.

It was not that the presence of Greek clerics or prelates necessarily provoked resentment or tension, and relations between Greek and Bulgarian were not always hostile. Greek bishops mediated successfully between disputing Bulgarian guilds, and if the Greek ecclesiastical authorities were suspicious of teaching in Bulgarian they were equally set against teaching in demotic Greek. Aprilov himself believed that Bulgarian should be taught not in place of but in addition to liturgical Greek, and both he and the first teacher at the Gabrovo school, Neofit Rilski, remained faithful members of the Greek patriarchate.

It is undoubtedly the case that in the first half of the nineteenth century, Paiisi's latent message notwithstanding, many Bulgarians who regarded themselves as cultured or educated preferred to speak Greek, believing this to be the mark of the enlightened person; and given the philhellenic hysteria in western Europe and the United States this was hardly surprising. But Greek also had its advantages in the Balkans as a widespread medium of commerce, and many guilds and trading concerns continued to use it and even keep their records in it into the second half of the nineteenth century. It was not until the 1850s that mounting disagreements over educational and religious issues forced the powerful Plovdiv guild of *aba* makers to split into separate Greek and Bulgarian sections.

The main area of friction between Greek and Bulgarian was the church. Originally this was because the Greek-dominated church was also widely corrupt. The practice of selling office and the percolation down of corruption which this had engendered were still very much in evidence at the end of the *kûrdjaliistvo*. In the 1820s many Bulgarian villages were paying to the church twice that which they were required to hand over in state taxes. As early as 1784 a Serb, Gerasim Zelić, had argued the need for Slav rather than Greek clerics, but it was not until the 1820s that action was taken in this regard. In 1820 the inhabitants of Vratsa refused to hand over their church taxes on the grounds that the local bishop, Metodi, was incorrigibly corrupt. There were few who would have disputed this contention but neither the Porte nor the patriarchate could tolerate such insubordination and the leaders of the Vratsa protest, most of them local merchants, were sentenced to long terms in exile by the Ottoman authorities. In 1825 a similar protest against the Greek bishop of Skopje was equally unsuccessful.

In the 1830s the nature of this incipient conflict began to change. A growing number of Bulgarian priests were being educated in Russia and their Slav consciousness was greater than those who had remained in the hellenist world of the Orthodox seminaries in the Balkans. When the see of Tûrnovo fell vacant in 1835 there was a concerted move to secure the nomination of a Bulgarian-speaking bishop. The move failed. Although it was supported by the Porte, it was opposed by the patriarchate. In 1839 the former issued the Hatt-i-Sherif, a declaration of intent which promised religious equality between Muslims and Christians; many Bulgarians chose to interpret it as also promising equality between themselves and the Greeks. In the 1840s the Bulgarians' protest became quite clearly one not against corrupt Greek bishops because they were corrupt; it was against Greek bishops because they were Greek. In 1841 there was an outburst of social unrest focused on Nish in the north-west of the Bulgarian lands; the demands produced by the rebels included one for 'bishops who at least can understand our language'. By the end of that decade there had been protests against Greek bishops in Rusé, Ohrid, Seres, Lovech, Sofia, Samokov, Vidin, Tûrnovo, Lyaskovets, Svishtov, Vratsa, Tryavna and Plovdiv.

The patriarchate refused to heed any of these demands, and it was increasing frustration at the obduracy of the church's rulers that forced Bulgarian communities into demanding the right to administer their own churches and appoint their own clergy. The movement was led by Neofit Bozveli and Ilarion Makariopolski, first in Tûrnovo and then in Constantinople. Initially they made little progress and both leaders were incarcerated, Neofit eventually dying in prison, but in 1849 came the first real breakthrough when the Porte agreed that the Bulgarians should be allowed to build a church in the Ottoman capital on land donated by Stefan Bogoridi, a wealthy local Bulgarian who had risen high in the Ottoman civil service and was a nephew of Sofronii Vrachanski. The church, St Stephen's, was dedicated the following year and was to become the focal point of Bulgarian cultural and political activity for the next two and half decades. The original church was replaced in 1890 by a building which is still to be seen in the Balat district of Istanbul, and which remains the cause of intermittent wrangles between the patriarchate and Bulgarian ecclesiastics.

The church established in 1848 was to be subject to the patriarch-ate in matters of dogma and ecclesiastical jurisdiction, and it was still to be a part of the Orthodox *millet* whose head, the patriarch, still represented the Orthodox community in its relations with the Ottoman authorities. The church, however, was to be the property of the Bulgarian people, was to conduct its services in Bulgarian, and was be to administered by a twenty-strong governing council which could appoint priests for the church. This governing council was the first new and specifically Bulgarian organisation to receive official recognition in the Ottoman empire since 1393.

There were few nationally conscious Bulgarians who did not now believe that the next step should be towards a fully separate Bulgarian church, an idea which was reinforced in 1850 when the Protestants, thanks to strong diplomatic support from Great Britain, had been granted their own *millet*. Much more importantly, in 1850 the patriarchate had finally been forced to recognise the Orthodox church in the Greek kingdom as an autocephalous institution. In 1851 the Bulgarian colony in Bucharest reflected a widespread feel-ing when it ended a circular letter to other Bulgarian communities with the phrase, 'Without a national church there is no salvation'.

The creation of the Protestant *millet* and the recognition of the church in Greece had shown that hopes for change were not unreal-istic, and these hopes were further encouraged by the widespread restructuring of Ottoman social and political institutions which had come about as a result of the dissolution of the *spahi* system. As part of its reforming programme the Porte expected the patriarchate to initiate changes, in particular to increase the influence of the laity within the Orthodox church. In predominantly Bulgarian areas an increase in lay influence could only mean an increase in Bulgarian influence. The patriarchate, however, was not disposed to give way to reformist pressures and would never contemplate a split in the Orthodox community, even more so after its defeat over the church in Greece controversy.

If they were to make any progress towards ecclesiastical independence it seemed the Bulgarians would need foreign sponsorship similar to that which the British had given to the Protestants. For many Bulgarians, especially those educated in Russia, the tsar seemed the obvious source of such backing, not least because Russia had consistently supported the call for the appointment of Bulgarian bishops to Bulgarian sees. But Russia, like the patriarch, did not want divisions in Orthodoxy, the purported right to protect whose adherents had since 1774 provided the justification for Russian diplomatic intervention in the Ottoman empire. Many Bulgarians were puzzled by the Russian position. To some degree their conundrum about Russia was eased by the latter's defeat in the Crimean war of 1854–6.

The war lessened Russian power and influence and it left the Bulgarians with a choice between pressing ahead on their own or finding an alternative sponsor. The former was always the more popular strategy. And it was one encouraged by the Hatt-i-Humayoun, the Porte's declaration of intent, issued at the conclusion of the war, to further reform the imperial administration.

In 1856 enthusiasts for the Bulgarian church cause decided to act alone, and presented the sultan with a petition asking for a separate church; the petition claimed to represent the 6.5 million Bulgarians living in the empire. In the same year, the Bulgarian communal council in Constantinople circulated a letter to all large Bulgarian communities asking them to send elected delegates to Constantinople to join in pressing for an independent church. These delegates, when they met in the imperial capital, constituted the first remotely representative body in modern Bulgarian history, and included in their number were many who were to achieve prominence in Bulgarian national affairs both before and after the liberation of 1878.

In 1857 the Porte ordered the patriarchate to institute a reform programme. In 1858 the patriarch agreed to call a council which was to include three Bulgarians; it was the first of seven such councils, all of them equally unproductive, to meet between 1858 and 1872. The Bulgarians suffered from a number of disadvantages. Despite the overwhelming popularity of their cause amongst the Bulgarian laity there were small but powerful elements in the Bulgarian clergy who were not prepared to split the Orthodox church; they included the abbot of the Rila monastery and two of the four Bulgarian bishops recently nominated by the patriarchate. Secondly, no official body created by the patriarchate would ever contain anything but an overwhelming Greek majority, and reform through official channels was therefore an illusion. Thirdly, the recognition of this truth strengthened for a while the minority who had always favoured the alternative strategy of seeking new forms of foreign sponsorship.

In 1860 matters came to a head. It was a time of further change in Europe, the Balkans and the Ottoman empire, a time which saw the emergence of a unified Italy, the unification of the Danubian provinces of Wallachia and Moldavia into Romania, and the intervention of the great powers to secure autonomy for the rebellious Ottoman provinces in Syria and Lebanon. In Constantinople 1860 witnessed a virtual declaration of ecclesiastical independence by the Bulgarian church. It happened on Easter Sunday in St Stephen's. According to a pre-arranged plan the congregation interrupted the priest, Bishop Ilarion Makariopolski, at that point in the service where he was to pray for the patriarch. The patriarch's name was omitted and Ilarion prayed directly for the sultan's welfare; this direct prayer was an implicit rejection of the patriarchate which was still legally the body through which all Orthodox Christians were represented to the imperial ruler. In the evening service, for which the customary patriarchal permission had not been secured, the Gospels were read in eleven different languages; Greek was not one of them.

Ilarion's bold move won widespread support amongst the Bulgarian communities. Thirty-three towns petitioned the sultan in support of Ilarion, as did over seven hundred merchants who had

Plate 4.5   Ilarion Makariopolski.

gathered for the annual fair in Uzundjovo. A number of bishops immediately aligned with the Constantinople church, including Gideon of Sofia who, though Greek, dared not offend the feelings of his flock. The events of Easter 1860 undoubtedly emboldened the Bulgarians. Veles broke away from the patriarchate, whilst the towns of Lovech, Samokov, Shumen, Preslav and Vidin all rejected bishops nominated by the patriarchate, even though those bishops were Bulgarian; in later years many Bulgarian communities refused to pay taxes to the patriarch, and by 1870 almost all the dioceses in Thrace, Macedonia and Bulgaria had committed some act of disobedience towards the patriarch.

The Easter declaration of independence in 1860, despite the widespread support it rapidly gained, did not bring official recognition of a separate Bulgarian church. The Porte did not wish to hasten to a conclusion a dispute which conveniently divided two of its major subject groups; the Russians remained reluctant to see any division in the patriarchate; and the patriarch himself was as adamantly opposed as ever to the loss of his Bulgarian flock, and, of course, the revenue he derived from it. Much more important, however, was the impact recognition of the Bulgarian church would have upon other non-Greek Orthodox communities. The Ottoman *millet* system had made cultural identity a consequence of religious affiliation; the Bulgarians wanted to reverse that order and make religious affiliation a consequence of national allegiance. Such a doctrine, if accepted, would fragment the Orthodox church in the Ottoman empire with Romanians, Vlachs and Albanians, as well as Serbs, making similar claims. Understandably, the status of the Bulgarian church now became the central theme in the seemingly endless councils and other discussions held in the higher ranks of the Orthodox church.

Those amongst the Bulgarians who had advocated internal action, the Bulgarian *fara da sè*, had hoped that a bold move such as that Ilarion had made would cut the Gordian knot, force St Petersburg to come off the fence, and free the Bulgarian church from its ties with the patriarchate. That Russia still did not back the call for an independent Bulgarian church inevitably strengthened the confidence of those who all along had believed that the Bulgarians would be better off finding alternative foreign sponsorship. The sponsor they had in mind was the Roman Catholic church; behind the Roman church stood the Habsburg empire and, more significantly, the France of Napoleon III whose taste for foreign adventures and entanglements had not yet been dulled by the Mexican fiasco. The association with Rome would be achieved by joining the Uniate church, which allowed former Orthodox communities to worship in their own language with rites identical to those of the Orthodox church; in return those communities would acknowledge the pope as head of the church.

Uniate propaganda had grown steadily in the 1850s, encouraged in part by Polish refugees in Constantinople and in part by the French and Sardinian successes in the Crimean war, and also by the support of Dragan Tsankov, an influential Bulgarian activist and Ottoman civil servant. In December 1860 a group of Bulgarians in Constantinople signed an act of union with Rome, and nominated as their leader an illiterate octogenarian, Josef Sokolski, who was soon to be personally invested with his new office by Pope Pius IX in Rome. It did not last. Within a few months Sokolski had reneged on his flock, reverting to Orthodoxy and taking ship at dead of night for Odessa. By June 1861 there was no-one in Constantinople who could perform the Bulgarian Uniate services, a situation not remedied until 1863 when Raphael Popov was appointed to the vacancy. He was thirty-five years of age.

The Uniate option was in later decades to be chosen by some Bulgarian communities in Macedonia but after 1861 it was a *non possumus* in Constantinople. The Sokolski fiasco forced the former advocates of Uniatism back to the conclusion that they had to find some form of compromise between the Bulgarians and the patriarchate. After years of hopeless debate a breakthrough came in 1867 when Patriarch Gregory VI offered the Bulgarians an autonomous church within the patriarchate; the church would be headed by an exarch, an ecclesiastical rank between that of archbishop and patriarch. For the first time the patriarch had recognised the Bulgarians' right to a church of their own and the settlement would have found favour with them but for its territorial provisions. The 1867 proposal confined the Bulgarian exarchate to the area north of the Balkans, and it made no mention of where the exarch would have his headquarters. This was an issue of cardinal importance because if the exarch were confined to the area north of the Balkans he and his church would have no influence amongst the Bulgarians of Macedonia and Thrace. The plan was rejected by the Bulgarians. It seemed like a return to square one.

The situation had however changed, primarily because of external developments which alarmed the Porte. There had been signs in the early and mid-1860s of an emergent Bulgarian political movement which was prepared to resort to arms to achieve its goals; the Austro-Prussian war had created instability which could easily spread into the Balkans and Prince Michael Obrenović of Serbia was busy trying to fashion a Balkan alliance in case it did; should the war spread that projected alliance might easily be founded on the territorial ambitions of Serbia, Montenegro and Romania, many of which could be fulfilled only at the cost of the Ottoman empire. Most important of all, however, was the 1866 insurrection in Crete. This fanned Greek territorial aspirations and rapidly led to a serious deterioration in Greek–Ottoman relations. This factor more than any other pushed the Porte towards the Bulgarians, whilst Russia moved reluctantly in the same direction because of its own worsening position in Athens and its fear that if the Bulgarians were much longer left unsatisfied they would turn again to Uniatism. In February 1870 the sultan issued a *firman*, or declaration of intent, to recognise a separate Bulgarian church headed by an exarch.

The rights of the new Bulgarian church, the exarchate, were not unlimited. Its liturgy still had to mention the patriarch, to whom it had to defer in matters of doctrine, and whose right to procure Holy Oil it had to respect. The territorial division was also of great importance. In 1869 Gavril Krŭstevich, a prominent Constantinople Bulgarian who worked in the Ottoman civil service, had submitted a plan for the division of the dioceses between the two churches. According to his scheme the exarchate would take twenty-five of them whilst the rest would remain within the patriarchate. The Bulgarian dioceses were generally to be larger than the patriarchist and were to cover almost all of Macedonia. Though Krŭstevich's scheme was used as the basis for the divisions contained in the 1870 *firman* the Bulgarian share had by that time been reduced to fifteen, namely Rusé, Silistra, Shumen, Tûrnovo, Sofia, Vratsa, Lovech,

Vidin, Nish, Pirot, Kiustendil, Samokov, Veles, Varna, and Plovdiv, although the latter two cities (the Virgin Mary quarter of Plovdiv excepted) were to remain within the patriarchate. Of the remaining fifty-nine dioceses fifty-one were to stay in the patriarchate and eight were to be divided. The 1870 settlement provided that a diocese should be allowed to transfer to the exarchate if two-thirds of its population voted in favour of such a move, but it said nothing on the question of where the exarch was to reside and have his headquarters. The Bulgarians, not for the last time in their modern history, could not rejoice over the territorial terms of a major settlement.

The 1870 declaration was rejected by the patriarch. Impasse had returned and it was to remain until 1872. In that year the patriarch called a patriarchal assembly to condemn the Bulgarians. In response the latter set about choosing an exarch, the choice falling on Bishop Antim of Vidin who was to reside in Constantinople. On 23 May 1872 he celebrated the liturgy in St Stephen's and then read a long proclamation of the independence of the Bulgarian church. In September the patriarch proclaimed a schism. The exarchate was condemned for the sin of phyletism, that is maintaining that ecclesiastical jurisdiction is determined not territorially but ethnically; the kernel of the problem was the seat of the exarchate because canon law contained the principle of there being only one prelate in any city.

In the struggle for the establishment of a separate Bulgarian church the modern Bulgarian nation had been created. The process had begun when, in conformity with the then largely unknown injunction of Paiisi, Bulgarians began to know their own nation and to study in their own tongue. They had since then developed a nation-wide educational system, they had produced their own intelligentsia, and they had pitted themselves against the Greek-dominated clerical hierarchy. The exarchate could now represent the interests of the Bulgarian nation in the Ottoman corridors of power; more importantly it could defend Bulgarian Orthodoxy against the patriarchate and against Uniatism in Macedonia, and sponsor Bulgarian churches and schools in the mixed dioceses and even in some which were still in the patriarchate.

Yet as the cultural revival moved towards its culmination in 1870 there was already a small body of Bulgarian activists for whom the political struggle had already become supreme. For them the goal was not simply the creation of a Bulgarian cultural nation represented in its church. Their aspirations were towards a political nation represented by its own political institutions within its own political borders.

THE STRUGGLE FOR POLITICAL INDEPENDENCE AND THE LIBERATION OF 1878

When Patriarch Gregory VI made his proposals for an autonomous Bulgarian church in 1867 he noted, 'With my own hands I have built a bridge to the political independence of the Bulgarians.' It was a prescient remark but one which would have puzzled his contemporaries, including the Bulgarians amongst them, because the political side of the Bulgarian national movement was little developed.

There had been political action by Bulgarians in the past. A number of Bulgarian volunteers fought with the Serbs between 1804 and 1814, and even more joined with Greeks in their war of independence in the 1820s. In May 1835 there was a small outburst against the Ottoman authorities in the Tûrnovo region but this so-called 'Velchov Rising' was easily suppressed and left little legacy behind it. In the 1840s and 1850s there were outbursts of social unrest in the north- and south-west of the Bulgarian lands, with serious clashes in Nish in 1841 and around Vidin a decade later, but again the outbursts were contained.

It was not until the 1860s that the first real signs of concerted political action were discernible. In 1862 the Serbs used force to drive the last Ottoman garrison, that in Belgrade, from their country. Taking part in the action was a small Bulgarian Legion led by Georgi Rakovski. Born in Kotel in 1821, Rakovski had attended a local cell school before receiving higher education in Constantinople. By the early 1840s he was already trying to form secret societies first in Athens and then in Braila. For the latter the Romanians sentenced him to death, but he escaped. In the Crimean war he tried to raise a Bulgarian force to assist the Russians but had little success, though during this period he did begin writing and publishing, fields in which he was soon to be prolific. After the Crimean war he wandered through Hungary, Romania and southern Russia before settling for a while in Belgrade. There he continued writing, particularly for the periodical *Dunavski Lebed* (Danubian Swan), and scheming to bring political liberation to the Balkan Christians; his vision was of a Balkan Christian federation. At the same time he formed the Bulgarian Legion which, however, was disbanded by the Serbs after the action against the Ottoman garrison in 1862.

Rakovski then moved to Bucharest where he continued his journalistic activities and also began organising small armed bands, *cheti*, of dedicated revolutionaries. His belief had always been that Ottoman power in the Balkans would be destroyed only by an armed uprising by its Christian subjects; the *cheti* would in the meantime harass Ottoman officials and raise national consciousness. In 1867 Rakovski also established a second Bulgarian Legion but it was to have little success, not least because Rakovski himself died that year, struck down by tuberculosis.

A more lasting creation of Rakovski's was the Bulgarian Secret Central Committee (BSCC) founded in 1866. The BSCC made the first sustained attempts to organise and equip *cheti* and early in 1867 two such bands crossed the Danube under the leadership of Panaiot Hitov and Filip Totiu. In 1868 more followed, this time led by Hadji Dimitûr Asenov and Stefan Karadja. They were soon dispersed. The BSCC meanwhile combined political pressure with military action. In 1867 it submitted a petition to the sultan suggesting a Bulgarian–Ottoman compromise on the model of that just reached between the Austrian and Hungarian components of the Habsburg monarchy. It was this combination of attempted military action and political sophistication which alarmed the Porte and made it more anxious to conclude a settlement of the Bulgarian church question.

Rakovski's greatest achievement was to establish the practice of conspiracy for political rather than cultural or ecclesiastical objectives. He left behind some accomplished followers, and leadership of the nascent revolutionary movement passed eventually to three of them: Liuben Karavelov, Vasil Levski and Hristo Botev.

Liuben Karavelov arrived in Bucharest in 1869. Born in 1834 in Koprivshtitsa he was educated there and in Plovdiv before making his way to Russia where he attended lectures in Moscow on history. In 1866 his association with the narodniks or 'populists' brought about his expulsion from Russia; in 1868 he fell foul of the Habsburg authorities who locked him up on suspicion of involvement in the murder of the pro-Austrian Prince Michael Obrenović of Serbia. By this time Karavelov had established himself as one of the foremost Bulgarian men of letters, having published numerous tracts and essays as well as a number of novels. Like Rakovski, Karavelov dreamed of a Balkan republic, and, again following Rakovski, he believed that Ottoman power could only be removed by a revolution of the Balkan Christians, but he dissented from Rakovski's view that the *cheti* would be the means by which that revolution would be brought about. Following the precepts of some Russian narodniks Karavelov argued that before a successful rising the people had to be educated, and this task could only be performed by a small number of trained and dedicated 'apostles'.

Vasil Levski not only shared this view; he acted upon it. Levski was a native of Karlovo in the foothills of the Balkan mountains where he was born in 1837. After initial schooling in his home town he went to Stara Zagora where he received training for the priesthood; in 1858 he entered a monastery. He remained there scarcely two years and after a short period as a teacher went to Belgrade where he joined the Bulgarian Legion and took part in the action of 1862. After the dissolution of the Legion he reverted for a short while to the monastic life, before resuming teaching and then returning to revolutionary activity as the standard bearer in Hitov's *cheta*. At the end of the 1860s he had become one of the most experienced and influential of the small group of Bulgarian political revolutionaries. By now he had also formulated his ideas clearly. He followed Karavelov in urging the need for apostles to prepare the people for their historic task, but he differed from most of his contemporaries when he insisted that it was hopeless to dream of foreign sponsorship or assistance: Bulgaria's liberation could be achieved only by the Bulgarians. Levski became a leading member of the Bulgarian Revolutionary Central Committee (BRCC) when it was established in April 1870, and he spent the next two years primarily occupied in setting up a network of secret organisations in Bulgaria. In 1872 he was arrested together with an accomplice. The latter, in an effort to prove he was a political prisoner, revealed details of the conspiracy in which he and Levski were involved. In February 1873 Levski was hanged in Sofia. He had once written, 'If I succeed, I shall succeed for the whole nation: if I fail, then I alone shall die', words which are now carved in huge letters on the monument outside the National Cultural Centre (NDK) erected in Sofia in the 1980s.

Hristo Botev was born in Kalofer in 1848, the son of teacher. He received his basic education at home before winning a scholarship to study in Odessa. He, like Karavelov, became influenced by and associated with the populists, and after a brush with the tsarist police returned to Kalofer in 1867. He taught in a number of schools and was profoundly influenced by the Paris Commune. In 1872 he was in Bucharest where he became involved with the Bulgarian revolutionaries. He never attained the same prominence in the organisational structures as Karavelov or Levski, but he was soon widely known and admired for his writing, above all for his poetry. He was to lose his life in the struggle for liberation in 1876. Of the three most notable heirs of Rakovski only Karavelov, who died in the second half of 1878, lived to see an independent Bulgaria.

The death of Levski was a shattering blow to the revolutionaries in Bucharest. Karavelov and the left-wing Botev could not cooperate and when the BRCC was reconstructed in 1875 Botev was not a member. A new figure in its inner circles was Georgi Benkovski, a brilliant organiser who had been born in Koprivshtitsa in the early 1840s. The Bulgarian lands were now divided into four revolutionary districts based on Tûrnovo, Vratsa, Sliven and Plovdiv.

In 1875 the Ottoman empire was facing difficulties in Bosnia where a revolt had broken out over changes in the taxation system. In the following year the disorders spread and were soon to lead to war between the empire and Serbia. To the Bulgarian revolutionary conspirators this seemed too good an opportunity to miss. In April 1876 leaders of the fourth revolutionary district met in Oborishte in the woods between Pangiurishte and Koprivshtitsa. After three days of discussion it was agreed that a simultaneous rising should be staged in all four districts; it was to begin in May. However, the Ottoman authorities learned of the preparations and sent an armed unit to Koprivshtitsa. The revolutionaries had decided at Oborishte that were this to happen the revolt would be brought forward and action was taken on 19 April. The April Uprising had begun. The

Plate 4.6 The greatest of Bulgaria's national activists and martyrs, Vasil Levski, born in Karlovo in 1837. This photograph is said to have been taken in 1870, three years before his execution in Sofia.

Plate 4.7   A wooden cannon captured from the Bulgarian insurgents by the Turks, January 1877.

insurgents had few arms and no heavy weapons, though some rudimentary cannons were fashioned from cherry trees.

In terms of its immediate achievements the April Uprising can hardly be judged other than a disastrous shambles. In the Sliven district no more than sixty men rallied to the revolutionaries' call, whilst in Tûrnovo there was little or no response except in a few monasteries. In the Vratsa district no-one at all joined the uprising. The major action here was when Botev, having hijacked an Austrian steamer on the Danube, landed with his *cheta* and advanced about twenty kilometres southwards. They were soon surrounded and slaughtered by *bashibazouks*, or Ottoman irregular detachments, many of whose members were Bulgarian Muslims, and who were being used extensively because the main body of the regular army was deployed against the Serbs.

If the rising in Sliven, Tûrnovo and Vratsa may be seen as farcical tragedy, in Plovdiv the tragedy was unalloyed. Here Benkovski and his flying column had been active and had persuaded a number of villages to throw in their lot with the revolutionaries. But Benkovski and his men were no match for the local *bashibazouks*. The latter wreaked a terrible vengeance on villages which had joined the rebels, particularly in Bratsigovo, Perushtitsa, and above all Batak

Plate 4.8   A contemporary Russian periodical described this as 'The peaceful visit of the *bashibazouks* to a Bulgarian village'.

where five thousand Bulgarian Christians, mostly women and children, were said to have been killed, many of them being herded into the local church and burned alive.

The April Uprising was over. It had not dislodged Ottoman power but it had irreversibly changed the nature of that power in Bulgaria. National consciousness which, in the political sense, had been at a low level was immeasurably raised; the moral power of the Porte, such as it was, had been destroyed. Furthermore, the nature of the Bulgarian question had been transformed. European newspapers had relayed the stories of the massacres in graphic detail and opinion had been outraged. In Russia, Britain, and elsewhere there were increasingly loud calls for action to prevent any further outrages. The Bulgarian question had become a European one.

In December 1876 the ambassadors of the European powers in Constantinople met to discuss a programme of reforms to be introduced into the Ottoman empire. Agreement on the contents of such a programme was not difficult to achieve, but it proved impossible to persuade the sultan to consent to European supervision of its application. In April 1877 Russia declared war on the Ottoman empire.

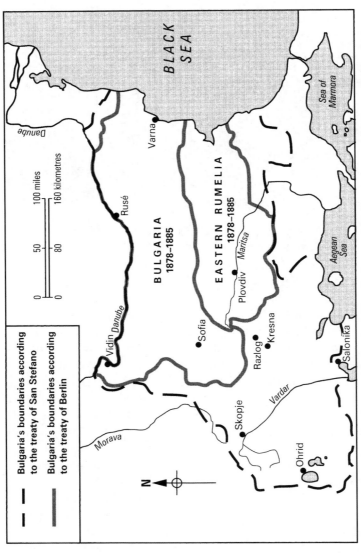

Map 4.2   Bulgaria according to the treaties of San Stefano and Berlin.

Most observers had expected an easy Russian victory but it did not come about. The Ottoman forces dug in in Pleven to the north of the Balkan mountains and could not be dislodged for five months. An advanced detachment of the Russian army under General Gurko did manage to take Tûrnovo and then force its way through the Balkan range only to be repulsed at Stara Zagora by a large Ottoman force recently returned from the war against Serbia. The Russian forces retreated to the Shipka pass where they were subjected to ferocious enemy attacks. The Russian commander was helped by the newly formed Bulgarian militia, the *opûlchenie*. When Pleven finally surrendered the Russians could advance with ease. In January 1878 Sofia was taken and in the following month a truce was signed at Adrianople. On 3 March a preliminary peace was signed at San Stefano.

The peace of San Stefano envisaged a vast new Bulgarian state stretching from the Danube in the north to the Rhodopes in the south, and from the Black Sea in the east to the Morava and Vardar valleys in the west; San Stefano Bulgaria included some of the Aegean coast, though not Salonika, and the inland cities of Skopje, Ohrid, Bitola and Seres. In territorial terms this was as much as any Bulgarian nationalist could have hoped for or even dreamed of.

It was, however, just what the statesmen of Britain and Austria-Hungary had feared. They saw the new Bulgaria as an enormous wedge of potential Russian influence in the Balkans and they demanded that the boundaries be redrawn. The treaty of Berlin of July 1878 satisfied British and Austro-Hungarian demands. San Stefano Bulgaria was dismembered. The Bulgarian principality was to be confined to a small area between the Balkan mountains and the Danube; the region between the Balkan mountains and the Rhodopes, southern Bulgaria, was to form a new autonomous unit of the Ottoman empire to be known as Eastern Rumelia; Macedonia was to return to Ottoman rule with a promise that its administration would be reformed; and the Morava valley in the north-west, including the important towns of Pirot and Vranya, was to go to Serbia.

The Bulgaria of the treaty of Berlin was 37.5 per cent of the size of the San Stefano variant. For every Bulgarian, however, the real Bulgaria remained that of San Stefano. The new Bulgarian state was to enter into life with a ready-made programme for territorial expansion and a burning sense of the injustice meted out to it by the great powers.

The peace of San Stefano and the treaty of Berlin differed little in their provisions for the internal structure of the new state. Bulgaria was to be a principality with a Christian prince who was to be elected by the Bulgarians and confirmed by the powers; he was not to be a member of a major ruling European dynasty. Bulgaria was to remain a vassal state of the sultan whose suzerainty it was required to acknowledge. The principality was to be allowed a militia but it was not to construct fortresses; it was to assume all the international obligations previously entered into by the Ottoman empire in terms of foreign debt payments, railway building, tariffs and the protection of foreign citizens through the so-called Capitulations. Before the prince was elected an assembly was to be convened at Tûrnovo to devise a new constitution for the principality.

Eastern Rumelia was to remain under the direct political and military authority of the sultan, though the latter was not allowed to billet *bashibazouks* in the province, nor was he to quarter passing Ottoman troops on the population. The maintenance of order was to be the responsibility of an Eastern Rumelian gendarmerie whose ethnic composition was to reflect that of the local population and whose officers were to be appointed by the sultan. The senior official in Eastern Rumelia was to be the governor general who was also to be appointed by the sultan, subject to confirmation by the signatory powers; his period of office was to be five years.

With the signing of the treaty of Berlin, despite its many shortcomings from the Bulgarian point of view, the modern Bulgarian state had been born. Unlike the Bulgarian church it was the creation more of external than internal forces.

5

The consolidation of the Bulgarian State, 1878–1896

THE CONSTITUENT ASSEMBLY AND THE TÛRNOVO CONSTITUTION

The assembly which was to devise Bulgaria's political system met in Tûrnovo in late February 1879. It contained a mixture of elected and nominated deputies, the latter including representatives of the Turkish, Greek and Jewish minorities.

The assembly also contained deputies from Bulgarian lands outside the new principality. This indicated that the great passion over borders had not subsided. Indeed, there had been attempts to rekindle the struggle in Macedonia. Activists in Bulgaria staged a rising in the Kresna-Razlog region of eastern Macedonia, but it was not well coordinated and was suppressed with ease. The territorial question, however, was still the first preoccupation of the delegates when they assembled in the mediaeval capital, and a vocal faction amongst them urged that they disperse and the assembly be disbanded; better, they argued, unity under Ottoman authority than a division of the nation between the free and the enslaved. Others supported this argument with suggestions that Bulgaria should seek a compromise similar to that granted to the Hungarians in 1867. A more moderate view urged that the Tûrnovo assembly be postponed rather than dissolved, and that the breathing space be used to draw up a petition which a delegation should then take around the European capitals. The Russians were embarrassed by all this. They feared that any postponement of the assembly might lead to international

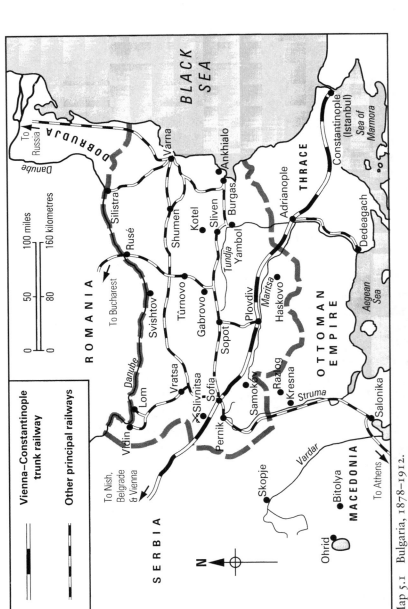

Map 5.1 Bulgaria, 1878–1912.

complications which, in their enfeebled post-war condition, they could not afford. The Bulgarians were told that it was not in the assembly's power to communicate directly with the governments of the great powers, though there was no reason why private messages should not be sent to the powers' consuls in Tûrnovo.

Such messages were sent after the constituent assembly had debated the issue of national unity. That debate took up the first week of the assembly's deliberation and focused upon a report drawn up by a special commission appointed by the delegates to study the national question. The report favoured the moderate faction which had argued that the disbandment of the assembly would only anger the powers and make matters worse. The week-long debate was intense but the report's recommendations were finally approved. The highpoint of the proceedings had been a speech from the Exarch Antim who quoted Jeremiah chapter 31, verses 16 and 17:

Thus saith the Lord; refrain thy voice from weeping and thine eyes from tears; for thy work shall be rewarded, said the Lord; and they shall come again from the land of the enemy.

And there is hope in thine end, saith the Lord, thy children shall come again into their own border.

Before the constituent assembly convened, Sofia had been chosen as the capital of the new principality. Although small, Sofia had two advantages: it was at the crossroads of the north-east to south-west and north-west to south-east routes across the Balkans, and it offered easy access to the coveted lost lands of Macedonia and the Morava valley.

With the territorial issue decided early in March the constituent assembly began work on defining the principality's political system. The draft constitution was presented by Prince Dondukov-Korsakov, the head of the Russian Provisional Administration which had governed Bulgaria since the war. His draft was amended by a commission elected by the assembly which presented its recommendations early in April. Two tendencies immediately became apparent. Those later to be grouped under the label 'conservative' argued for a system which placed real power in the hands of the small number of wealthy Bulgarians. The peasant masses who made up 90 per cent or more of the population, the conservatives argued, were too immature to be entrusted with real power; after five centuries of Ottoman domination they were too suspicious of the state as an institution and would too easily treat their new one as they had their old. This was anathema to the other group, the 'liberals'. They believed the peasants and the village councils were the repositories of national political wisdom; they rejected outright the paternalism of the conservatives and stressed that the equal distribution of political power throughout the nation was a natural consequence of its basic social homogeneity.

These opposing attitudes were fully developed during the debate on the nature of Bulgaria's parliamentary system. The conservatives wanted a second chamber to reinforce the power of the wealthy minority; a senate, they said, would check the enthusiasms of the lower chamber. The liberals saw no need for a second chamber. It would be needlessly divisive and it would be a dangerous dilution of natural, healthy, peasant democracy.

Although the two hundred and thirty or so delegates included only twelve from the villages so beloved of the liberals, liberal views enjoyed massive support in the assembly. The second chamber was rejected. The single-chamber parliament (sûbranie) was, however, to have two variants. Copying the example of the Serbian constitution, there was to be an ordinary and a Grand National Assembly. The ordinary assembly was to meet every year in October, after the harvest had been taken in, was to sit for two months, and was to be elected for a three-year period. The Grand National Assembly (GNA) was to have twice as many elected deputies together with prominent members of the church, the judiciary and local government. The GNA was to be called to elect regents, choose the head of state, to sanction changes in the state's boundaries, or to change the constitution, a two-thirds majority being necessary in the latter case.

All sane male citizens over twenty-one were allowed to vote for both assemblies, and all literate males over thirty were eligible for election. The obligations of each citizen were to obey the law, to pay taxes, to send all children to school for at least five years, and to send all healthy males to the army for two years.

Executive power was to lie with the prince but was to be exercised via a council of ministers or cabinet chosen from the assembly. The prince could appoint and dismiss ministers; he nominated the chairman of the council of ministers, or prime minister, and he could prorogue the assembly.

An important section of the constitution dealt with the church. The general convention in the Orthodox church is 'One Church, One State', but if that were now applied the exarch would have to leave Constantinople and settle in the principality. Were he to do that he would lost contact with the members of the exarchate in Macedonia, Thrace, the Morava valley and even Eastern Rumelia. This would be an immense blow for the Bulgarian nation, one equal to that inflicted by the tearing up of the San Stefano treaty, because in 1878 members of the exarchate living outside the confines of the principality outnumbered those within it. The Tûrnovo constitution therefore decided that the church in the principality was to be an inseparable part of the Bulgarian exarchate, and that the highest body of the Bulgarian church, the holy synod, was to have its seat in Sofia. The exarch, however, was to remain in Constantinople.

The constitution also decided that the prince must confess the Orthodox faith, only the first prince being exempt from this ruling. That first prince, the assembly decided, was to be Alexander of Battenberg, a candidate whom all the great powers found acceptable. Alexander arrived in Bulgaria early in July 1879.

CONSTITUTIONAL CONFLICTS, 1879–1883

Alexander had much to commend him to the Bulgarians. He was young, he was handsome and above all he had served with the tsar's forces in the war of 1877–8. Unfortunately, his paternalist instincts made it almost impossible for him to work with the liberals who dominated Bulgarian politics, and who had now organised themselves into the Liberal Party. The liberals won the first elections held in September 1879 and the second which took place early in 1880 after Alexander had dissolved the first sûbranie. Constitutional issues arising from this contest between the executive and legislature were to dominate Bulgarian politics for the first five years of the new state's existence.

After the second elections Alexander had little choice but to nominate as prime minister Dragan Tsankov, the erstwhile champion of Uniatism who was now a fierce russophile and leader of the Liberal

Party. There was sufficient truce between prince and prime minister to enable the latter to begin the construction of the new state and its apparatus. Tsankov therefore introduced a national currency based on the lev (lion), he regulated the national system of justice, and he took measures to control brigandage which had plagued the mountain areas since liberation. But it was not long before friction arose between him and the prince on constitutional issues. Alexander insisted on using for his title a Bulgarian word to which the liberals took exception, and he greatly offended the majority party by dissolving the city council in Sofia; not even the Ottomans had done such a thing, the liberals declared. On the other hand, the liberals frightened Alexander by bringing forward plans for a citizens' militia which was to compete with if not replace the army.

Tsankov resigned in November 1880 and was replaced by Petko Karavelov, brother of Liuben. The prince's preference would have been for a change of constitution rather than of prime minister, but to this the Russians would not consent, fearing it might excite demands for west European interference in Bulgarian affairs. The Russian veto, however, was withdrawn in March 1881 when Tsar Alexander II was assassinated. His successor, Alexander III, was more reactionary. He raised no objections in May when his namesake in Bulgaria dismissed the Karavelov government and announced he would convoke a Grand National Assembly to meet in Svishtov later in the year to consider changes to the constitution. The liberals were not unduly perturbed. They believed they had the nation with them, that this would be reflected in the election results, and that they would therefore easily dominate the GNA. Anxiety began to assail them when Alexander published his proposals for constitutional change, for these bore great resemblance to the conservative ideas expressed at Tûrnovo. Liberal fears intensified when the Russians gave Battenberg's plans their blessing. The Russians also backed the prince in the elections held in July; Russian soldiers were available at the vote to 'help illiterates' and preserve order, though they placed little restraint on the pro-Battenbergist thugs who also congregated around the voting points. Only two electoral districts returned liberal deputies and not all of them reached the assembly. It would have made no difference if they had. The Svishtov GNA which met on 13 July was overwhelmingly conservative in outlook, and in less than two hours it

Plate 5.1   Alexander Battenberg, prince of Bulgaria, 1879–86.

passed all the prince's proposals: a state council was to be introduced, the franchise was to be made indirect, the sŭbranie was to be reduced in size, and civil liberties were to be restricted. Prince Alexander had in effect carried out a *coup d'état*.

After the coup many liberals left Bulgaria for exile in Eastern Rumelia, though Tsankov remained hoping to influence Alexander's authoritarianism from within the principality. In fact the authoritarian regime was from the beginning weak and insecure. The fundamental political reality of Bulgaria remained unaltered: the great majority of the politically conscious part of the nation, the intelligentsia, backed the liberals and would not cooperate with the conservatives or the prince. The latter was soon to face another difficulty because when a sûbranie was elected in the autumn of 1882 its conservative majority – the liberals had boycotted the poll – showed a surprising degree of independence. This spirit of independence was to be shown primarily against the Russians.

In the spring of 1882 the prince, desperate to find ministers who would be generally acceptable, had imported two Russian generals, Sobolev and Kaulbars, who were given responsibility for the major share of internal administration. This seemed a sensible move in that the Russians remained widely respected and popular, particularly amongst the liberals. Yet there were dangers in such a policy. Alexander's own relations with the Russians were equivocal at the best of times, the main points of friction being on matters affecting the army. Alexander was determined to strengthen his influence over the ministry of war and the officer corps, yet the ministry was by convention held by a Russian and all officers above the rank of captain in the Bulgarian army were Russians. The appointment of Kaulbars as minister of war did nothing to improve relations in this area.

Whilst the prince and the Russians competed for influence within the army, there were serious disagreements between the Russians and the conservatives over railways. Since 1879 the Russians had been pressing the Bulgarian government to allow them to construct a railway from the Danube in the north-east to Sofia. This would have great strategic importance in any future Russian military operations in the Balkans, but the suggestion was embarrassing for the Bulgarians. The treaty of Berlin obliged Bulgaria to complete that section of the Vienna to Constantinople trunk line which passed through Bulgarian territory. This was an expensive obligation which would more than absorb whatever funds the Bulgarians had for railway construction. The Russians nevertheless urged that the Berlin obligation be placed second to that of the Danube–Sofia line; at the same time they strove hard to secure control of the national bank which the Bulgarians had decided to establish. The two issues were obviously connected because Russian control of the bank would ensure funds were made available for the Russian railway project. These arguments the Russians pressed in the state council and the sûbranie but both bodies refused such pressures and in April 1883, with full support from the prince, the sûbranie enacted that the trunk line be built.

The Russians were enraged but there was nothing they could do, not least because the moderate liberals shared conservative attitudes on this issue. The liberals believed that Russia, as the liberating power, had the right to dominate Bulgarian foreign policy, one liberal even arguing that Bulgaria had no need of a foreign ministry because its external affairs should be left in Russia's hands. But the liberals did not expect Russian interference in Bulgaria's internal affairs. After the 1883 decision on the trunk line the conservatives, the moderate liberals and the prince combined to contain Russian pressures. In September Sobolev and Kaulbars left Bulgaria and Tsankov formed a coalition government.

The internal comprise reached in Bulgaria was based on liberal acceptance of the April 1883 railway agreement, and conservative acceptance of a return to the Tûrnovo constitution, together with the acknowledgement that any future constitutional changes could only be brought about by constitutional means. In December 1883 the sûbranie passed a constitutional reform bill which reintroduced much of the 1881 system. The conservatives then left the coalition government, believing they had secured their constitutional objectives. They had not because the December 1883 bill had been passed by very dubious means and it was repealed in the following year before it had been put into effect.

THE NATIONAL QUESTION AND UNION
WITH RUMELIA, 1884–1885

The passing of the December 1883 bill embarrassed the liberals. Their ranks were already divided, particularly between those who had remained in Bulgaria in 1881 and those who had gone into exile, the latter being headed by Petko Karavelov. These divisions were sharpened early in 1884 when Tsankov announced the government had agreed to purchase the British-owned Rusé–Varna railway. Purchase of the line was another obligation laid upon Bulgaria by the treaty of Berlin and no-one could object to the government's decision. They could, however, object to the price. And this the Karavelov wing of the Liberal Party did with some energy. When elections were held in June 1884 they were a contest not between the conservatives and the liberals but between the tsankovist and karavelist wings of the Liberal Party.

The karavelists won and their leader formed the next government. His first act was to repeal the December 1883 constitutional legislation after which he went on to introduce two vitally important bills. The first placed the new Bulgarian National Bank (BNB) under state ownership. The second nationalised the railways; all existing and future lines in the country were to be the property of the Bulgarian State Railways (BDZh); plans were also drawn up to determine the shape of the future national rail network. By this time the split between the two wings of the Liberal Party had been formalised. The karavelists formed the new Democratic Party, Tsankov's group retaining the title of the Liberal Party.

By the end of 1884 most of the constitutional issues raised in 1879 had been settled. The prince's political wings had been clipped after his too rapid ascent in 1881; the conservatives had become a minor factor in the political equation; and the Russians had been rebuffed by Karavelov's nationalist legislation on the bank and on railways. The decline of the constitutional questions meant that attention could once again focus on the issue which had been at the forefront of discussion before the constitutional debates: that of national unity.

Ever since 1878 there had been a sizeable Macedonian presence in Bulgaria. Some Macedonians were economic migrants, many of them taking part in the construction work which liberation spawned in Sofia and other cities. Others, however, were fugitives or refugees. Most if not all Macedonians in Bulgaria at this period regarded themselves as ethnically Bulgarian and the refugees were a potential political lobby of considerable size. After the end of authoritarian rule they became more active and by 1884 had moved some distance towards forming effective organisations. Movement in this direction was encouraged by the first signs of emergent Serbian propaganda in Macedonia where the exarchist/Bulgarian cause already had to meet strong competition from the patriarchist/Greek faction. In 1885 two *cheti* crossed from Bulgaria into Macedonia, one of

Plate 5.2   The sûbranie (parliament) building, Sofia. Its motto means
'Unity is Strength'. The building dates from the 1880s and replaced one
destroyed by fire in 1883. The building in the left background is the
Aleksander Nevski cathedral, built largely with Russian money in
commemoration of the war of 1877–78 and finally completed in the early
1920s.

them equipped with arms taken from a Bulgarian military installa-
tion with the obvious connivance of local officials. Both bands were
soon rounded up or dispersed by Ottoman forces but alarm signals
had been clearly sounded, particularly in Russia. They were heeded
by Karavelov. He retained enough of the liberals' original pro-
Russian attitudes still to believe that Bulgaria must do nothing in
its foreign policy to anger or alienate St Petersburg. And at this
period the focus of Russian diplomacy was on central Asia; it was
made abundantly clear to Sofia that complications in the Balkans
would be most unwelcome as they would make it much more
difficult to secure Russian objectives in Asia. Karavelov therefore
acted swiftly. In 1885 a number of known Macedonian activists
were moved away from the western border areas and settled in
central or eastern Bulgaria.

Karavelov's firm line on Macedonia focused attention on Eastern
Rumelia. The internal administration of Eastern Rumelia, it had
been decided in Berlin, was to be under the control of a governor

general but he was to rule through an elected assembly whilst a permanent council of that assembly was to function as a form of cabinet. It had been intended by the Berlin powers that the permanent council would contain representatives of the Turkish and Greek minorities in Rumelia and an elaborate system of proportional representation had been devised for when the regional assembly elected the permanent council from its own membership. These plans were scuppered by one Bulgarian deputy who had a doctorate in mathematics from Prague. He lectured, drilled, and rehearsed his colleagues so effectively that when the vote was held the maximum possible number of posts in the council were taken by Bulgarians. Though minority rights were safeguarded in Rumelia the election of a predominantly Bulgarian permanent council meant that the province's political machinery was entirely in Bulgarian hands.

There was an understandable desire to emphasise the Bulgarian nature of the province. To that end the Bulgarian flag and the Bulgarian national anthem were used on every permissible occasion and as many of the province's official institutions as possible were modelled on their equivalents in the principality. Thus the school system in Rumelia was similar to that north of the border; the literary alphabets were the same; and military training was again taken directly from the Bulgarian example.

However, the party system which emerged from the constitutional debates in the principality did not appear in Rumelia where the dominant political elements were small, conservative oligarchies consisting of wealthy merchants and former Ottoman civil servants. Provincial politics, and not least its press, were enlivened by the arrival of the liberal refugees after the coup of 1881 but that coup acted as a hindrance to the development of political links with Bulgaria. Rumelia's economy was more developed than Bulgaria's and its merchants did not want the sort of upheavals which in two years had given the principality seven cabinets and two general elections; even more importantly, serious disturbances or political changes might invoke that clause of the treaty of Berlin which stated that Ottoman troops could be reintroduced into Rumelia if there were a serious threat to its internal stability and if the signatory powers of the Berlin treaty had been informed beforehand. Rumelia could not contemplate union until the principality had returned to an orderly, constitutional life.

Another hindrance to any attempts at union between Bulgaria and Rumelia had been the attitude of the western and central European powers. Initially they had seen Bulgaria as a dependency of Russia and had therefore feared that any expansion of Bulgaria would mean an extension of Russian influence. By 1884 this view was changing. The prince's disagreements with the Russians over the army and above all the decisions on the railway and bank questions had shown Europe that Bulgaria was not a Russian satrapy.

As his reaction to the *cheti* of 1885 showed, Karavelov was not willing to anger the Russians, but there were conspiracies afoot which had no such inhibitions. Early in 1885 a Bulgarian Secret Central Revolutionary Committee (BSCRC) had been established. It advocated extremist methods and had maximalist aims. It wanted to bring about a mass rising of all Bulgarians under foreign rule and to unite them in a single state, to recreate in fact San Stefano Bulgaria. It was a hopelessly ambitious aim and Karavelov's reaction to the 1885 *cheti* showed that the maximalist path would lead nowhere. With Macedonia denied to them the activists of the BSCRC concentrated instead on what seemed the easiest of their objectives: Rumelia where Bulgarians already dominated the machinery of local administration. The BSCRC became the Committee for Union; it abandoned its call for a mass uprising, deciding instead that the local, Bulgarian-dominated militia should carry out a coup. This would be rapid and could be effected before international diplomacy could be rallied to defend the *status quo*.

The coup was duly carried out on 18 September 1885, although the scheduled date had been a little later. It was enthusiastically welcomed amongst the general Bulgarian population both north and south of the Balkans. Karavelov and Prince Alexander were less sure. Karavelov dithered, caught between his obvious desire to see unification and his reluctance to do anything which would anger the Russians.

Alexander was equally concerned at Russian reactions. He had been informed of the conspiracy and of the date it was due to be carried out. But there had been endless similar rumours over the last few years and he took this one no more seriously than those which

Plate 5.3   A group described by the contemporary caption as a Volunteer Detachment of Schoolboys, 1885; the figure second from the left is clearly no schoolboy and could be a teacher. Detachments such as these helped to secure the military victory against Serbia in 1885.

had preceded it; in August he had even assured the Russian minister for foreign affairs that there was no reason to expect any dramatic developments in the Balkans in the foreseeable future. Initially, Alexander also dithered. His mind was made up for him by Stefan Stambolov. Stambolov had been born near Tûrnovo in 1854 and had won a scholarship to a seminary in Russia. There, however, he had become involved with the narodniks and had been expelled. He had taken an active part in the 1876 rising and in the attempted Kresna-Razlog revolt in 1878. After liberation he had been elected to the sûbranie, although technically he was too young. Despite this he was made chairman or speaker of the assembly in which position he had established a reputation for toughness and efficiency. These qualities he showed again in 1885. He told Alexander that if he did not go to Plovdiv and accept the union he would be totally discredited and might as well return to Germany. Alexander went to Plovdiv. At the same time he ordered the Bulgarian army south to garrison the border with the Ottoman empire in case the sultan should try to move his army into Eastern Rumelia.

The Union of 1885 created a major diplomatic crisis. The Russians were furious, seeing Alexander's conduct, in the light of his recent assurances, as duplicity. In retaliation the tsar ordered all Russian officers and military advisors to leave Bulgaria; the Bulgarian army was left with no officer above the rank of captain. The dangers for Bulgaria were obvious and were made greater by Greek and Serbian reactions. Both states demanded territorial compensations if Bulgaria were to be allowed to increase in size. The Greeks were contained but the Serbs were not. King Milan declared war on Bulgaria on 13 November and moved his troops towards and across Bulgaria's unguarded north-western border. The Bulgarian forces were now required to race from one end of their country to the other; they had no senior officers to organise them, few railways to transport them, and no organised commissariat to feed them or their animals. Despite this the transfer was accomplished mostly on foot and on horseback, Bulgarian troops and Rumelian militiamen being fed *en route* by local inhabitants. In mid-November they faced the Serbs at Slivnitsa on the road to Sofia and in a two-day battle put the Serbs to flight. So complete was the rout that had not Austria-Hungary intervened diplomatically the Bulgarian army would have entered Belgrade.

The battle of Slivnitsa was a remarkable achievement for an untested army shorn of its senior officers. It was equally an achievement of the nation as a whole, and it is worth recalling that the highest incidence of medals for gallantry was amongst Muslim troops. More than any other event the battle of Slivnitsa welded the Bulgarians north and south of the Balkan mountains into one nation.

The diplomatic settlement of the union crisis was effected in the treaty of Bucharest of April 1886. It was a distinct disappointment for the Bulgarians. It stated that the governor general of Rumelia should henceforth be the prince of Bulgaria, but it recognised no more than the personal union of these two offices, and the governor general of Rumelia was still required to seek reapproval every five

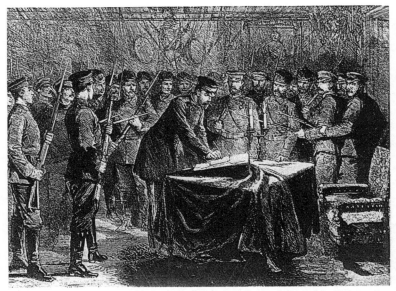

Plate 5.4   A contemporary woodcut showing Prince Alexander's forced abdication in 1886.

years from the sultan and the powers; nor was any mention made in the text of Prince Alexander. The Russians were leaving the door open for his removal.

Alexander did little to help his own cause. He placed no check on the insensitive treatment of Eastern Rumelia by officials in Sofia. This naturally caused resentment, particularly in Plovdiv which, even in 1885, was a larger and more sophisticated city than Sofia. Even worse, Alexander frittered away the support the war had given him in the army. A large number of the Russian trained officers had always been suspicious of Alexander's German origins and his attempts, most of them futile, to subject the army to German methods of training and organisation. After 1885 Alexander committed the fatal error of promoting only those whom he thought politically reliable, even though this meant discrimination against some of the heroes of the recent war.

The prince could ill afford to alienate so powerful a group. By the spring of 1886 he was being criticised in public meetings for the meagre rewards offered by the treaty of Bucharest and for the deterioration in relations with Russia. In May a new sûbranie was elected in which many of these criticisms were energetically voiced. Even more important in the new assembly was the reappearance of the Rusé–Varna railway question. The recent upheavals had delayed consideration of this issue and in the interim the British shareholders had raised the asking price. When Karavelov, who was still prime minister, announced that he was now willing to pay a sum much higher than that which he had denounced as exorbitant in 1884, there was pandemonium in the assembly.

The Russians watched all this with relish. Their agents had for some months let it be known that they would not be opposed to the removal of the prince. In August 1886 a group of army officers acted and deposed Alexander who fled across the Danube. Stambolov, however, was not prepared to tolerate such intervention by the military and their Russian backers. He rallied loyal garrisons, seized Sofia, and induced Alexander to return to Bulgaria. He did not stay long. He was not willing to hold office in the face of Russian hostility and he therefore telegraphed to St Petersburg asking for Alexander III's endorsement of his return to Bulgaria. This the tsar refused. He could not forgo the chance to be rid of Battenberg at the latter's own suggestion. The prince had sacrificed himself. On 7 September 1886 he left Bulgaria for the last time. He died in 1893 aged only thirty-six, and was buried in Sofia.

THE REGENCY AND THE ELECTION OF PRINCE FERDINAND, 1886–1887

After Alexander had left Bulgaria the country was governed by a regency of Karavelov, Stambolov and Stambolov's brother-in-law, Mutkurov, who had done much to rally loyal troops in August. A government was formed under Vasil Radoslavov, a young liberal who had no russophile inclinations. The strongest force in the land was Stambolov.

Stambolov's priority was to find a new prince. The first step towards this goal was to call a Grand National Assembly. There were immediately problems with the Russians. The tsar decided to send a special advisor to Bulgaria, appointing General Nikolai Kaulbars, brother of the former minister of war, to the post.

Kaulbars demanded the release of those imprisoned for their part in the coup of August, the lifting of the state of siege Stambolov had declared, and the cancelling of the elections for the GNA. The elections could not be valid, Kaulbars insisted, because they were called by the regency which itself had not come to office through due constitutional process. Kaulbars carried his message around the country in a rather shambolic attempt to discredit Stambolov and the regents. There were more sinister threats. In October Kaulbars talked of Russian warships being sent to Varna to protect Russian subjects, and this was widely but incorrectly seen as opening the way to a military coup which would depose Stambolov. The latter made a number of concessions, releasing most of those imprisoned and lifting the state of siege, but he would not give way over the elections to the GNA which took place in September.

The convening of the GNA did not bring about any immediate improvement. For Kaulbars the fact that the assembly had met was a severe rebuff and in November he left Bulgaria, citing as his justification an alleged insult to a Russian consular official in Plovdiv. Relations between Bulgaria and its liberating power were completely severed and were not to be restored for almost a decade.

If the convocation of the GNA had been a defeat for Kaulbars it was hardly an immediate victory for Stambolov because it made no progress towards the election of another prince; in fact most delegates would have reappointed Alexander of Battenberg had that option been open to them. To make matters worse there was an almost constant threat of subversion by Russia or its supporters. In 1887 a Russian adventurer, Nabokov, made a second incursion into Bulgaria with the hope of raising a revolt; as on the first occasion he had no success and was soon captured, only to be released because, as a Russian subject, he enjoyed protection under the Capitulations. He was to return for a third pathetic attempt at the end of 1887 but this time the Bulgarian forces of law and order made sure that he was killed rather than captured.

In March of the same year a much more serious threat to Bulgarian stability had been discovered. Dissident officers seized the garrison in Silistra and those in Varna and Rusé soon joined them; the rebels also had support in the country's largest military base, that in Shumen. The plot was suppressed but only with great brutality. Eight of the leaders were shot and in disaffected regiments one in twenty of the compliment were chosen at random to be executed by their comrades. Another victim of the Silistra affair was Karavelov who was clapped in jail without any hard evidence that he had been involved in the conspiracy.

Stambolov's ruthlessness had understandable causes. He needed to attract a prince to Bulgaria but this could hardly be done unless it could be shown that he could guarantee that prince internal order and security. The GNA had nominated a three-man delegation to tour Europe in search of a new prince and any sign of internal instability would make their task much more difficult. Nor had Stambolov or the delegation been helped by the fact that shortly before the latter's appointment Karavelov had left the regency having come to the conclusion that the crisis could be overcome only by accepting whatever terms Russia chose to dictate.

It was not until the mid-summer of 1887 that Stambolov or the delegation had any reason for celebration. It then became known that Prince Ferdinand of Saxe-Coburg-Gotha was considering taking the Bulgarian throne. His main concern was over the attitude of Russia. Adequate assurances were given on this account, another GNA was convened in July to elect him, and on 26 August he arrived in Bulgaria. The tsar, however, refused to recognise him as the lawfully elected prince and the other powers, not wishing to endanger their relations with Russia over a state as small as Bulgaria, followed suit.

THE *STAMBOLOVSHTINA**, 1887–1894

Ferdinand was to stay in Bulgaria for thirty-one years. That he survived his first three years there was largely due to the man who had brought him to the country: Stambolov. Ferdinand immediately appointed Stambolov as prime minister, Stambolov having in the meantime formed his own National Liberal Party on which he could rely for support in parliament. But despite the assurances given to Ferdinand, Russian opposition to him continued, and there were strong fears that Russian agents, particularly after the failure of

---

* In Bulgarian the suffix -*shtina* attached to a personal noun means the times, attitudes, atmosphere and events associated with that person.

Plate 5.5   Stefan Stambolov. A young revolutionary in 1876–8, he became speaker of the sûbranie in the early 1880s. After the deposition of Alexander Battenberg he became the strong man of Bulgaria who resisted Russian intrigues and secured Prince Ferdinand upon the Bulgarian throne.

Nabokov's third and fatal incursion, might sponsor conspiracies by Bulgarian politicians in exile. Foremost amongst these was Tsankov who had taken refuge in Constantinople and Russia before moving to Belgrade. His move to the Serbian capital had been made possible by political changes in Serbia which brought a pro-Russian monarch to the throne and gave the Russians, for the first time in years, a secure base in the Balkans. From Belgrade Tsankov could easily intrigue in his homeland.

There was little Stambolov or Ferdinand could do. They expanded the army, nearly doubling its size, in the hope that this would give them more protection and would cauterise discontent amongst the officer corps by enhancing promotion prospects. Ferdinand also made empty and rather foolish boasts about raising Macedonia to a man if the Porte did not reform the administration there in accordance with article 23 of the treaty of Berlin. The first crumb of comfort for Ferdinand and his prime minister came from Britain which at the end of 1888 agreed to lend Bulgaria 46.7 million francs. The loan was to enable the Bulgarians to purchase the Rusé–Varna railway and therefore did not bring real economic benefit to Bulgaria, but it broke the financial ice and other more substantial loans from German and Austrian banks soon followed. At much the same time as agreeing to the loan the British began tariff negotiations with Bulgaria, an agreement being signed in January 1889. In a few months similar agreements were concluded with Germany, Austria, France, Italy, Switzerland and Belgium. Once again the agreements were of little intrinsic economic value to Sofia but a number of European states had dealt with Bulgaria as if it were a fully independent and recognised state.

The turning point for Ferdinand and Stambolov came in 1890. The year began badly. In 1889 another military conspiracy was hatched, this time around the central figure of Major Kosta Panitsa, a talented but flamboyant young officer of Macedonian origin and a hero of the 1885 war. Panitsa had been a close friend of Alexander Battenberg, the prince being godfather to Panitsa's son. Panitsa had no great affection for Stambolov and, as a Battenbergist, none at all for Ferdinand. More importantly, however, Panitsa had by 1889 come to the conclusion that Bulgaria had no hope of advancing its cause in Macedonia as long as it remained estranged from Russia. He therefore resolved to assassinate the prince; the deed was to be done at a court ball on 2 February 1890. Panitsa was far too indiscreet a character to make an effective conspirator. The police were soon informed of the plot, much of their information coming from Panitsa's own valet. The day before the ball all leading conspirators were arrested. Once again retribution was fierce. After due investigation and legal process Panitsa was tied to a tree and shot by a firing squad drawn from Macedonians amongst his own regiment. The government's victory, however, was hedged with anxiety because the investigations into the plot revealed that it had been far more widespread and popular than Stambolov and his associates had originally thought.

Despite this Stambolov used the plot to great effect. In doing so he concentrated on the Macedonian aspects of the conspiracy's origin and strength. If he could do something to advance the Bulgarian cause in Macedonia he would greatly weaken his opponents and greatly bolster his own and Ferdinand's position. He therefore insisted in Constantinople that Ferdinand was in danger from further conspiracies which were likely to use the Macedonian issue as one of their chief recruiting arguments. Should one of those conspiracies succeed, its architects would have to pay off its supporters by demanding concessions in Macedonia. This could only destabilise the Balkans and weaken the Ottoman empire. It would be much better, said Stambolov, if the Porte voluntarily granted concessions to the Bulgarians in Macedonia; this would increase Ferdinand's internal standing and thereby lessen the dangers of an anti-Ottoman faction seizing power in Sofia. The argument worked. In the summer of 1890 it was announced that the Porte intended to issue decrees promising the exarchate the three major Macedonian bishoprics of Skopje, Ohrid and Bitola. The exarchate was also to be allowed to publish a newspaper in the Ottoman capital, and to establish direct relations with the Bulgarian communities of the Adrianople province.

These were the most important concessions received by the exarchate since 1872 and they greatly increased Stambolov's and Ferdinand's popularity. Since 1885 and the union with Rumelia the Porte had tended to favour the Greek and Serbian churches in Macedonia at the expense of the exarchate with the result that a number of dioceses which had originally voted to join the Bulgarian church were still under patriarchist control and many of their parishes were without priests. Matters had been made worse by a breach between the church in Bulgaria and the government, a breach which had led the government in Sofia to suspend the subsidies it had previously given to the exarchate.

Stambolov had never been on good terms with the higher clergy who feared his radicalism; they had good reason to do so because in 1886 he prevented a meeting of the holy synod and adjusted clerical salaries – downwards. By the time Ferdinand arrived in Sofia matters had worsened. Ferdinand made few attempts to underplay his Catholicism; his mother, who came with him and exercised great influence over him, made fewer. The Bulgarian clergy refused to pray for him in their services and it was for this that Stambolov suspended the annual payments from the Bulgarian government to the exarchate. The low point in church–state relations came in January 1889 when Stambolov closed a meeting of the holy synod which had produced a series of complaints against the prince. Gendarmes were used to escort the bishops back to their sees.

The concessions of 1890 in Macedonia transformed the situation. The church agreed that prayers for Ferdinand should now be included in the liturgy in Bulgaria, and a synod in November 1890 settled nearly all outstanding issues between church and state; Ferdinand even felt able to invite four leading bishops to his palace, and, equally surprisingly, they accepted. Meanwhile the government had agreed to provide three million leva a year for exarchist schools in Macedonia.

Stambolov's victory was consolidated in general elections held later in 1890. A certain amount of influence was used at the polls but Stambolov would have achieved his victory without it. Even the seemingly irreconcilable tsankovists now recognised that the new regime must be accepted; henceforth their criticism was directed not at its existence but at its methods of governing.

These had of necessity been harsh but any hopes that they might be relaxed were dashed by continuing violence on the part of the regime's enemies. In March 1891 the minister of finance was gunned down in mistake for Stambolov and a little under a year later the Bulgarian representative in Constantinople was murdered. Not even the secret police network, greatly expanded after the Panitsa plot, could prevent such outrages.

Stambolov believed that Ferdinand might be safer if he were married and produced an heir; then, even though an assassin might remove the prince, the Russians would not be in a position to nominate his successor. A suitable bride was found in Princess

Marie-Louise of Bourbon Parma who, however, would consent to marry Ferdinand only if any children of the union were brought up as Roman Catholics. This would contravene the article of the constitution which demanded that all but the first prince belong to the Orthodox church, an article which according to some commentators Ferdinand had already breached. In February 1893 Stambolov convened a Grand National Assembly and secured the changes in the constitution necessary to satisfy Princess Marie-Louise's conditions, though he did so only at the cost of renewed and serious disagreement with the church hierarchy.

Stambolov had rightly believed that popular enthusiasm for the marriage would outweigh displeasure at the changes in the constitution, and his belief was reinforced by the rejoicing which followed the birth of a son, Boris, nine months after the royal marriage.

By now Stambolov's own position was weakening. He had in effect fulfilled his function: he had brought Ferdinand to Bulgaria and established him on his throne. Despite these successes he was unable to go further and achieve the international recognition for which the prince now craved. That no movement in the Russian position followed the defeat of Panitsa and the granting of the Macedonian bishoprics in 1890 convinced Ferdinand that Stambolov would never secure recognition; this being so Stambolov had to be replaced, and by 1893 the prince was moving towards open conflict with his prime minister. In that year a new opposition group, soon to be known as the Nationalist Party, was formed of dissident liberals, some conservatives, and unionists from southern Bulgaria; they were led by Konstantin Stoilov, a former secretary of Alexander Battenberg. The new opposition exploited the mounting social unrest caused by the decline in world agricultural prices, a danger which the Stambolov regime found difficult to comprehend or contain; the Greek minority was offended by educational laws which forced all Christian, but not Muslim, children to receive their primary education in Bulgarian; and most important of all in 1894, Ferdinand secured the appointment of his own nominee to the war ministry. That nominee was also chief of the general staff and by his appointment Ferdinand secured greater control over the military in Bulgaria than anyone had yet enjoyed.

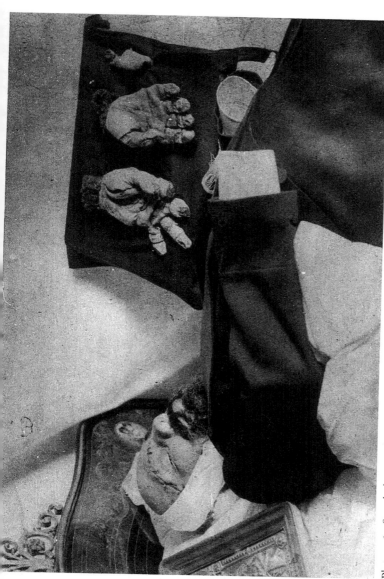

Plate 5.6 Stambolov was brutally attacked in the streets of Sofia in 1895, dying a few days later. His assailants severed his hands.

Shortly after this Stambolov was accused of having an affair with the wife of a ministerial colleague, something which Stambolov vehemently denied. It was no use. In May Stambolov was engineered into a position in which he had to resign. A year later he was brutally murdered in the streets of Sofia.

THE RECOGNITION OF PRINCE FERDINAND

The new prime minister was Stoilov. He began his period in office by relaxing some of the strict controls which Stambolov had imposed. Amongst those who benefited from this policy were the Macedonians in Bulgaria who were now able once more to equip bands for operation in the Ottoman empire, much to the displeasure of the Russians. This displeasure Stoilov could ill afford. If it were not his immediate objective, Stoilov had to achieve some progress towards recognition; he had to succeed where Stambolov had failed. Movement towards this goal was made much easier by two external events. First, in Asiatic Turkey a series of massacres of Armenians made some believe that the Ottoman empire had entered its final death throes. Second, Tsar Alexander III died in November 1894. His successor, Nicholas II, was more pliable and both Russian and Bulgarian statesmen realised that the two states must cooperate if they were to maximise their gains from any collapse of the Ottoman empire. In 1895 the first sign of a thaw in Russian attitudes appeared when a sûbranie delegation was given permission to visit Russia to lay a wreath on the grave of Alexander III. From this visit it became clear that in return for the recognition of Ferdinand the Russians would make one major demand: that Prince Boris be received into the Orthodox faith.

This faced the Bulgarian regime with a difficult choice. Conversion would be immensely popular amongst the Bulgarian people as a whole, as would reconciliation with the Russians who had liberated them: how could a Bulgarian government refuse a price which the people were eager to pay for an item which they all wanted to purchase? And, it was pointed out, the king of Romania had recently agreed to the conversion of his son. The difference was that the king of Romania was a Protestant. He did not have the pope to answer to, nor did he have staunchly Catholic families, his own and his wife's, to contend with. Stoilov wisely left the decision to Ferdinand. Ferdinand's was not a conscience frequently troubled but in this case he felt a genuine dilemma, pulled in one direction by his feelings for his mother and his wife and, no doubt, his own immortal soul, and in the other by the obvious political advantages to be gained from accepting Russia's terms. He decided in favour of the latter. He knew that recognition and reconciliation with Russia would bring greater internal cohesion. He knew too that with the situation in the Ottoman empire deteriorating the Macedonian question was bound to become more acute, and should it become critical and his freedom of action be restricted because he had not mended his fences with Russia, he would have failed his adopted nation and would personally be in grave danger of deposition or worse. On 3 February 1896 it was announced that Prince Boris would receive an Orthodox baptism on 14 February; Tsar Nicholas II, though he would not attend in person, would stand as godfather. Two weeks later, on the anniversary of the signing of the peace of San Stefano, the sultan, with Russian backing, recognised Ferdinand as prince of Bulgaria and governor general of Eastern Rumelia. Within a few days all the great powers, Russia included, had done likewise.

ETHNIC AND SOCIAL CHANGE AFTER THE LIBERATION

Before the outbreak of the April uprising about a third of the population of what was to become Bulgaria and Eastern Rumelia were ethnic Turks, almost all of whom were Muslim. The atrocities of 1876 naturally created amongst the Christian Bulgarians an urge to take revenge. This was to some extent gratified during and immediately after the war of 1877–8. A number of Muslims fled during the conflict and there was some destruction of Muslim buildings and cultural centres; a large library of old Turkish books was destroyed when a mosque in Târnovo was burned in 1877, and Sofia, which one Russian soldier had described as 'a forest of minarets', lost most of its mosques, seven of them in one night in December 1878 when a thunderstorm masked the noise of the explosions arranged by Russian military engineers. In the countryside a number of Turkish villages were burned and there were many instances of ethnic Turks being driven from land which was coveted by local Bulgarians.

Such events are the depressing feature of wars in the Balkans and elsewhere, but they were not repeated in peacetime Bulgaria. The treaty of Berlin insisted upon freedom of worship for all faiths and outlawed discrimination on the basis of religion. It also guaranteed the property rights of Muslims who chose to reside outside the principality whilst retaining land within it.

After 1878 Bulgaria and Eastern Rumelia abided by the letter of these international laws. But no amount of legislation could prevent Muslim emigration from both areas. There was some cultural pressure on Muslims. A decree of the Russian Provisional Administration, for example, had declared the rice-paddies of the Maritsa valley a health hazard because they were breeding grounds for malaria-carrying mosquitoes. This was no doubt true but Muslims could not help but see the decree as an attempt to make more difficult the growing of their staple food.

More important were laws regulating land tenures and taxation. Regulations affecting land unworked for three years, a period later extended, meant that absentee Turks forfeited their property, whilst in Eastern Rumelia in 1882 the imposition of tax on land owned rather than on the produce it yielded again hit many Muslim landowners; they were accustomed to leave part of their land fallow and if taxes were levied only on produce this had no financial penalty which it obviously did have when a tax based on ownership increased the amount to be paid without any compensating increase in the amount earned. Many of the Muslims left simply because they could not adjust psychologically to living in a Christian state and society. They did not comprehend the way in which women appeared unmasked in public or, even worse, mingled in society at mixed dinner parties, theatrical excursions, balls or picnics. Many Muslims resented the fact that a number of mosques were taken from them. Some of these were reverting to Christian places of worship, but others were given over to secular usage; some became storehouses, one a printing-house, and one even a prison. Even more distasteful to many Muslim families was conscription into a Christian army. Muslim soldiers did not have to wear the cross on their uniforms but they did have to obey Christian officers, observe

Christian festivals, and in many cases eat Christian food. In later years exemption from military service for Muslims was made easier but conscription was in force for the first ten years after 1878, a time of maximum disorientation and demoralisation for the Turkish and Muslim population. This makes the loyalty and courage of the Muslims during the war of 1885 all the more remarkable.

Many Muslims, however, had not stayed long enough in Bulgaria to be involved in that war. There was a steady stream of emigration and by 1900 the Turkish element, as measured by mother-tongue, had declined from about 33 per cent in 1875 to 14 per cent of the total population. In absolute terms the Turks were 728,000 in 1880/84 (the figures being for the principality in 1880 and Rumelia in 1884) but only 540,000 in 1900. In the same years the number of Greeks increased from 53,000 to 71,000.

The liberation produced great economic and social as well as ethnic change, and this affected all communities. The majority of the population remained rural and for many villages the departure of Muslims and the relaxation or non-observance of laws forbidding the ploughing up of village communal land or forests meant that there was no land shortage in Bulgaria and an increasing population could be absorbed without any significant increase in agricultural productivity. This perpetuated the small self-sufficient peasant holding which had characterised most of the Bulgarian lands before liberation.

The Bulgarian peasant farmer continued to feed himself and his family but the liberation did bring him nearer the European market and European manners. In the early 1880s most inhabitants of Sofia still had a cow or two grazing on nearby meadows under the care of the cowherd whom most city districts employed; they had all but disappeared by the turn of the century. At liberation the only form of street cleansing in the new capital were the packs of wild dogs which roamed the city and which killed three people in 1882. The dogs were put to the sword in 1884 and by the turn of the century Sofia had modern amenities such as municipal transport and abundant fresh water piped in from the nearby mountains.

Other towns did not fare so well. The traditional textile producing centres along the foothills of the Balkan mountains withered when they were exposed to greater competition. In Sopot in 1883 women burned bales of imported cloth and attacked the home of the importer. The traditional, workshop-based producers, organised into their old-fashioned and protectionist guilds, could not survive. In 1880 there had been seventy lace-making workshops in and near Gabrovo; in 1900 there were twenty-three, and Gabrovo had survived the post-liberation whirlwind better than most areas.

Cheap, high-quality imports from Europe were one cause for the decline in traditional manufacturing. Another was the loss of traditional purchasers such as the Ottoman army; Samokov had supplied cloth for two army corps and had had a flourishing metal-working industry, but by 1900 it had declined from being a major Balkan city to a small and depressed provincial town. Some traditional industries were crippled because the new political frontiers separated them from sources of raw materials or from established markets. Vidin declined because its natural hinterland was in that part of the north-west of the Bulgarian lands assigned by the treaty of Berlin to Serbia. Kotel, which had grown rich by fattening sheep and goats in the Dobrudja and then driving them to market in Adrianople and Constantinople, now found its grazing grounds cut off by the new Bulgarian–Rumanian border, and its markets beyond the Bulgarian–Rumelian and then the Bulgarian–Ottoman frontiers.

Changes in social habits and customs also weakened traditional industries. Many of these new habits were the result of conscription which gave many of the younger generation of peasants their first experience of urban life. And the changes were more pronounced in the Bulgarian than in the Turkish or Pomak communities. That leather-making workshops survived in a healthy state only in Sliven and Haskovo was because there were sizeable Turkish populations in those areas and they continued to wear the traditional footwear and the broad leather belts which Bulgarians were discarding as old-fashioned. The casting off of the belt damaged the knife-making industry. This was already suffering because it was facing competition from small, cheaper Austrian and German products, because it had been excluded by new tariffs from its established markets in Romania and the Ottoman empire, and because the suppression of brigandage in the 1880s lessened the need to carry a knife for self-protection; now the adoption of western-style belts meant that anyone attempting to carry the old-style large knife would not be able to keep his trousers in a socially acceptable position. The processors and workers of precious metals had relied chiefly on local wealthy Turks for their purchasers; when the latter departed the industry was ruined. The same fate befell the slipper-makers; Christian Bulgarians were not likely to adopt Muslim foot-wear. Western porcelain became popular and, having the additional advantage of being cheap, soon replaced, in the towns at least, the copper tableware which most Bulgarians had previously used. Beds too became more modish, very much to the cost of the craftshops which for generations had produced the carpets and cushions on which the Bulgarians had until then been content to sleep.

Some manufacturers were able to adapt to changed conditions. Some aped western styles in products such as clothes or furniture, whilst a few even moved over to factory production, importing German or British machinery in order to do so; between 1888 and 1893 seven new textile mills and ten new leather works were opened in Gabrovo, three of them joint stock companies. Another saviour for some depressed areas was to begin producing goods to cater for the new tastes. When, during the war of 1885, a German revisited the Bulgaria he had last seen in 1878 he rejoiced to find that now beer was available; by the mid-1890s there were twenty-nine breweries in the country and commercial distilling was also being developed.

In a country as backward and as poor as Bulgaria industrial advances could not come without government help. Under the early liberal administrations there had been attempts, few of them successful, to make civil servants wear clothes made of local cloth, and the government had drawn up a strategic plan for the development of the railway network. This developed only slowly; in the winter of 1888 Stambolov found that the quickest way to get from Tûrnovo to Plovdiv was to take a ship from Varna to Constantinople. By the mid-1890s the trunk line had been com-pleted, Yambol had been linked to Burgas, and the mines at Pernik joined to Sofia, but there was still no line across the Balkan moun-tains and the roads remained in a woeful state. Any improvement in either form of transport would require massive investment. There were no internal sources of capital; there was no financial infra-structure and the few wealthy merchant concerns were found in a limited number of urban centres; if any peasant made money he was less likely to invest it in productive concerns than to set himself up as a moneylender because here the largest profits were to be made. And external sources of credit would be almost as meagre as long as Bulgaria remained an international outcast.

6

Ferdinand's personal rule, 1896–1918

Because the early liberal governments had been preoccupied with constitutional issues and Stambolov's first concern always had to be internal security, it was not really until the Stoilov administration came to power that a systematic attempt to develop the Bulgarian economy could be made. Stoilov, who had once declared that he wished to make Bulgaria 'the Belgium of the Balkans', was eager for the task. In 1894 his government passed the encouragement of industry bill. Industries which were included within one of nine defined categories and which had capital of 25,000 leva and at least 20 employees were to receive state encouragement; the chief beneficiaries were mining and metallurgy, textiles and the construction industry. State encouragement was to take the form of free grants of land for factory building together with financial help for the construction of any necessary road or rail links, preferential rates on the state railways for finished products, free use of state or local authority quarries and water power, tax advantages, preference in the awarding of state contracts even if the native products were more expensive than imported ones, and a monopoly in supplying certain items within specified geographic limits. Further acts in 1905 and 1909 both widened the scope of industries eligible for encouragement and lowered the qualifications necessary to receive it.

If home industries were to be stimulated, however, they would need protection from cheap western imports. Any substantial alteration in the Bulgarian tariff regime had been impossible whilst Ferdinand was unrecognised but in 1896 Stoilov was able to raise the general import duty from 8 to 14 per cent; in 1906 it rose to almost 25 per cent. There were a number of exceptions, particularly if the imported items were ones which would help domestic industrial growth, but the only goods allowed in completely duty free were equipment for making silk, coke-fired samovars, and, somewhat mysteriously, church bells.

Stoilov also helped stimulate commerce. In 1894 the government began work on developing the harbours at Varna and Burgas, work which was completed in 1903 and 1906 respectively. Regulations which had frustrated the development of local banking had already been relaxed by Stambolov in 1893, and in the following year Stoilov hoped further to stimulate local commercial activity by the creation of chambers of commerce. In 1897 commercial law was codified.

Stoilov's efforts to modernise the Bulgarian economy enjoyed some success. In 1894 there were 72 factories with 3,027 workers in encouraged industries; in 1911 there were 345 factories employing 15,886 workers, and between 1904 and 1911 the value of production in this sector trebled. On the other hand, the number of workers per factory changed very little and only just before the first world war did it begin to move ahead of the 1894 figure; this showed the tenacity of the small unit of production. Nor was there any significant change in the structure of industry. Food, drink and textiles completely dominated Bulgarian factory production, and even if this were also the case in all other Balkan countries, it indicated that progress towards a modern industrial economy was quantitative rather than qualitative. Railway building also continued with the total track rising from 220 kilometres in 1880 to 1,566 kilometres in 1900 and 2,109 kilometres in 1912, by which time the basic network as outlined in Karavelov's legislation of 1884 had been completed. Trade too increased and by 1911, with a total value of 384,000,000 leva, it was 60 per cent above the level of the early 1890s. At the same time government expenditure had risen nine-fold from 20,000,000 leva in 1880 to 181,000,000 in 1911. Internal sources could not support such expenditure and the shortfall was covered by foreign loans, the sums borrowed rising by 70 per cent in the decade after 1900. Yet at 149.25 leva Bulgaria's per capita debt was lower than any of its neighbours.

THE ESTABLISHMENT OF FERDINAND'S PERSONAL RULE

The recognition of Prince Ferdinand in 1896 was a turning point in Bulgarian history. The constitutional preoccupations of the first years of statehood and the insecurity caused by non-recognition could now be set aside. Order and stability, it seemed, had been achieved and Bulgaria could now progress to economic restructuring and the pursuit of its foreign policy objectives. But the stability of the late 1890s was apparent rather than real and had been bought at considerable cost.

Between 1879 and 1884 the executive and the legislature had competed for dominance. The executive had made a major advance with the coup of 1881 but had failed to capitalise on its advantages. Alexander Battenberg did not use to the full the powers he had secured for himself, not least because he was restrained by fear of Russian disapproval. In 1883 and 1884 the legislature seemed to recapture the high constitutional ground and with the formation of the Karavelov government the liberals appeared to be in a commanding position. But the liberals had been damaged in the struggle of the past five years and their weaknesses began to appear at their moment of victory with the split between Karavelov and Tsankov.

In subsequent years the executive rapidly regained the ground it had lost. The events of 1886 had shown that the army had to be kept under control if it were not to become the dominant factor in Bulgarian political life. And it was much easier for the executive than the legislature to exercise this control.

After the departure of Alexander Battenberg only the inveterate russophiles would contest the need to increase executive power. Stambolov did not create but he greatly elaborated on the existing police and informer networks and once boasted that a bee could not cross the coast at Varna without his knowing about it.

By the mid-1890s it was established practice for an incoming government to fill administrative posts with its own supporters. This trafficking in political office, which was by no means confined to Bulgaria, was known in Bulgarian as *partisanstvo*. But by the

Plate 6.1   Ferdinand of Saxe-Coburg-Gotha, prince of Bulgaria, 1887–1908, King of the Bulgarians, 1908–18.

mid-1890s there were, for the first time, more young men qualified for civil service posts than there were jobs available for them. This unemployed intelligentsia tended to drift towards opposition groups which promised them jobs when that group was included in government. Parties thus became less and less organisations dedicated to the pursuit of political principles than mechanisms for satisfying the lust for office.

This aspect of *partisanstvo* also encouraged the splintering of parties: if there were ten rather than three opposition parties there were ten rather than three groups offering the prospect of high office. Whereas in the 1880s the liberals had split on constitutional issues and in 1886 Stambolov had formed his National Liberal Party to distinguish himself from the pro-Russian liberal groups, in later years splits in all parties were to occur over trivial issues or over personalities. And the more parties there were the easier it was for the executive to play one off against the others.

The executive had also learned well the art of electoral management which had been practised since liberation. Turn-out was generally low in Bulgarian elections and control could easily be exercised at the polling station or in the processing of the results. Elections by the turn of the century were seldom exercises to measure public opinion and to tailor a government's composition to it; they were more often carried out simply to provide a newly appointed cabinet with a dependable majority in the assembly. And by 1900 it was the prince who determined when the composition of a government should be changed and an election held.

Ferdinand had established control over the ministry of war in 1893 and because he had always insisted he should supervise foreign policy he had equal control over the ministry for foreign affairs. When he considered it time to change government he simply had to instruct one or both of these dependent ministers to resign and the incumbent cabinet would be paralysed and forced out of office.

In 1881 Alexander had engineered a coup and given himself powers he failed to use. Ferdinand simply operated the existing system to construct his personal rule. But that rule did not go unchallenged.

SOCIAL CRISIS AND THE EMERGENCE OF THE
AGRARIAN MOVEMENT, 1895–1908

After the union of Bulgaria and Eastern Rumelia in 1885 the railways in the latter remained under the ownership of the Oriental Railway Company (ORC) rather than being incorporated into the

BDZh. The main route involved was the Rumelian section of the Vienna–Constantinople trunk line. This became an increasingly irksome factor because the ORC's tariffs were twice as high as those of the BDZh, this seriously disadvantaging the exporters of southern Bulgaria when world agricultural prices were falling disastrously. When the encouragement of industry act was passed the ORC refused to agree to the preferential rates which the BDZh was required to offer encouraged industries; once again southern Bulgarians, this time the industrialists, were greatly discriminated against *vis-à-vis* their northern colleagues. Stoilov was dependent on the votes of southern Bulgarian unionist deputies for his majority in the sûbranie and he had to act.

He could not, however, nationalise the ORC lines as this was diplomatically too dangerous. Nor could he purchase it. The ORC's chief shareholder was the Deutsche Bank and given the growing interest in Germany in the Berlin to Baghdad railway project there was no prospect of the line being sold. Stoilov had to bypass the ORC with a parallel line.

The parallel line was a disaster. Work had not been long in progress when it was realised that there would never be enough money to complete it. An attempt to purchase the operating rights on the ORC in Rumelia was frustrated by Germany and the German banks, and by 1899 the government in Sofia had been forced into a humiliating agreement under which it promised to build no line in southern Bulgaria which would compete with the ORC. The latter was also to take over the Yambol–Burgas line, in clear contravention of the December 1884 railway act which had stated that all lines in the principality should be state owned. The ORC's assumption of control over the Yambol–Burgas line showed that the company did not consider southern Bulgaria to be part of the principality; it was another unwelcome reminder of the imperfections of the 1886 treaty of Bucharest and the inadequacies of the personal union which it sanctioned. In return the ORC did promise to grant preferential rates in conformity with the encouragement of industry act.

The embarrassments caused by the parallel line had excited more public anger than any issue except Macedonia. Part of that anger was caused by the fact that the government had been forced to borrow relatively large sums of money on the foreign markets to finance a project which came to nothing. And the loans had to be paid for, despite the fact that the government was already in desperate financial straits. Internal revenues had to be increased. Industry and commerce had recently been marked out as recipients rather than providers of government revenue and therefore the burden was to fall upon the land. In November 1899 the government announced that for the years 1900–4 the land tax, which had been introduced in 1894 as part of Stoilov's modernising programme, would be replaced by a tithe in kind.

This infuriated the peasants. The tax burden on them had almost doubled in the years 1887 to 1897 whilst in the towns, where most of the taxes were spent, the increase had not been as great. Taxation on land had see-sawed between cash and kind and, the peasants suspected with justification, the type levied was that which would yield more revenue for the government; now, just as world wheat prices seemed at last to be moving upwards, the peasant would have less grain to sell. The peasants were in desperate need of cash, many of them having been forced into the hands of the usurer because they could not repay the loans they had taken out to purchase vacant Muslim land. The north-east of the country, with its concentration on grain production, was the most severely hit by the decision to levy the tax in kind, and it was here that the reaction against the new tax regulations was most intense.

There had already been stirrings of new organisations in this area and a number of local activists called a meeting in Pleven in December 1899. From this meeting was to emerge the body which soon became the Bulgarian Agrarian National Union (BANU) which was the most original and important political body to emerge in post-liberation Bulgaria. Its ideology had not been clearly formulated and as yet its leaders would not allow that it was anything more than a pressure group; it was not, said its leaders, a political party and it had no objectives other than to 'raise the intellectual and moral standing of the peasant and to improve agriculture in all its branches'. But it could not be anything but a political phenomenon, and within months Stoilov acknowledged that it was the true representative of the peasant and the strongest political force in the land.

Such a powerful body was bound to come into conflict with the established order. In series of clashes between agrarian supporters and the police in the spring of 1900 in the Dobrudja villages of Daran Kulak and Trûstenik a number of peasants were killed. A summer of intense agitation followed and when the second congress of the new organisation met in December there was a much sharper political edge to its proceedings.

Stoilov's credibility had been destroyed by the parallel railway fiasco and the agrarian movement. In December 1900 he resigned. In February 1901 one of Bulgaria's few genuinely open elections took place. In the new sûbranie were twenty-eight agrarians. The established parties still dominated the assembly and a government was formed with Karavelov, the leader of the Democratic Party, as prime minister. His minister for foreign affairs was Stoyan Danev, the leader of the Progressive Liberals (tsankovists) who were the other main party in the new coalition. One of the first acts of the new administration was to abolish the tithe in kind.

Of the twenty-one agrarian deputies elected in 1901 sixteen soon defected to established parties. This strengthened the growing pressure within the movement for a more open commitment to political activity, and in a congress convened in October 1901 this faction had its way; the title of Bulgarian Agrarian National Union was now adopted. In 1908 BANU polled one hundred thousand votes and took twenty-three seats, the next largest non-government party having forty-six thousand votes and five seats. The growth in agrarian support had two main causes. At the local level the agrarian movement was becoming increasingly associated with the intelligentsia, primarily teachers, priests and agricultural advisors, and also with the burgeoning cooperative movement which was rescuing the peasant from the clutches of the usurer and therefore gaining great respect in the villages. Second, in 1906 Aleksandûr Stamboliiski was appointed editor of the party newspaper, *Zemedelsko Zname* (Agrarian Standard). He soon became the dominant figure in the movement.

In the party paper Stamboliiski codified agrarian ideas for the first time. The movement's objective was justice for all in a society devoid of extremes and excesses; this applied especially to landed property, and land was to be taken from those who had too much to be given to those who had too little. Stamboliiski believed that human nature had two aspects, the individual and the social, the former requiring private property and the second developing as society became more complex. This rejected the marxist notion that economic development simplifies social relationships, and marxism was also rejected when Stamboliiski argued that society was divided not into classes based on the ownership of the means of production, but into estates or occupational categories, the most important of which was the agrarian. There was some anti-urbanism in agrarian ideology, and particular scorn and hostility were directed to those whose labour was unproductive: the bureaucracy, the legal profession, the church hierarchy, the monarchy, and the army. Stamboliiski was not overtly republican, that would have invited too much interference from the authorities, but his republicanism was implicit. In foreign affairs he showed little interest in territorial acquisition and looked forward to the solution of Balkan national problems through the creation of a Balkan agrarian federation.

Radical opinion was not confined to the agrarian movement. In 1892 the Bulgarian Social Democratic Party was founded and in 1894 it won four seats at the general election. In 1897 it secured six seats and in 1901 eight, though five of the latter were immediately disqualified. In 1903 the party split. The extremists, known as 'narrows', rejected cooperation with the established political parties, called for the subjection of the trade unions to party needs, and demanded the confiscation of all private property including that of the peasant. The moderates, or 'broads', were prepared to work with the radical bourgeois parties in the sûbranie, to tolerate some private property, and to open membership of trade unions to all, irrespective of their political affiliations. The party split was replicated in the trade unions and did much to weaken the socialists in the years before the first world war.

The splits in the socialists' ranks meant that they could not take full advantage of the urban discontent which followed the rise in the cost of living in the 1900s. This discontent was registered in a number of strikes, including those by printers and miners in 1905 and by railwaymen in 1906–7, but industrial action secured few positive gains. There was also action on the streets by students. They rioted in 1905 in support of the revolutionaries in Russia, and in January 1907 they joined with striking railwaymen to pelt Ferdinand with snowballs when he opened the new national theatre in Sofia. The university was then closed and all its academic staff sacked.

The most serious outburst of unrest in the 1900s was not social, however, but ethnic. In 1906 the arrival in Bulgaria of Neophytus, the newly appointed patriarchist bishop of Varna, sparked off a series of anti-Greek riots, the worst of them being in Anhialo (Pomorie). Much of the anger directed at the Greeks had its origins in events in Macedonia.

THE MACEDONIAN CRISIS AND THE DECLARATION OF INDEPENDENCE, 1900–1908

The Macedonian problem was nothing if not complex. By 1900 it was dominated by two factors. The first was the international situation. In 1897, after yet another crisis in Crete, the Ottoman empire and Greece had gone to war, and within a few weeks the Greek army had been smashed in the plains of Thessaly. The war had two main results as far as Macedonia was concerned. The first was that it reversed the opinion which had been gaining ground since the Armenian massacres of 1894 that the Ottoman empire was about to dissolve; a crisis in the Balkans was not, after all, inevitable. The Russians sighed with relief and turned their attention to their internal problems and to the Far East, agreeing with Austria-Hungary that the Balkans should be kept 'on ice'. The second result of the 1897 war was that the Porte now felt that it had little to fear from Greece and, loyal to its traditional practice of dividing its potential opponents, began to favour the patriarchist cause in Macedonia at the expense of the exarchist and Serbian.

The other dominating factor in the Macedonian problem was that two rival Macedonian organisations had appeared. The first had been founded in Macedonia in 1893 and is best known to history by the name it later assumed, the Internal Macedonian Revolutionary Organisation, or IMRO. IMRO's objective was an autonomous Macedonia to be achieved by a mass uprising; some factions in the organisation hoped that an autonomous Macedonia would then become part of a Balkan, socialist federation. The second organisation was the Supreme Committee established in 1894. It also called for an autonomous Macedonia but wanted this to be the prelude to the incorporation of the area into Bulgaria in much the same way that autonomous Rumelia had joined Bulgaria in 1885. The supremacists had no faith in a mass uprising and planned instead to use *cheti* which would produce such disorder that the Porte would have to cede autonomy, probably after intervention by the great powers, much in the way they had after 1876; in 1895 one supremacist band captured the town of Melnik and held it for two days.

The activity of the supremacist bands, which was connived at by Ferdinand and his officials, threatened to melt the ice in the Balkans and therefore angered the Russians. Between 1900 and 1902 the Bulgarian government was in negotiations with St Petersburg for financial help. When Danev, who had become prime minister in January 1902, went to the Russian capital in the following month he was told that such help would be forthcoming only on certain very harsh conditions. The Bulgarians were to put an end to the incursions into Macedonia, and they were to agree to the appointment of a Serb to the critical post of administrator of the Skopje diocese. The Bulgarians had no choice but to accept, even though the latter condition was a huge blow to their cause in northern Macedonia. Danev returned to Sofia and took some measures against the Macedonian activists. They were not enough and in October, on the twenty-fifth anniversary of the victory in the Shipka Pass, the celebrations of which were attended by a number of prominent Russians, a supremacist band crossed into Macedonia and tried to raise a rebellion in Gorna Djumaya, the present-day Blagoevgrad.

Russian and Austro-Hungarian diplomacy now went into action. A reform scheme for Macedonia was drafted and the Russian foreign minister, Count Lamsdorff, appeared in Belgrade and Sofia to demand once more an end to the incursions. This time the Bulgarian government had to bite the bullet. In February 1903 Danev introduced into the sûbranie a bill dissolving all Macedonian organisations and calling for the arrest of their leaders. After two days of intense debate the bill was passed. Shortly thereafter Danev resigned and a new administration was formed by the National Liberal Party, the stambolovists, though the premiership went not to the party leader, Dimitûr Petkov, but to the non-party General Racho Petrov who was a close confidant of Prince Ferdinand.

With the dissolution of the organisations inside Bulgaria the focus of the Macedonian question was entirely on Macedonia itself. In January 1903 the central committee of IMRO, meeting in Salonika, had taken a fateful decision: their long-planned mass uprising would be staged in the coming summer. The central committee had been hustled into this decision. The supremacists had not yet been dissolved and the central committee feared further incursions from their bands would frighten the Ottoman forces into a more advanced state of readiness. The central committee also feared that the reform scheme produced by Austria-Hungary and Russia would be implemented and improve the situation in Macedonia to such an extent that there would be no response to calls for a mass uprising. In April the Ottoman forces were put on their guard by a series of anarchist bomb outrages, and in May IMRO suffered a devastating blow when it lost its most able leader, Gotse Delchev, in a chance encounter with a group of Ottoman soldiers.

Despite these setbacks the rising took place as planned on 15 August, St Elijah's Day, or Ilinden in Slavonic. A few days later, on the Feast of the Transfiguration, Preobrazhenie, a rising was staged in the Adrianople province. The Ilinden-Preobrazhenie rising attracted more support than previous attempts to incite the Christians of the Ottoman Europe and administrative centres were established at Krushevo in Macedonia and Strandja in eastern Thrace. But the rebels could not survive without foreign help. And that help could only come from Bulgaria because IMRO was seen as essentially pro-Bulgarian by the Serbs and Greeks. But Bulgaria dared not act alone. To do so would alarm the other Balkan states and would enrage Russia and Austria-Hungary, besides which after the 1897 war no Balkan state was anxious to face the Ottoman armies alone. The rising therefore proceeded to its inevitable, grim conclusion. The embryonic administrations of Krushevo and Strandja were suppressed, and the rebellion's supporters savagely punished. Many exarchist villages were destroyed, their crops burned, their cattle seized, and their teachers and priests packed off to exile in Asia Minor. Thousands of weary refugees trudged into Bulgaria, some of them going on from there to the New World; those who had remained in Macedonia could often find shelter and sustenance only from patriarchist or Serbian organisations. It was a blow from which the exarchist cause in Macedonia never fully recovered.

The stambolovist government made the best of this dismal situation by the traditional stambolovist means of controlling the

Macedonians at home and seeking concessions from the Porte abroad. In a treaty signed in March 1904 the Bulgarians promised to take further steps to control the Macedonian organisations, and the Ottoman government granted an amnesty to most of those arrested after the uprising; the Bulgarians were also to be allowed to appoint commercial agents in important Macedonian towns.

In the same month Petrov's cabinet also concluded an agreement with Serbia. It was basically a military convention aimed at combatting any external interference in Macedonia. It was not of lasting importance because the basic problem was not external interference but clashes between Bulgarian, Serbian and Greek supporters inside Macedonia. This was in part because the Austro-Russian reform scheme called for the redrawing of Macedonian administrative boundaries to produce units of greater ethnic homogeneity. The Greek, Bulgarian and Serbian factions interpreted this as an invitation to use ethnic cleansing to create zones of influence.

It was anger at the activity of Greek bands which did much to fuel the anti-Greek outbursts of 1906 in Bulgaria but in other respects the importance of the Macedonian question in Bulgarian politics subsided. Many people were tired of an issue for which they could see no solution. The Macedonian organisations did not help. Within Macedonia they continued to levy taxes on the remaining and impoverished exarchist communities, whilst in exile their leaders fell to unseemly and frequently violent feuding; a series of spectacular assassinations in Sofia in 1906 and 1907 did little to enhance the image of the Macedonian organisations. Meanwhile the stambolovist government argued that the Macedonian issue would be settled either by international diplomacy or, failing that, by armed action. But it would be the armed action of modern states and armies, not of feuding guerilla units, and this being the case, the most appropriate tactic was to wait patiently and prepare assiduously a modern and effective army.

The stambolovists were allowed to wait only until January 1908. The student riots of 1907 had angered Ferdinand and he replaced General Petrov with the stambolovist party leader Petkov, but the latter was assassinated in March. His successor, Petûr Gudev, did little more than fill his own pockets from the public purse. He was replaced in January 1908 in an operation typical of Ferdinand's personal rule. The stambolovist cabinet was destabilised and then replaced by one headed by Aleksandûr Malinov who had become leader of the Democratic Party when Karavelov died in 1903. After the formation of the new government an election was held to manufacture a comfortable sûbranie majority, the Democratic Party having had only two deputies in the outgoing assembly.

Malinov's Democratic Party had no more taste for this way of proceeding than any other of the parties, and one of his government's most notable legislative achievements was to introduce a graduated shift towards proportional representation under which it would be much more difficult to fix electoral returns. For most of its time in office, however, the Malinov government was preoccupied with external affairs, and in particular with the declaration of full independence in October 1908 and its consequences.

The declaration of independence arose from unexpected causes. In July the Young Turks had seized power in Constantinople and announced that they intended to modernise and unify all Ottoman territories; that included, by their book, the provinces of Eastern Rumelia, or southern Bulgaria, and Bosnia-Hercegovina, the latter having been administered by Austria-Hungary since 1878. The first sign of trouble had been when the Bulgarian minister in Constantinople had been treated not as the representative of a foreign government but as the governor of an Ottoman province. More serious was a strike by ORC workers in Constantinople which spread to the company's lines in southern Bulgaria. The Bulgarians were enraged that at a time of international tension the railways in half the country could be paralysed by a strike in a foreign state. On 19 September, the anniversary of the Union of 1885,* the Bulgarians nationalised ORC property in their country. On 5 October Ferdinand declared full independence. The restrictions

---

* The Union of 1885 had taken place on 6 September according to the Julian calendar then used by most Orthodox Christian states; in the nineteenth century the Julian calendar was twelve days behind the Gregorian calendar used in western and central Europe. In the twentieth century the Julian calendar was thirteen days behind the Gregorian, the anniversary of 6 September therefore occurring on the 19th rather than the 18th in the western system. Stoilov's modernising impulses had led him to try and switch to the Gregorian calendar for state business, but conservative, religious opposition defeated him. The change was eventually made in 1916.

of vassaldom had not in recent years been great but they had been much resented. Austria-Hungary annexed Bosnia-Hercegovina on 6 October.

The declaration of independence was not universally popular. The Macedonian lobby resented the fact that it had been issued before union with the lost territory had been secured, whilst some thought there were dangers in Ferdinand's being so closely associated with this measure. The most striking expression of such feelings was seen in 1911 when a Grand National Assembly met in Tûrnovo to register the constitutional changes the declaration had made necessary. When Ferdinand opened the GNA Stamboliiski led fifty-odd agrarians out of the hall in protest. It was a symbolic gesture and did not frustrate the GNA's real tasks which were to declare Ferdinand 'King of the Bulgarians', and to enact a constitutional amendment stating that the king and the cabinet should have the right to conclude foreign treaties.

Ferdinand's personal power had been strengthened and secret diplomacy had become possible. It was soon to produce dramatic results.

BALKAN DIPLOMACY AND THE BALKAN WARS, 1908–1913

Shortly before the GNA met in Tûrnovo a new government had been formed under Ivan Geshov who had succeeded Stoilov as leader of the Nationalist Party. Ferdinand was known to loathe Geshov deeply primarily because the Nationalists were amongst the fiercest critics of the prince's personal rule. If the king so mistrusted the Nationalists on internal affairs their elevation to office must mean that the king approved of their views on foreign policy. Geshov's first priority in this area was better relations with Russia, and as Russia had been calling for some time for a Bulgarian–Serbian alliance it was widely believed that Geshov had been appointed to bring that about.

There was reason enough for the two Balkan states to move closer together. Young Turk rule had not brought peace to the peninsula and in particular had angered the Albanians; these former loyal servants of the sultan were now subjected to more central government in the form of taxation, conscription and an attempt to disarm them. They rebelled every summer from 1909 to 1912. This increasing disorder raised two great dangers for the surrounding Balkan states. The first was that the powers might intervene to impose reforms which would work and which they would supervise. The second was that one or more powers might itself occupy part of the peninsula, and when Italy declared war on Turkey in 1911 over territorial disputes in North Africa this danger became more ominous. In either case the door would be closed on expansion by the Balkan states. But if two or more of those states could form an alliance they would make intervention by any external power more difficult. Russia meanwhile feared Austro-Hungarian rather than Italian encroachment and saw in a Balkan alliance the best barrier against it.

When negotiations between Belgrade and Sofia began Russian diplomacy was under the illusion that the two states were aiming for a defensive alliance. The Bulgarians and Serbs knew full well that the alliance could only have an offensive purpose. They wanted to seize the Ottoman empire in Europe before there was time for reform or intervention by the powers. The negotiations were not easy. The Bulgarians, obviously hoping for a second Eastern Rumelia, pressed that Macedonia should be given autonomy; the Serbs insisted on partition. To this the Bulgarians eventually agreed but it proved impossible to draw final lines of division and the central area around Skopje was declared the 'contested zone' whose fate would, if necessary, be submitted to the tsar for arbitration.

A treaty on these lines was signed in February 1912. In the spring the situation in Macedonia deteriorated yet further and the Greeks hastily concluded a treaty with the Bulgarians, so hastily in fact that there were no clauses regulating the division of any conquered territory. The Greeks also concluded an alliance with the Serbs. Montenegro was not to be left out and concluded verbal agreements with the other three states.

By the summer of 1912 Macedonia was in chaos. The annual Albanian revolt spilled over into the Vardar valley and reached as far as Skopje, forcing the Young Turk government to resign. The Bulgarians faced mounting pressure at home for action to defend the exarchists in Macedonia, pressure which culminated in a huge, pro-war rally in Sofia on 5 September. Two days later the king and cabinet decided upon war and set about making the final arrangements at home and with their allies. Montenegro declared war on the Ottoman empire on 8 October; the other allies followed suit ten days later.

For the Bulgarian army the main task was to drive back the enemy on the plains of eastern Thrace, although other small forces were sent to join the Serbs in Macedonia, and to race down the Struma valley in the hope of reaching Salonika before the Greeks. In their main campaign the Bulgarians were stunningly successful. By the first week of November the Ottoman forces had been driven back to the Tchataldja lines around their capital.

The king and most politicians wanted to push forward and attempt to take Constantinople; Ferdinand was even said to have ordered a sumptuous uniform for the occasion. The general staff was less enthusiastic; the troops were exhausted and there had been an outbreak of cholera in some units. The civilians prevailed but the soldiers' caution proved justified, and on 17 November the attack was abandoned. Within days an armistice had been signed and all the belligerents had agreed to meet in St James's Palace, London, to determine the terms of a peace settlement. The great powers had in the meantime let it be known that an independent Albania must emerge from the wreckage of the Ottoman empire in Europe.

Whilst the discussions in London were in progress fighting broke out again on 3 February 1913 in Thrace when the Bulgarians launched an attack on Adrianople, one of the few fortresses left in Ottoman control. The fighting lasted until the surrender of the garrison on 26 March; during the siege Bulgarian aeroplanes carried out the first aerial bombardment in European history. Despite their success in Adrianople the Bulgarians were faced with a diplomatic problem for which no satisfactory conclusion could be found. The Romanian government had demanded territorial compensation for the gains of its neighbours and, it said, as a reward for its good behaviour during the war. Such compensation could only come from Bulgaria and after an ambassadorial conference in St Petersburg the Bulgarians were forced to concede the southern Dobrudja to a line from Silistra to Balchik.

The general settlement of the war came later with the signature of the treaty of London on 30 May 1913. The treaty stated that an

Plate 6.2   Bulgarian and Ottoman representatives meet to discuss the signing of the armistice after an unsuccessful Bulgarian assault on the defensive lines around Constantinople, November 1912. Note the ORC carriage in the background.

Albanian state should be created and its borders defined by an international commission; the rest of the former Ottoman possessions, north of a line from Enos to Midia, were to be divided amongst the allies as they saw fit. This was not going to be easy. The loss of the southern Dobrudja intensified Bulgarian determination to secure its full share of the Macedonian spoils. Sofia pressed for 'proportionality', arguing that as Bulgaria had contributed the major share of the fighting it should receive the largest gains. The Greeks and Serbs invoked the notion of 'balance', stressing that the future peace of the Balkans could only be secured if the victors emerged from the war more or less equal in strength. The core of the problem was the contested zone. When the Bulgarians suggested that the question be submitted to Russia for arbitration the Serbs refused, insisting instead on direct negotiations in which the Greeks must take part. The talks were as futile as the Bulgarians had feared. When they collapsed Geshov gave up and was succeeded as prime minister by Danev.

Geshov was much discouraged by the powerful war lobby then forming in Sofia, a lobby greatly bolstered by the knowledge that a

Greek–Serbian alliance had been signed. In the war party were to be found most Macedonian groups, the non-socialist and non-agrarian opposition parties, the general staff, the king and finally Danev who was at last persuaded that nothing acceptable could be expected from Russian arbitration. On 29 June the Bulgarian army attacked its former Serbian and Greek allies.

At first all went well for the Bulgarians but after two weeks of fighting news came that the Romanians were mobilising, shortly after which the Ottoman army crossed the southern frontier and took Adrianople. The northern borders were undefended which meant there was nothing to stop the Romanians entering Sofia and the Bulgarians therefore sued for peace. In the treaties of Bucharest (10 August) and Constantinople (13 October) they lost much of the territory recently acquired. They retained only Pirin Macedonia to a point half way down the Struma valley and a strip of Thrace which included the Aegean port of Dedeagach.

The second Balkan war had caused more casualties than the first; it had witnessed horrific crimes against civilians; and it had produced a second partition of San Stefano Bulgaria. It was in every respect a disaster for Bulgaria. The loss of the southern Dobrudja, confirmed in the treaty of Bucharest, deprived Bulgaria of its most advanced agricultural areas and the chief source of its grain exports; the territories acquired were by contrast backward and expensive – even Dedeagach was useless because the railway to it wound in and out of Ottoman territory. If full advantage were to be taken of this new territory on the Aegean coast a new line to and harbour facilities at Porto Lagos would have to be constructed. Furthermore, the new masters of Macedonia were not the Ottomans whose *millet* system allowed the exarchists cultural autonomy, but aggressive, assertive nationalist states which would impose their own culture on all Macedonians.

During the disastrous second war Danev had resigned on 17 July to be succeeded by a coalition of liberal factions under the premiership of Vasil Radoslavov. In November Radoslavov went to the polls but, in a legacy left by the Malinov administration, was forced to conduct the elections under proportional representation. He did not secure a dependable majority and therefore called another election in April 1914. This time he allowed the new territories to vote,

Map 6.1   Territorial changes after the Balkan wars.

but he did not permit the opposition parties to campaign there. The new territories had little political experience and fell easy prey to Radoslavov's electoral managers. He secured his desired majority.

BULGARIA AND THE FIRST WORLD WAR

The most pressing task facing the Radoslavov government after the elections of April 1914 was to find money to pay for the recent wars and to develop the newly acquired territory. In July 1914 a loan of 500 million gold leva was granted by a consortium of German banks. As war clouds gathered in Europe a loan of this size inevitably had international significance, and many believed that it was Radoslavov's pro-Austrian and pro-German attitudes that had led to the German loan. There was some substance to these allegations. The French had also been approached but they had insisted that if they lent the money Bulgaria must follow a policy favourable to the western powers. Ferdinand and Radoslavov refused such conditions and when war broke out in Europe declared 'strict and loyal neutrality' and introduced a state of emergency.

In a Bulgaria exhausted by the recent wars neutrality was popular but the loan was not. This was in part because its conditions, many believed, amounted to a virtual contradiction of neutrality. The Bulgarians were required to earmark a series of state revenues to service the debt; they were obliged to grant the contract for the construction of a railway to Porto Lagos to a German consortium; and the Germans were to take over the running of the state mines in Pernik and Bobov Dol. There were rowdy scenes in the sûbranie when the issue was debated, at one point Radoslavov waving a revolver above his head, and few of the neutral witnesses present believed the government when it claimed the loan had been approved by a show of hands.

The loan did not, however, commit Ferdinand to the German cause, and both sides to the European conflict courted him. Bulgaria, despite its war-weariness, still had a large and well-equipped army, and it commanded a strategic position in the Balkans; through it the allies could reach Serbia, whilst it was also the vital link between the central powers and the Ottoman empire which had joined them in October; and from Bulgaria

Constantinople and the Straits could be controlled. Ferdinand and Radoslavov listened to suitors from both sides but made no commitment until the late summer of 1915, mobilising and declaring 'armed neutrality' on 21 September and joining in the central powers' renewed offensive against Serbia on 11 October.

Two factors determined this fateful decision. The central powers could offer more, and by the summer of 1915 it seemed they would win. What the Germans could offer was all of Macedonia and much of Thrace; they even persuaded the Porte to allow Bulgaria full control of the railway line to Dedeagach. The allies, on the other hand, would talk only of Thrace up to the Enos-Midia line, whilst for them what Bulgaria could be allowed in Macedonia would depend on how much the Serbs were prepared to relinquish. And the Serbian leader, Nikola Pašić, said he would not concede one square inch. The Russians backed the Serbs. In early 1915 Russian and allied intransigence on Macedonia was increased by military success; the Russians took the vital fortress of Przemyśl, the allies established themselves in Gallipoli whence they could reach Constantinople, and in May the Italians joined the war on their side. Two months later the position had been reversed. The Italian intervention had had little impact, other than to make the Serbs, who feared Italian designs on Dalmatia, more determined to hold on to Macedonia, allied troops were pinned on the murderous beaches of Gallipoli, and the Russians had lost Przemyśl and huge swathes of territory in Russian Poland together with its important industries. Furthermore, allied diplomacy in Bulgaria had been less adept than that of the central powers. The allies tended to court opposition politicians whereas the Germans paid much more attention to Ferdinand and his immediate advisors. Given the nature of Ferdinand's personal rule, his control over foreign affairs, and the state of emergency which limited the opposition's freedom of manoeuvre, the central powers were backing the stronger horse.

The opposition parties did not welcome mobilisation. They all declared themselves 'resolute partisans of peace' and all of them, with the exception of the narrows, joined together in a United Bloc to demand that the sûbranie be allowed to debate and decide upon the issue of war or peace. Radoslavov refused such a debate. Ferdinand, however, did agree to receive a delegation consisting of

Plate 6.3   Bulgarian soldiers on Belassitsa mountain during the first world war, just over a thousand years after their predecessors were defeated by the Byzantine emperor, Basil the Bulgar Slayer.

leaders of the opposition. The meeting ended in a furious row between the king and Stamboliiski and when the latter published details of this he was thrust into gaol. No parliamentary debate on the war took place until December. By then the opposition parties had decided to rally to the cause of the nation and all of them, again with the exception of the narrows, voted in favour of war credits.

For the Bulgarian forces the first world war was for most part not a war of rapid movement. Serbian Macedonia had been occupied in 1915 and in 1916 they advanced into Greek territory as far as Fort Rupel, and later in the year, following a Greek attack, took Drama, Seres and Kavalla; in the same year Bitola was lost after a ferocious battle on mount Kaimakchalan. Also in 1916 Romania had entered the war on the allied side only to suffer huge defeats; the Bulgarians, accompanied by Ottoman units, took the southern Dobrudja and later moved across the Danube into Romania proper. Thereafter the military fronts, especially in the south and south-west, remained more or less stable until the late summer of 1918.

Despite general rejoicing at the reacquisition of Macedonia problems soon began to appear on the home front. In Macedonia itself the military became more and more concerned at the nature of the civilian administration. Too many free-booters and incompetents had been given office in the new territories. By August 1916 the military were seriously concerned lest maladministration destabilise the area immediately behind the front line, and they attempted to seize control of the Macedonian administration. They failed and the problems intensified.

These problems were not confined to the new lands. Almost from the beginning of the war there were difficulties with supplies. By 1916 there were shortages even of bread. The deterioration in supplies was reflected in the inflation rate. Taking the cost of living in 1914 as a base of 100, by the end of 1916 it stood at 200, and by July 1918 was 847. And these were official figures which took no cognisance of the black market where prices were even higher and which was often the only source of supply. By the late summer of 1918 these difficulties were so severe that they entirely undermined civilian and military morale, and were a major factor in Bulgaria's collapse in September.

The roots of the supply problem were varied. In 1915 mobilisation had had some impact on the distribution if not the gathering of the harvest, and far too much of that harvest had been requisitioned for the army. As the war went on future sowing and harvesting were hit by the mobilisation both of men and of draught animals, the latter being needed in huge numbers to transport supplies to the army in Macedonia where the terrain was mountainous, the roads primitive and railways almost non-existent. There was also competition between civilian and military procurement agencies. The evil of corruption was omnipresent; and the requisitioning agencies became increasingly unpopular as their personnel took commodities such as sugar and salt which they had no right to take but which they could sell at high prices on the black market. An aggravating factor was the presence of German and Austrian troops in Bulgaria. They were better paid than the Bulgarians and they bought increasing quantities of food to send home, frequently exceeding the quotas officially allowed them. In this they were much aided by the facts that the Germans controlled both the railway and the telephone systems, and that after December 1915 German and Austrian currency was legal tender in Bulgaria. Official German and Austrian

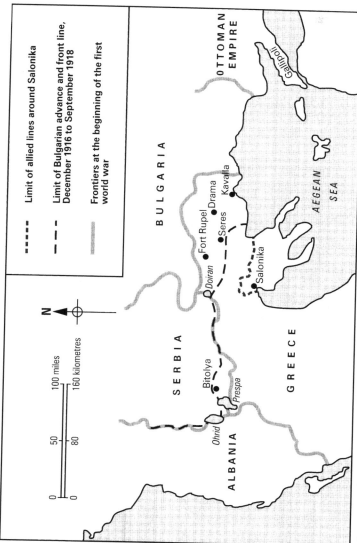

Map 6.2   The southern Balkan front during the first world war.

procurement agencies were equally rapacious, often having no consideration for local requirements or for the long-term needs for fodder and seeds; in 1917 three-quarters of the immensely fertile arable area of the Dobrudja was reported to be untilled because so much of the previous year's harvest had been taken that there was no seed. Nor was the problem of supplying civilian and military markets helped by changes in administrative responsibility. In March 1915 the public welfare act had given the government the right to control the price of deficit goods in time of war. In 1916, as the situation worsened, a central committee for economic and social welfare was established, again under civilian control. It had hardly had time to organise itself when, in April 1917, most of its powers were transferred to the newly established directorate for economic and social welfare which was under military domination. The military body was no more successful than the civilian.

Inevitably there was reaction, particularly in the occupied areas where deprivations were at their worst. The Morava valley saw a series of outbursts against Bulgarian occupation, even in villages which were purely Bulgarian. Protest was encouraged by events in Russia. In March 1917 Stamboliiski, writing from his prison cell, declared that the fall of tsardom would allow the USA to enter the war on the allied side and that the central powers were therefore doomed. By the summer soldiers on the front opposite the Russians in Romania were forming 'soviets' and five hundred troops, many of them agrarian supporters, had been gaoled for political agitation. The Russian revolution also produced the call for a peace 'without annexations or indemnities', calls which were echoed in March 1917 by the leader of the Radical Democratic Party in Bulgaria, Tsanov, who publicly questioned the right of Bulgarian troops to occupy parts of Romania which had no Bulgarians amongst their population. By the end of the year public pressure was much stronger, and the narrow socialist leader, Dimitûr Blagoev, could attract over ten thousand to a rally in Sofia to call for an end to the war and to the political system which had made it possible. Early in 1918 there was a mounting tide of social unrest with protests in Gabrovo and riots in Stanimaka and Samokov, whilst in May a woman was killed in Sliven while taking part in one of the many meetings called throughout the country in what came to be known as the 'women's revolt'.

As the internal situation deteriorated Radoslavov was faced with unexpected and unusual difficulties on the diplomatic front. In May 1918 the treaty of Bucharest regulated the northern Dobrudja. The Bulgarians had confidently expected that they would be given responsibility for this area but they were to be disappointed as it was placed under joint German, Austrian and Bulgarian administration. Radoslavov remarked that his country had been treated more like a defeated enemy than a victorious ally, and on 20 June 1918 he resigned.

Malinov, the leader of the Democratic Party, now formed a government. He had hoped to include Stamboliiski in it but the latter would accept office only if the war were ended, and to this Ferdinand would not consent. Malinov did manage to wrestle sole control of the northern Dobrudja from his allies, but it was a hollow victory. Bulgaria's capacity to continue fighting was exhausted; to use a figure of speech almost too literal for comfort, the Bulgarians had no more stomach for war.

The people, particularly those in the towns, were on the verge of starvation, and some in Macedonia had gone beyond it with deaths from malnutrition being reported in Ohrid and other centres. Soldiers, who at the front were already suffering shortages of food, ammunition and clothing, came home on leave or to help in the harvest and found that their loved ones were in no better and perhaps even a worse condition. Their morale collapsed and when the French and British launched an offensive on 15 September resistance broke. Within a week Franco-British troops had entered Bulgaria. The government sued for peace and on 29 September 1918 signed an armistice in Salonika.

On the day allied troops entered the country Stamboliiski was released from prison. It was hoped that he would contain a military revolt centred on Radomir between Sofia and the advancing allies. There was no need for him to do so. When the armistice was signed the soldiers gained their principal demand – peace – and the revolt fizzled out. For the second time in half a decade Ferdinand's personal regime, it was alleged, had led the nation to humiliating defeat. He abdicated and left the country on 3 October 1918. He was succeeded by his son, Boris III.

7

Bulgaria, 1918–1944

The peace treaty with Bulgaria was signed at Neuilly-sur-Seine on 27 November 1919. Bulgaria was required to relinquish all lands it had occupied during the recent conflict and it was also deprived of three small pockets on its western border, despite the fact that the vast majority of the local population was Bulgarian. Bulgaria also lost those parts of Thrace it had gained in the Balkan wars, although this loss was tempered somewhat by article 48 of the treaty which guaranteed Bulgaria 'economic access' to the Aegean; however, there was no indication of how that access was to be achieved. In peacetime it never was. The Neuilly settlement ruled that the Bulgarian army was to have a maximum effective strength of twenty thousand men, all of whom were to be volunteers. Reparations were to be paid both in kind and in money. Deliveries of coal, livestock and railway equipment were to be made to the governments of Greece, Yugoslavia and Romania, whilst Bulgaria was required to pay 2,250 million gold francs to the allies over a period of thirty-seven years. It was a preposterous sum and was soon recognised as such. In 1923 it was reduced to 550 million to be paid over sixty years, and in 1932 it was scrapped altogether.

Compared to Hungary, Germany and Austria the territorial provisions of the peace settlement were not harsh for Bulgaria. It lost just under nine thousand square kilometres of territory and ninety thousand more Bulgarians now found themselves under foreign rule.

The total number of Bulgarians living outside the national state was in the region of one million or about 16 per cent of all Bulgarians. Another and indirect effect of the peace settlement did, however, much affect Bulgaria. The reversion of Macedonia to Serbian and Greek rule produced yet another wave of refugees. Many of these lived in appalling conditions on the south-western borders of Bulgaria, their upkeep placing a substantial burden on the Bulgarian exchequer.

AGRARIAN RULE, 1919–1923

The domestic factors which played a major role in Bulgarian politics during the inter-war years were the agrarians, the communists, the old sûbranie parties, the Macedonian organisations, the army, and the throne.

Immediately after the war the two dominant factors were the agrarians and the communists. At the end of hostilities an interim cabinet had been formed under Teodor Teodorov of the People's Liberal Party. Its actions were closely observed by representatives of the allies who had troops stationed in Bulgaria. Its main duty was to preserve order until elections could be held in August 1919.

Those elections registered massive popular anger with the system which had taken Bulgaria into the war and approval of those parties which had opposed it. The agrarians took 31 per cent of the vote; the narrows, who had become the Bulgarian Communist Party (BCP) in May 1919, 18 per cent, and the democrats, the most left-wing of the old parties, 10 per cent. Stamboliiski formed a coalition with the democrats but his initial instinct had been to work with the communists; they, however, spurned him. They did not intend to form a coalition with anyone; they wanted and believed they could seize unadulterated power. The agrarians had the same ambition and an equal self-confidence.

The communists and the agrarians were in fact competing for the vacancy created by the collapse of the old parties. Open confrontation was to come at the turn of the year. The communists were full of confidence. As living standards in the towns continued to plummet their support increased, particularly in the trade unions, and on 24 December they joined with the social democrats, the former broads,

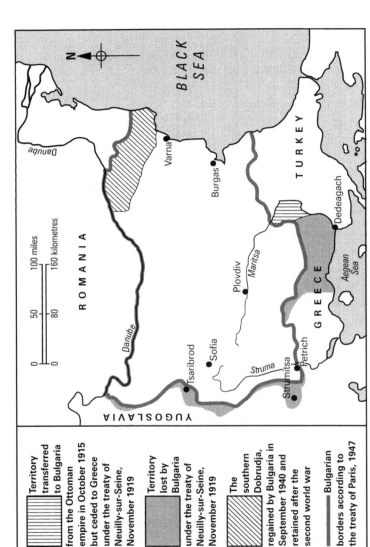

Map 7.1 Bulgaria's borders after the first and second world wars.

to stage a day of protest in Sofia. It was the first time the two socialist factions had cooperated since the split of 1903, and that cooperation continued when the transport and telegraph workers went on strike. Two days later a general strike was called. Stamboliiski reacted toughly. Strike leaders were arrested, their families' ration cards were withdrawn, and some were evicted from their homes. To enforce these measures Stamboliiski used the army, allied troops, the police and the Orange Guard. The latter, armed with clubs, had been set up recently by BANU to counteract the semi-armed groups established by the social democrats and the communists. On 5 January the general strike was called off, although some transport workers and the miners in Pernik continued the struggle for another six weeks.

Having defeated the communists on the streets Stamboliiski called a general election for 28 March 1920 to register popular endorsement of his victory. It produced a not entirely comforting result. One in three of the electorate voted for BANU but another one in five voted for the BCP. BANU returned 110 deputies and the BCP 51. Stamboliiski was just nine seats short of an absolute majority and therefore annulled the returns of thirteen deputies, nine of whom were communists and who were now replaced by agrarians. Stamboliiski had secured his absolute majority in a fashion worthy of the old sûbranie parties he so despised.

The agrarians were now in a position to implement their ideology and, in the words of the great Anglo-Irish journalist and friend of Bulgaria, James Bourchier, to transfer power 'from the political coteries of the towns, the office seekers and the parasites of the court, to the honest hard-working tillers of the soil, the bone and sinew of Bulgaria'. The agrarians' programme, which had not been drawn up until 1918, wanted to create a society in which all held enough but none too much land, and which was dominated by tidy, modernised villages with paved streets, clean water, proper sanitation, good schools, adequate libraries, and cinemas. The peasant proprietor was to be helped by the cooperatives which would provide credit, store crops and find markets; the cooperatives would fit the square peg of peasant proprietorship into the round hole of commercialised, capitalised agriculture.

Despite his parliamentary majority there were limitations on Stamboliiski's freedom of action. Reparations complicated matters not only because revenue had to be diverted to meet payments, but also because the government was forced to requisition draught animals for delivery to Bulgaria's neighbours. This impaired productivity and created yet another opportunity for corruption. Meanwhile, the allies remained suspicious of so radical a government, and in September 1921 they intervened to insist upon the dissolution of a government grain purchasing consortium which had restricted merchants' sphere of operations, to say nothing of their profits.

The grain consortium had been intended to restrict such profits and was part of BANU's offensive against those whom it considered parasites. Lawyers were even more in the firing line. They were denied the right to sit in parliament or on local councils, and were barred from major public office. The agrarians also established new lower courts to deal with issues such as boundary disputes, and in these courts peasants were to plead their own cases before judges elected by the local populace. The agrarians also greatly limited the king's power to make appointments, and they required banks to help fund credit cooperatives. BANU's main objective, however, was to redistribute land.

In June 1920 a bill was passed to establish a state land fund. Into this would go excess property. All Bulgarians were allowed four hectares of inalienable land but absentee owners were to lose anything above that amount. For those working their land the maximum holding was to be thirty hectares in arable areas and a little more in forest regions; there was to be an extra five hectares for the fifth and every subsequent member of a family. For those who lost land there was to be compensation in the form of government bonds, with payment being on a sliding scale which reduced the amount per hectare as the number of hectares increased. In April 1921 a second act was passed clamping down on the corruption which had allowed some owners to escape the first bill. The 1921 act also stated that monastic lands were now to be included within the act's provisions, and it made it easier for dwarf-holders and the few landless peasants to purchase more land. The agrarians had hoped to redistribute over a quarter of a million hectares but they were to be disappointed. The process of redistribution was slow and still open to corruption but most important of all there were very few individuals who owned

Plate 7.1   The old and the new in the Bulgarian peasantry; Aleksandûr Stamboliiski with his father.

large estates, and institutional owners were more difficult to tackle. By June 1923 only 82,000 hectares had changed hands, and in 1926 only 1 per cent of all the land held in the country had been acquired as a result of redistribution. On the other hand, after the fall of the agrarian government almost all of their land legislation, including the principle of maximum holdings, remained in force. This did not apply, however, to the extension of the maximum property regulations to urban areas and the ruling that all families should have only two rooms and a kitchen, with extra rooms for larger families. This legislation was repealed as was that placing limitations on office space.

Another major item of BANU legislation which survived the fall of the regime was the compulsory labour service introduced in June 1920. This required all males between twenty and forty to perform a total of eight months labour, whilst unmarried females between sixteen and thirty were to perform four months. The labour service was usually carried out on public works such as road or school building, and until October 1921 it was impossible to purchase exemption. The compulsory labour service no doubt benefited the nation but it aroused suspicion amongst the allies not least because it was organised along military lines, used military terms for its officials, and originally had a former general as its director.

The BANU government carried out many other reforms. A progressive income tax was introduced. Dwarf-holders who received land were required to consolidate separate strips into one holding before they were allowed to purchase more land from the state land fund. Secondary schooling was made compulsory, its vocational content was increased, and a massive school-building programme produced over eleven hundred new schools. At the same time the teaching profession was purged of communists.

In foreign policy Stamboliiski sustained his pre-war lack of interest in territorial expansion. This pleased the victorious allies, as did the fact that he kept well away from Lenin's revolutionary regime. After Stamboliiski had toured European capitals in 1920 Bulgaria became the first defeated state to be admitted to the League of Nations.

Also pleasing to the allies was the agrarian leader's desire for good relations with his western neighbour. The main problem was that posed by the Macedonian organisations. These had become fragmented but one of them, that led from October 1923 by Ivan Mihailov, had established a virtual state within the state at Petrich where the Bulgarian, Greek and Yugoslav borders met. From here the mihailovists launched raids into Greek or Yugoslav Macedonia. There was little Stamboliiski could do to contain these irreconcilables but he did attempt to purge the frontier police of Macedonian sympathisers. In November 1922, when he was at last allowed to visit Belgrade, he used the Yugoslav capital as the venue for a vehement denunciation of the Macedonian extremists, and in March 1923 he signed the Nish convention by which Bulgaria and Yugoslavia agreed to cooperate in the struggle against those extremists; in the following month the Bulgarian government banned all organisations suspected of terrorist activities, suppressed their newspapers, and confined their leaders to internment camps.

Naturally the Macedonians were greatly angered by these measures. Nor were they the only ones dissatisfied with agrarian rule. All sections of the nation suffered from the corruption which, though always a feature of Bulgarian life, reached enormous proportions under the agrarians, especially amongst the petty officials appointed by BANU to administrative posts in the villages. But it was in the urban areas that resentment was most bitterly felt.

The working class could not escape the effects of inflation which by 1923 had reduced the leva to a seventh of its 1919 value; and the tough action taken against the strikers of 1919–20 and other measures to limit communist activities increased resentment. For the more wealthy townspeople the regulations limiting personal and business accommodation were intensely hated. Amongst professionals the lawyers had clear reasons for dissatisfaction but they were not the only ones to bear grudges or harbour fears. Doctors were alarmed by agrarian talk of forcing many of them to work in remote villages. Teachers resented action taken against the communists in their ranks and even more so the rule that all teachers had to be periodically reelected; academics so resented governmental interference with the autonomy of the university that in 1922 they went on strike; even the Academy of Sciences was angry, not least because of the minister of education's obsessive and eventually unfulfilled desire to reform the alphabet. The church, too, had a number of causes for complaint. The religious content of the school curriculum had been reduced, church property had been subjected to the land redistribution acts, and the holy synod had been moved to Rila, its Sofia headquarters being turned into an agronomy institute. The professional civil servants meanwhile were disturbed by the propensity of the government to bypass official, state channels in favour of BANU party organisations which were becoming a byword for corruption. The Orange Guard, for example, were taking over some of the functions of the police; local BANU organisations, the *druzhbi*, rather than local government officials were told to draw up the fine details of the land reform scheme; and the *druzhbi* rather than the village or urban district councils were given the major role in the periodic reelection of teachers.

An extremely important element of the discontented in the towns were the former army officers who had been decommissioned as a result of the treaty of Neuilly. They had lost status as well as their careers and their livelihood. They knew that there had been little Stamboliiski could do to ameliorate the terms of the treaty but they greatly resented his apparently dismissive attitude towards the military profession, and even more so the fact that he did not even maintain the army at the permitted level of 20,000 men. Nor did they like the increasing use of the Orange Guard for state rather than purely party purposes. In 1922 a number of discontented officers formed the Military League. There was another military force in Bulgaria in the early 1920s. Over thirty thousand refugees from the Russian civil war under the command of General Wrangel had entered the country and they brought with them a quantity of heavy weaponry. In May 1922 Stamboliiski dissolved their organisation; amongst the population at large this was a welcome measure but Stamboliiski had created yet another group with cause for resentment.

The old political parties were also fearful and angry. They had established an electoral alliance, the Constitutional Bloc, and some leaders had formed a smaller, closer-knit organisation, the National Alliance. They feared Stamboliiski intended to establish a republic and a one-party state, their fears being greatly fuelled late in 1922 by the forcible disruption of the National Alliance's plans for a series of rallies culminating in a march on Sofia; Mussolini had 'marched' on Rome that October. Their fears increased when Stamboliiski abolished proportional representation and called an election in April 1923. BANU romped home with 212 deputies to the BCP's 16 and the Constitutional Bloc's 15.

After the election a conspiracy was formed consisting of some mihailovists from Petrich, the National Alliance, the Military League and even some social democrats. The conspirators informed the king of their intentions and, calculating correctly that the communists would remain inert, acted in the early hours of 9 June 1923. The agrarian regime was dismantled in hours, though it was not until 14 June that Stamboliiski was found and brutally tortured to death by his Macedonian captors. A new government was formed under the premiership of Aleksandûr Tsankov, an academic economist.

The Bulgarian communists had stood idly by in June 1923 but for so doing they were severely criticised by Moscow and told to redeem their honour. This led to an abortive communist uprising in September 1923. The Tsankov government had no difficulty in suppressing it and used it as an excuse to impose further restrictions on individual rights and political liberties.

Within less than four months the two most radical factors in the Bulgarian political arena had been immobilised. In effect the left had been dealt a seemingly crippling blow.

THE RULE OF THE DEMOCRATIC ALLIANCE, 1923–1931

After seizing power Tsankov fashioned a new grouping, the Democratic Alliance, to provide him with reliable support in the sûbranie. The Democratic Alliance was a coalition of the National Alliance, the Military League, the mihailovists, and a motley collection of factions from the Democratic and Nationalist Parties.

Initially Tsankov's rule was firm but tinged with attempts at consensus. A defence of the realm act was passed in November 1923 which once again banned terrorism and gave the government powers which it used to influence the elections held that month. The act was also used in April 1924 to ban the BCP, confiscate its property, and dissolve its trade union; using the same legislation the eight BCP deputies elected in November 1923 were deprived of their seats in March 1925. Yet at the same time the government repealed very little of agrarian legislation and continued with the programme of land reform enacted by Stamboliiski.

Any pretence at conciliation ended in 1925. On 16 April a bomb planted by the communists exploded in the roof of Sofia's Sveta Nedelya cathedral during a state funeral due to be attended by the king and the entire political establishment. Amazingly no prominent figure was amongst the one hundred and twenty or so fatalities. The bomb unleashed a ferocious reaction. Martial law was declared and thousands of left-wing activists were detained. Many of the detainees disappeared and there were rumours that some of them had been fed into the furnaces of the Sofia police headquarters. The fate of others was all too clear: they were executed in public.

Violence was not a communist or a government monopoly. In the early 1920s there had been further divisions in the ranks of IMRO with one faction calling for cooperation with the communists. This led to more feuding and consequent assassinations in Sofia and elsewhere. The mihailovists meanwhile retained their hold on the Petrich enclave and continued their guerilla activities in Serbia and Greece. After one raid in October 1925 the Greek army moved into southern Bulgaria; that it withdrew without further complications was one of the League of Nations' more notable successes.

Despite this help from the League of Nations the internal excesses which Tsankov had allowed were making Bulgaria into a pariah state. The king had already suggested to leading army officers that changes had to be made, but as yet his political standing was weak and his words went unheeded. International bankers were more effective. By 1925 Bulgaria was in desperate need of a loan. In an astute move it asked for one to help finance welfare schemes for the thousands of Macedonian refugees most of whom were still living in abject poverty. The refugees, the government argued, were a fertile recruiting ground for communist or Macedonian extremism, and could only be kept immune from such viruses by an injection of welfare spending, particularly if that spending were directed towards providing them with land of their own. The League of Nations was persuaded but in London where the bulk of the cash would be raised there were doubts. It was made clear that a government headed by Tsankov would never be in receipt of such a loan. In January 1926 therefore he resigned and was succeed by Andrei

Plate 7.2   Sveta Nedelya cathedral, Sofia, after its bombing by the communists on 16 April 1925.

Lyapchev, the leader of the Democratic Party and himself a Macedonian. The loan was then granted and over 650 village communes used the funds received from it to provide land for Macedonian refugees.

Lyapchev relaxed many of the restrictions imposed by Tsankov. Trade unions were allowed to function again and in 1927 the communists reformed under the title the Bulgarian Workers' Party (BWP) and had soon established attendant trade union and youth organisations. The Macedonians were also allowed to continue their often murderous activities.

By 1926 the tsankovist terror was over, the Bulgarian left had been eliminated, and the right had not, outside the ranks of the mihailovists, produced any significant movement. The moderate centre was therefore in control. It did not acquit itself well. The Lyapchev government had no great legislative programme and it fell into a form of aimless drift. This applied to the political scene as a whole. The agrarians, deprived of power and of the leader who had dominated them, splintered to such a degree that it was later said they had fragmented not into wings but feathers. Even the communists, renowned for their cohesion and discipline, showed signs of division. On the right a group around the journal *Lûch* (Ray) called for cooperation with other parties, a view strongly opposed by the 'left sectarians' who seized control of the party in 1929. The old sûbranie parties split even more. In 1926 there were nineteen identifiable factions within the assembly; by 1934 there were twenty-nine. Lyapchev took one step to counter drift in this sector. He introduced an Italian-style bonus system whereby the faction securing most of the votes in an election was awarded an automatic majority in the sûbranie. This system was in place in time for the 1927 elections which the Democratic Alliance won, albeit with a reduced majority.

By the end of the decade and in the early 1930s there were increasing calls for radical action. One such call came from Zveno (Link), an organisation founded in 1930 with a small membership associated with a newspaper of that name. The zvenari were of the intelligentsia and were avowedly élitist. They were also étatist, advocating increased power for a centralised and rationalised administration. They were authoritarian and saw in the political parties the origin of most of the ills besetting the country, believing that the present system encouraged politicians to put party before country. In foreign affairs they wanted better relations with Yugoslavia and were therefore hostile to the Macedonian organisations. They had powerful support from a number of republican-minded army officers and members of the Military League.

The hour of the zvenari had not yet come. When general elections were held in June 1931 the electorate was preoccupied with the intensifying economic crisis triggered by the world depression. It was an open election for which PR was reintroduced. Victory went to the People's Bloc which took 47 per cent of the vote and 150 seats as opposed to 31 per cent and 78 seats for the Democratic Alliance. The latter was now a broken force and it fell apart, Tsankov shearing away to form his own, avowedly fascist National Social Movement.

The People's Bloc consisted of factions from the Nationalist, Radical, and National Liberal Parties, together with one group of agrarians, the first time that any BANU faction had been back in office since the coup of 1923. The prime minister of the new government was the leader of the Democratic Party, Aleksandûr Malinov, but in October ill-health forced him to make way for his party colleague, Nikola Mushanov.

Any hopes entertained by the peasantry that the return to government of BANU, albeit only one faction of the party, would bring about an improvement in the peasants' lot were soon dashed. In part this was because the government had to weather the worst part of the great depression. In the five years from 1929 to 1934 peasant incomes fell by 50 per cent, urban unemployment soared, and even for those lucky enough still to be in work real wages fell by almost a third. The government took a number of steps to cope with the crisis. Debt obligations were reduced by 40 per cent and the repayment periods extended; Hranoiznos, a government grain purchasing agency, was introduced in 1930, and encouragement was given to crop diversification, particularly into higher-price export commodities such as fruit and vegetables. But setting these efforts aside, the People's Bloc ministers did little to endear themselves to popular opinion. Whilst the peasants were experiencing almost unparalleled hardships the ministers, the agrarians no less than the others, were engaged in a grotesque exercise of self-enrichment accompanied by the most unseemly squabbles over the spoils of office. It was against this background that the communists secured notable successes in the local elections of November 1931 and took control of Sofia city council in February 1932. The government waited a year before dissolving the council. Another beneficiary of the depression was Tsankov's National Social Movement which began to find an increasing number of adherents, particularly amongst the young of the towns and cities.

Bulgaria also faced difficulties abroad. A series of Balkan conferences in the early 1930s had failed to secure significant moves towards unity in the peninsula because Bulgaria could never accept that existing borders were permanent, a condition upon which the other states insisted if Bulgaria were to be included in any agreement. For this reason Bulgaria was not included when the Balkan entente was signed in Athens in February 1934. The combination of Turkey, Greece, Yugoslavia and Romania had an ominous similarity to the hostile coalition of the second Balkan war. Foreign relations were further complicated by the mihailovists who became even more extreme in their utterances. In June 1933 Mihailov himself called for an attack on the Yugoslav embassy in Sofia which he called a 'nest of vipers'. In the following month a convention in London included in its definition of an aggressive state the support of or failure to suppress any subversive groups operating on that state's territory. Under this description Bulgaria could easily be branded an aggressive state and because of its isolation would then be in an extremely vulnerable position.

By the spring of 1934 external and internal tensions were rising. Tsankov had called a large rally for 21 May and confidently expected an audience of over fifty thousand; the rally was to coincide with a private visit to Bulgaria by Hermann Göring. There seemed no-one able or willing to curb the Macedonians or restrain the fascists. The agrarian left was too divided, the communists would be suppressed, the old parties were enfeebled, Zveno talked much but did little; only the army and the king were left.

On 19 May 1934 the army stepped into the breach. Taking advantage of yet another dispute amongst ministers as to who should have which cabinet office, pro-Zveno officers with strong connections to the Military League seized power. The coup was orchestrated by Colonel Damyan Velchev, but he chose not to become prime minister, this position being taken by his co-conspirator, Colonel Kimon Georgiev.

THE RULE OF THE *DEVETNAISETI*, MAY 1934–JANUARY 1935

The *devetnaiseti* (the '19thers'), as Velchev's group became known, ruled for only a short period but with considerable vigour and much in conformity with the ideas of Zveno.

They suspended civil rights and set up the directorate for social renewal which was given great influence over the press and other publications, over the arts, and in the organisation of youth activities; its objective was 'to direct the cultural and intellectual life of the nation towards unity and renewal'. One way in which unity was to be fostered was by changing Turkish topographical names to Bulgarian ones, and more such name changes took place under the *devetnaiseti* than at any other point in pre-war Bulgaria. Party political divisions were to disappear and the parties themselves were dissolved. So too were most existing trade unions, and in those that remained all officials had to be approved by the central government authorities. Plans to establish one large union, the Bulgarian Workers' Union, were drawn up and were implemented by the successor government. Although the Bulgarian Workers' Union was technically a voluntary organisation, by 1936 120,000 out of a total of 145,000 industrial workers had joined it. Membership was not by occupational category but by estate; the *devetnaiseti*, copying the Italian fascists, had divided society into seven estates: workers, peasants, craftsmen, merchants, intelligentsia, civil servants and members of the free professions. The estates were also to provide the basis for the election of three-quarters of the members of the new sûbranie, the existing one having been dissolved.

Rationalisation and centralisation, much championed by Zveno, were also very much a feature of the *devetnaisetis'* programme. In the central administration the number of ministries was decreased, as was the number of civil servants. Nearly a third of the latter lost their jobs, many of them being replaced by others of a more dependable political disposition. The banks were also rationalised and centralised in a series of reforms which included the amalgamation of nineteen commercial banks into the Bulgarian Credit Bank, one purpose of this reform being to establish greater central control over provincial banks.

Central control over local government was increased to a degree unparalleled since the liberation of 1878. The sixteen existing regions were reformed into seven provinces and the 2,600 village communes made into 837 units. Elected mayors were replaced by centrally appointed figures all of whom had to have either a legal training or a civil service rank equal to that of officer status in the army. The new local councils were to be half appointed and half elected, with the franchise for the latter being based on the seven social estates.

Since the fall of Stamboliiski Bulgarian foreign policy makers had tended to regard Italy as the great power most likely to provide the patronage a small state such as Bulgaria needed. The *devetnaiseti* wished to break away from this association. In July 1934 they recognised the Soviet Union, but their main hope was for an understanding with Yugoslavia. This would relax Balkan tensions and would make it easier to improve relations with Britain and France. The main obstacle to better relations with Belgrade was, of course, the mihailovist enclave in Petrich. The *devetnaiseti* took resolute action. They moved in the army. In what proved to be a surprisingly easy and immensely popular operation the mihailovists were dispersed. They did not disappear but they were no longer the formidable force they had been since the early 1920s. Furthermore, the feuding between various Macedonian factions which had taken over eight hundred lives in the decade before 1934 greatly subsided.

The *devetnaiseti* had proved effective conspirators and energetic rulers, but they were not expert politicians. There were divisions within Zveno on the advisability of creating a mass party organisation to sustain the government, one faction fearing that to do so would give new life to the party system. More importantly, there had been no decision as to what to do about the king, an issue on which both Zveno and the Military League were divided. Velchev was generally acknowledged to be in the republican camp and when rumours began to circulate that he was about to promulgate a new constitution it was assumed that this would greatly reduce royal powers.

Velchev and Georgiev, being preoccupied with the government's full programme of reforms, did not have time to guard their political backs. They were therefore relatively easy prey to a plot by their royalist opponents who in January 1935 manoeuvred them out of office and made General Pencho Zlatev prime minister. By April of the same year the royalists had removed Zlatev and installed a civilian, Andrei Toshev, in the prime ministerial chair.

THE PERSONAL RULE OF KING BORIS, 1934–1941

The king had been angered by the officers' intervention in the political arena in 1934 and he was determined that they should not dominate the country. But if he were to establish his own supremacy he had to find a means to build bridges with the nation and he had to secure himself against further action by the military.

When appointing Toshev in April 1935 Boris had issued a declaration promising to return the country to an 'orderly and peaceful life'. He also stated that there was to be no turning back and although the directorate for social renewal was to be abolished most of the reforms introduced since May 1934 were to remain. Toshev's task was now to contain the military, to work out a new constitution, and to construct a new popular movement. He made no progress on any of these fronts, and he resigned in November after it was discovered that Velchev had slipped back into the country with the intention, it was presumed, of conspiring against the king. Toshev's successor was Georgi Kioseivanov, a diplomat very much open to influence from his royal master.

The Velchev conspiracy made the containment of the military easier. Velchev himself was tried and sentenced to death in February 1936, his life being spared by that royal prerogative which he had wanted to abolish. The following month Boris used the revelations of the Velchev trial to justify his dissolution of the Military League. Immediately afterwards he toured the country's most important garrisons in an attempt to bolster his image amongst the office corps.

In the declaration of 1935 Boris had promised a return to constitutional government but under a new constitution which would correspond to 'the present complications and to the requirements of the times'. Amongst these complications were, it was believed, a potential threat from the left. The communists had been encouraged in 1931 and 1932 by their successes in local elections, and then in 1933 when their leader in exile, Georgi Dimitrov, had made a fool of Göring in the Reichstag Fire trial in Leipzig. In 1935 the Comintern had switched its strategy to the Popular Front making the communists more ready to cooperate with other parties. In 1936 there were enthusiastic celebrations of May Day, and the communists boasted that they had cells in every garrison in the country. Credibility was given to this chilling statement when army officers in Plovdiv showed support for the traditionally communist tobacco workers who had gone on strike. Meanwhile, after the January 1936 elections in Greece the small communist group held the balance of power in the Athens parliament. Nor had the fear of the right entirely disappeared. Tsankov's National Social Movement had not been classified as a political party and had therefore survived the ban on such bodies. At its 1936 congress it changed its statutes to make it more of a fascist organisation, and its public support seemed to grow with every fresh triumph Hitler recorded. The Nazis, like most Bulgarians, wanted to revise the peace settlement of 1919.

The old parties, though proscribed, continued to lead a shadowy existence and in May 1936 a number of them formed the 'Petorka', or group of five, to demand a return to the Tûrnovo constitution. Later this regrouped as the People's Constitutional Bloc which included some members of the Democrat Party, a radical agrarian faction and the communists.

By the beginning of 1936, sensing these and other dangers, Boris was in no hurry to rush into constitutional reform. He did not want to return to the old system and did not feel he could work with the older generation of politicians. He decided that there should be a slow return to 'a tidy and disciplined democracy imbued with the idea of social solidarity', that the constitution should be amended gradually, and that any changes introduced should be tested in local elections before a new sûbranie, due in 1937, was convened. Local elections were accordingly held in January 1937 after a number of changes had been decreed. Before voting all electors were to sign a statement attesting that they were not communists; voting was to be spread over three Sundays to enable the police to concentrate units where they were thought most needed; married women and widows were able to vote for the first time if they wished, though voting for males was to be compulsory; and rural voters were required to have primary and the urban electorate secondary education. The local elections went off to the government's satisfaction but it was not to be until March 1938 that a general election was held. Before then further changes had reduced the size of the sûbranie to 160 deputies and proportional representation had been abandoned in favour of carefully constructed single-member constituencies. Despite these measures the People's Constitutional Bloc still managed to win over sixty seats, though five communists and six agrarians were soon expelled from the assembly. That assembly, however, was never entirely pliable and at the end of 1939 Kioseivanov dissolved it, holding fresh elections spread over December 1939 and January 1940. Before the poll yet more restrictions were imposed on the

Plate 7.3 Boris III, King of the Bulgarians, 1918–43, with Princess Maria Louise, Crown Prince Simeon and Queen Giovanna.

opposition, particularly with regard to their freedom of movement during the short campaign, and the government vote rose accordingly. But having secured this majority Kioseivanov was sacked and replaced by Bogdan Filov.

Filov was an avowed pro-German and his appointment reflected the fact that in Bulgaria, as elsewhere in Europe, the overriding political problems were now in foreign rather than domestic affairs.

After the fall of Stamboliiski the strategy of Bulgarian foreign policy had been to redress Neuilly through 'peaceful revisionism' via the League of Nations with Italy as its patron within that body, the first objective being the implementation of article 48 giving Bulgaria economic access to the Aegean. The relationship to Italy had been symbolised by the marriage of Boris to an Italian princess in 1930, but in other respects reliance on Italy had not produced results. In the early 1930s Italy began to move away from Bulgaria whilst the League of Nations declined in effectiveness, particularly after the Nazis took power in Germany. By then Bulgarian policy makers were looking towards Yugoslavia as a means of avoiding isolation but with little hope of real success as long as the Macedonian enclave in Petrich continued to operate. That problem had been resolved by the *devetnaiseti* and Boris and his advisors were anxious to maintain the momentum towards better relations with their western neighbour. In 1936, as a gesture of goodwill to Belgrade, Kioseivanov banned all demonstrations calling for the dismantling of the treaty of Neuilly, and in January 1937 Bulgaria received its reward when a pact of friendship with Yugoslavia was signed. This was of little more than symbolic significance but it did procure Yugoslav diplomatic backing and in July 1938 the Salonika agreements allowed Greece to remilitarise Thrace and Bulgaria to disregard the arms limitation clauses of the treaty of Neuilly, which in fact the Sofia government had been doing for some time.

By 1938 all European diplomacy was dominated by the German resurgence. The Munich settlement in September and the Vienna award which followed it in November, by virtually destroying Czechoslovakia, ruined the little entente upon which Czechoslovakia, Yugoslavia and Romania had relied for their security; both Yugoslavia and Romania now became more conciliatory towards Bulgaria. But Munich had another effect. After the Vienna award Bulgaria was the only power defeated in 1918 not to have received back some of its lost territory. It was a point frequently made by the more vociferous of Bulgarian nationalists and especially by those amongst them who championed a pro-German foreign policy.

Boris would not listen to them, fearing that Germany might plunge Europe once more into war. Boris believed Bulgaria's best interests were served by peace or, failing that, neutrality without commitment to any great power; he once despairingly remarked, 'My army is pro-German, my wife is Italian, my people are pro-Russian. I alone am pro-Bulgarian.'

When war did come in September 1939 he immediately declared Bulgaria's neutrality. And for months he remained deaf even to the most alluring of siren calls. In October 1939 the Soviets approached him with the suggestion of a Soviet–Bulgarian mutual assistance pact and Soviet support for Bulgarian claims in the Dobrudja, but Boris refused. He did so again, this time to the Balkan entente powers when they offered Bulgaria membership in February 1940, Boris calculating that this would commit Bulgaria too much to the allied side.

Yet the pro-axis pressures were mounting, not least because the Nazi–Soviet pact of August 1939 meant that friendship with Germany would not mean offending Russia and therefore disturbing the majority of peasants who still revered the liberating power of 1877–8. Early in 1940 Bulgaria concluded a commercial treaty with Moscow which allowed the import of Soviet books, newspapers, and films, and in August of the same year the first visit for many years of a Soviet football team occasioned widespread popular pleasure.

In September 1940 Nazi–Soviet cooperation brought the Bulgarians their first territorial revision. After the Nazi conquest of Scandinavia and France Stalin demanded compensation in the east. This was made at the expense of Romania which was so much weakened that it also lost northern Transylvania to Hungary and in the treaty of Craiova signed on 7 September 1940, was forced to return the southern Dobrudja to Bulgaria.

Whilst these benefits were being reaped a number of internal changes appeared to bring Bulgaria closer to Germany, on which it was already heavily reliant for manufactured goods, including armaments. A youth organisation, Brannik (Defender) was established to instil discipline and patriotic sentiments; one of Bulgaria's very few outspoken anti-semites, Petûr Gabrovski, was made minister of the interior in February 1940; and in the summer the masonic lodges, to which most Bulgarian politicians belonged, were dissolved. In October the defence of the nation act consolidated these measures and others which had been taken against the communists. It also extended anti-semitic legislation enacted earlier in the year. At the same time steps were taken to increase Bulgaria's war-readiness. In May the compulsory labour service was placed under military control; a directorate of civilian mobilisation was set up which had the right to regulate manufacturing in time of war; and, again in the event of war, the ministry of agriculture was given much greater powers to requisition food and control prices.

Bulgaria had been placed on a potential war footing, but it was not yet known if it would go to war and, if so, on which side. After the fall of France and the treaty of Craiova, however, pressures from Germany, Italy and the Soviet Union outweighed those from the west. In October Mussolini offered Boris access to the Aegean if Bulgaria would join in the forthcoming Italian assault on Greece. Boris refused. In the following month another offer of a mutual assistance pact came from Moscow. This time the deal was for Bulgaria to take Thrace and the USSR the Dardanelles; the Soviets were also to have use of Bulgarian naval bases on the Black Sea. Boris knew that the Soviets had used different language in Berlin when talking of this deal, nominating Bulgaria as 'a Soviet security zone'. The Baltic states had been described in those terms shortly before they were incorporated into Stalin's empire a few months earlier.

The situation changed early in December when for the first time Hitler had a pressing reason for direct help from Bulgaria. Mussolini's attack on Greece had not prospered and Hitler, fearing an allied landing in the Peloponnese, had decided to occupy Greece, whence he could also harry British supply lines through the Mediterranean. His troops would need the right of passage through Bulgaria. On 8 December 1940 some forty German staff officers arrived in Sofia for secret discussions. Thereafter an increasing number of German tourists entered Bulgaria; they were all male, they all had short hair and shiny boots, and it was not the tourist season. The Americans made a last effort to persuade Boris that in the long run Britain, with the moral and material backing of the USA, was bound to win the war, but it was to no avail. In February Bulgaria consented to the construction of a pontoon bridge across the Danube and on 2 March agreed to allow German forces to cross Bulgaria *en route* to Greece. The day before Filov had travelled to Vienna to sign the agreement by which Bulgaria became a member of the German–Italian–Japanese tripartite pact.

Bulgaria was in effect now a member of the German alliance and the British minister left Sofia. Not until after the attack on Pearl Harbor, however, did Bulgaria declare what it chose to describe as 'symbolic' war on Britain and the United States. Immediately after the sûbranie ratified this declaration the king disappeared. He was found hours later deep in prayer in a remote and dark corner of Sofia's Aleksandûr Nevski cathedral.

BULGARIA AND THE SECOND WORLD WAR, 1941–1944

The Germans attacked Yugoslavia and Greece in April 1941. By the end of that month the Balkans had been partitioned between the axis powers, and Bulgaria's share was the western territories lost in 1918, western Thrace including the islands of Samothrace and Thassos, and Serbian Macedonia except for an undefined strip in the west under Italian rule. The Germans retained control of Salonika and Bulgaria was not given full ownership of its new territory lest it pocket its gains and leave the axis. The Bulgarians, however, saw this as the reunification of their nation, and if liking for the Germans was far from universal, British attempts to incite the Bulgarians to revolt against them met with no response whatever.

In Thrace the Bulgarian occupation produced terrible savagery. In September 1941 the local Greek population staged a rising and committed atrocities against Bulgarians; the latter took fearsome revenge in an effort, some believe, to drive the Greeks out of the region. There was no such confrontation in Macedonia. Here the Bulgarians were initially warmly received as they were a welcome relief to the centralising and serbianising policies of the Yugoslav government; a Bulgarian archimandrite officiated at the 1941 Easter service in Skopje cathedral and Bulgarian nationalists everywhere rejoiced that 'unified Bulgaria' had been recreated. The Bulgarians set about building schools and in Skopje opened Macedonia's first institute of higher learning, the King Boris University. The Bulgarian church did all it could to restore or introduce exarchist organisations, and all former exarchist priests were urged to forsake retirement and work in Macedonia or Thrace. Church leaders in Sofia hoped that now national unity had at last been achieved a patriarch might be elected for the Bulgarian church; all Bulgarian communities, acting through their church, would take part in the election of a patriarch who would remain as a symbol of national unity regardless of what political or territorial changes might come about. The king, however, feared an elected patriarch might be a potential rival and he and Filov therefore filibustered and the holy synod did not receive permission for the election of a patriarch, nor were bishops chosen for the sees of Macedonia and Thrace. This caused some frustration in the newly acquired lands which also felt resentment at the alleged insensitivity of Sofia-appointed administrators. By 1944 there was evidence of growing resentment at the over-centralisation practised by the Bulgarian authorities.

After the occupation of Thrace and Macedonia the dominant issue for Bulgaria's leaders, and in particular for King Boris, was not the nature of Bulgarian rule in the new territories but the degree to which Bulgaria would retain its freedom of action. This applied both to foreign and domestic affairs.

In foreign affairs the critical question was what Germany would require of Bulgaria in the military sphere. Boris was anxious that the Bulgarian army should not be deployed outside the Balkans, and this feeling was immeasurably strengthened when the Germans launched their attack upon the Soviet Union in June 1941. Boris argued that his army was not modern enough for a *Blitzkrieg*, and the peasant conscripts would not fight well far from home, particularly if they were pitted against their beloved Russians. Much better, said Boris, to keep the men in the Balkans where they could help deter a Turkish invasion or a Soviet descent on the Black Sea coast. The Germans did not object and agreed to supply the modern equipment which the Bulgarians insisted was necessary even for these limited tasks.

The German failure to take Moscow at the end of 1941 and the beginnings of partisan activity in occupied Yugoslavia changed the picture. The Wehrmacht had to call upon troops from the Balkans to reinforce the eastern front and pressed the Bulgarians to help garrison parts of German-occupied Yugoslavia. To this Boris agreed and a new Bulgarian army corps of three divisions was formed and placed under German command. The new Bulgarian army guarded railways, mines, ammunition dumps, and other strategic installations, and was later to take part in operations against the growing partisan movement; Bulgarian troops had not been deployed outside the Balkans but they had been used outside areas under Bulgarian political control in support of a non-Bulgarian civil authority. It was a qualitative change in Bulgaria's involvement in Germany's war.

This was not the end of German pressure for Bulgaria to extend its duties. In May 1943 Hitler asked the Bulgarians to take over an area in north-eastern Serbia to release more German troops for duty on the eastern front. He also wanted the Bulgarians to take over most of Greek Macedonia. Boris declined to accept all of the latter on the grounds that for Bulgaria to take Salonika would be too much of a provocation to the Turks and the Italians, but he agreed to help garrison Serbia on the grounds that the German troops so released might prevent a Soviet landing in Bulgaria, an eventuality which would bring about what Boris and Filov feared most: full Bulgarian involvement in the German–Soviet war. As a result of the May meeting Bulgarian soldiers assumed guard duties along the Belgrade–Salonika railway and replaced the Germans in northern Serbia and along much of the Aegean coast of Thrace. In August Hitler asked for two more divisions for northern Serbia to which Boris agreed.

Boris had succeeded in avoiding any commitment in the east beyond voluntary contributions to the *Winterhilfe* fund and the provision of one Red Cross train. He had refused to allow the recruitment even of a volunteer legion for duty on the eastern front and when the Germans asked for permission to use fifteen Bulgarian pilots trained in Germany Boris agreed only on condition that they served in North Africa, and even this permission was soon revoked. Boris was no doubt sincere in arguing that his forces were not equipped, materially or emotionally, for service in the Russian war, but there was another reason for this policy. He feared a victorious general might return

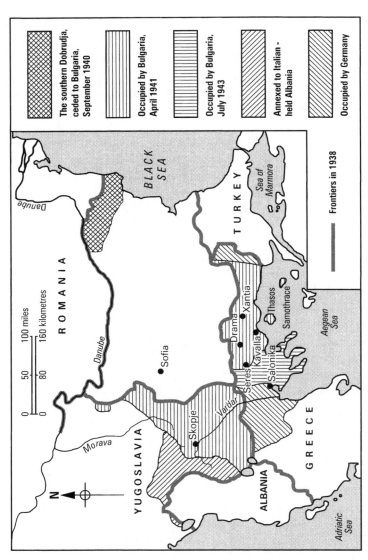

Map 7.2 Bulgaria and the second world war.

The southern Dobrudja, ceded to Bulgaria, September 1940

Occupied by Bulgaria, April 1941

Occupied by Bulgaria, July 1943

Annexed to Italian-held Albania

Occupied by Germany

Frontiers in 1938

ROMANIA

YUGOSLAVIA

ALBANIA

GREECE

TURKEY

BULGARIA

BLACK SEA

Aegean Sea

Sea of Marmora

Adriatic Sea

Danube

Morava

Vardar

Sofia

Skopje

Seres

Drama

Xantia

Kavalla

Salonika

Thasos

Samothrace

N

0   50   100 miles
0   80   160 kilometres

and, with German connivance, depose him. Right-wing groups which had the sympathy of German officials in Sofia had been very active in the spring of 1942, and in May Boris said he had heard from Berlin that Gestapo sources favoured a government led by General Lukov because the king was anti-German and the present administration was dominated by masons who were protecting the Jews. In September Boris refused General Lukov permission to travel to Berlin.

There was fear of the left as well as the right. The attack on the Soviet Union mobilised the communists in Bulgaria and exiled comrades were landed in an attempt to help them. The government clamped down hard, and in the next three years over eleven thousand people were detained as suspected communists, six thousand of them being sent to internment camps and the remainder to labour battalions. On 5 April 1942 communist conspiracies were unearthed in the 1st and 6th regiments of the Bulgarian army. Swift action was again taken against the conspirators and on 6 April it was decided to close the Soviet commercial mission in Varna.

There was, of course, no disagreement between the Bulgarians and the Germans on the need to contain any communist threat. Where German and Bulgarian views and jurisdiction did clash in domestic Bulgarian affairs was over the Jewish question. In October 1941 the German minister in Sofia, Beckerle, had begun pressing for more restrictions on the Bulgarian Jews. Further measures were introduced early in 1942 with a 20 per cent levy on Jewish property, the enforcement of the wearing of the yellow star, the compulsory sale of Jewish businesses with the proceeds being deposited in blocked accounts, and the disbandment of almost all Jewish organisations. Yet so unpopular were these measures amongst the general population that the press was forbidden to report on them immediately but had to let out the information gradually. After yet more pressure from Beckerle the sûbranie agreed in August 1942 to pass a bill depriving Jews in the occupied territories of their Bulgarian citizenship; it was a decision which was to cost most of those Jews their lives.

After the Wannsee conference and the decision to implement the final solution Nazi pressure intensified. A deputy of Eichmann's arrived in Sofia as assistant police attaché in the German mission with the brief to implement the next stage of the final solution. True to the agreement of the previous summer the Bulgarians did not

Plate 7.4   Jews detained in Bulgaria, 1943–4; they were incarcerated in labour camps in the provinces, but thanks to the intervention of the Bulgarian political establishment escaped deportation to the death camps.

impede the deportation in March 1943 of the Jews in the occupied lands. In the following months there was much less cooperation over the Jews with Bulgarian citizenship living in Bulgaria proper, at least 6,000 of whom the Nazis had wished to deport in the first wave of transports. The question was taken up by Dimitûr Peshev, a deputy from Kiustendil where preparations were being made to concentrate the putative deportees. He drafted a petition to the king which was signed by over forty deputies from the government party; Boris then forbade the deportations. In May of the same year the persecutions were fiercely opposed by the Orthodox Church and once again no deportations took place. The protests were backed by organisations representing every section of Bulgarian life from authoritarian, pro-fascist MPs to the trade unions and the illegal communist party. In the light of such strong and united feelings in the nation the king found no difficulty in standing firm against further pressure from the Nazis. The deportations never took place and Bulgaria's fifty thousand Jews survived the war.

Plate 7.5   King Boris's funeral, Sofia, September 1943.

The German minister in Sofia acknowledged in August 1943 that the Nazis would not persuade the Bulgarians to deport their Jews. At the end of that month the Jewish question faded into the background even for such a dedicated Nazi as Beckerle. On 15 August King Boris had returned exhausted and greatly depressed from a visit to Hitler. Sources close to the king indicate that there had been a terrible row when Hitler demanded a Bulgarian commitment to the eastern front, but no confirmation of this demand can be found in German documents. Whatever the cause of his dejection Boris hoped to dispel it by climbing Bulgaria's highest peak, Musala. He returned in a worse state and declined rapidly. On 28 August he died aged forty-nine. Mystery has surrounded his death ever since but there is no firm proof that it was due to foul play.

On the day before Boris's death a perceptive senior official in the German ministry in Sofia had noted, 'In the eyes of the Bulgarian people the king is less a monarch than a leader. He is a symbol of national unity and his disappearance could ... lead both to an internal crisis and to external realignments.'

Boris's successor, King Simeon II, was a minor and therefore a regency was formed, though without the constitutionally proper Grand National Assembly to confirm it. The dominant figure in it was Filov, the other members being Boris's brother, Prince Kiril, and a soldier, General Mihov. Filov chose the pliant Dobri Bozhilov as prime minister.

In the summer of 1943 the war was at a critical juncture for Bulgaria as for other powers. In the west Italy was facing collapse and was soon to surrender, whilst in the east the relaxation of German pressure on the Caucasus gave Turkey greater freedom of manoeuvre and made it more likely that it would join the allies. Towards the end of the year the war was brought to Bulgaria itself in the form of allied bombers. There had been some light raids on Sofia and other towns earlier in the war but in November the capital experienced its first heavy bombardment; on 9 January 1944 there was an even larger raid and in March Sofia was subjected to a series of incendiary attacks, culminating in a huge onslaught on 30 March. The raids had been intended to produce social chaos and push Bulgaria towards changing sides. At least in the first objective they were successful; after the January raid many Sofiotes fled in terror and the government had to order civil servants back to their posts.

By this time Bulgaria's urban population was facing privation similar in kind if not in intensity to that endured during the first world war, and for much the same reasons. Food shortages were causing inflation and a flourishing black market where in early 1944 goods were nine times their pre-war price. The shortages were caused by over-enthusiastic requisitioning, by German soldiers sending home more than they should have done, by peasants refusing to hand over to the official procurement agencies produce which they knew would command a much higher price on the black market, by widespread corruption, and by the general dislocation of the distribution system.

The growing plight of the cities together with a general war weariness encouraged the opposition forces. Of these there were two: the legal opposition, consisting of small groups of moderates and rightists from the old parties; and the Fatherland Front (FF). The FF had first been formed in 1941 but had made little progress because few parties were willing to cooperate with the communists who were demanding control of the organisation. In the summer of 1942 a second FF emerged, consisting of communists, zvenari, a social democrat faction, and the left agrarians under Nikola Petkov, son of the premier assassinated in 1907. The new FF broadcast regularly to Bulgaria from the Soviet-controlled Hristo Botev radio station. As relayed in these broadcasts the FF programme called for absolute neutrality on the part of Bulgaria, the withdrawal of Bulgarian troops from operations against the partisans in Yugoslavia, the removal of the army from royal control, a ban on the export of food to Germany, the guarantee of a decent standard of living for all Bulgarians, the full restoration of civil liberties, and a ban on all fascist organisations. In 1943 a new central committee was established which included Petkov, Kimon Georgiev, a communist and two social democrats. The loyal opposition, however, was still not ready to work with the FF. The democrats refused to work with the communists, and the non-petkovist agrarians could not cooperate with Georgiev and his associates who had been involved in the coup of 1923. Another weakness of the FF was that, despite its own propaganda, it had little in the way of military muscle, the partisan movement in Bulgaria not assuming any significance until well into the summer of 1944.

Within the political establishment the feeling that Germany had lost the war and that Bulgaria should therefore seek an accommodation with the western allies had been current since before Boris's death; indeed, Boris himself had shared that view. After his death approaches were made to the Americans in October 1943 but their terms were too harsh: unconditional surrender, the evacuation of all occupied territory, and an allied occupation. The allied raids on Sofia strengthened the desire to escape from the war. In February and March 1944 further approaches were made to the western allies but their terms were unchanged. Filov and Bozhilov continued to believe that the nation would not tolerate the loss of Macedonia and Thrace and that, in any case, there was no possibility of unconditional surrender with German troops still in the country. Bulgaria, said Bozhilov, would join the allies when the allies joined Bulgaria by landing in the Balkans. That illusion was finally dispelled on 6 June 1944 when the allies landed not in the Balkans but in Normandy.

By then Bulgaria had come under increasing pressure from the Soviets. They had refused a Bulgarian request to intercede with the allies for a cessation of the air bombardment, and instead launched a diplomatic offensive in Sofia. Notes from Moscow arrived in the

Bulgarian capital on 1 March, 17 April, 26 April and 18 May, insisting that Bulgarian territory cease being used by anti-Soviet forces. The Bulgarians were prepared to make some concessions over the construction of naval vessels in Varna and they also decided to turn down a German request that German troops be withdrawn westwards via the Bulgarian railway system. In April there were further concessions to the Soviets when Sofia accepted in principle their demands that Soviet consulates be opened in Burgas and Rusé. The consulates were the subject of the next Soviet note, that of 18 May, and this time Moscow threatened the breaking of diplomatic ties if the consulates were not opened, said Filov.

Soviet pressure, backed as it was by the rapid advance of the Red Army through Ukraine, raised the ultimate nightmare of the Bulgarian administration: involvement in the Russo-German war. What the Soviet pressure amounted to was that if Bulgaria did not break with Germany she would suffer Soviet occupation. But if she obeyed the Soviets and broke with Germany she would suffer German occupation; the experience of Hungary in March 1944 proved that beyond reasonable doubt.

Seeing these dangers Bozhilov resigned on 1 June 1944 to be replaced by Ivan Bagryanov, who had been educated in Germany and had served with the German army in the first world war, but who was generally regarded as pro-western. He was anxious to secure an armistice with Britain and the USA and to placate the Soviets before relations with them deteriorated any further. In the meantime a direct break with Germany could not be risked. Beckerle was informed on 18 June that Bulgaria would fulfil all its obligations under the tripartite pact but in order to avoid complications with the Russians the Germans should remove their troops from Varna. The Germans, suggested Sofia, could surely not wish another front to be opened in the Balkans by the Soviets, or by the Turks who were now pouring armour into Turkish Thrace. This was an argument which struck home and on 13 July the Germans signified their willingness to remove their steamers and hydroplanes from Varna to make it easier for Bulgaria to pursue 'a policy of peace, friendship and loyalty *vis-à-vis* the Soviet Union'.

As an indication of his goodwill to the allies, on 17 August Bagryanov declared strict neutrality, granted an amnesty to all political prisoners, repudiated the policies of his predecessors, and repealed all anti-Jewish legislation. It was too late. On 20 August the Red Army crossed into Romania and three days later King Michael locked Marshal Antonescu in a safe containing the royal stamp collection and changed sides. At a stroke the Russians were on the lower Danube and astride Bulgaria's northern frontier.

The pressures from the Soviets were now overwhelming and the Bulgarian government had to bend to them. On 25 August Sofia demanded the evacuation of all German troops and the following day the Bulgarian armies were ordered to disarm German forces arriving from the Dobrudja; there was little resistance and by 7 September over 14,000 German personnel had been interned in Bulgaria. The Soviets were not to be placated. On 30 August the Kremlin announced that it would no longer respect Bulgarian neutrality. Bagryanov was defeated and resigned to make way for Konstantin Muraviev, an agrarian.

Muraviev knew that he had to make the final concession to Moscow. On 5 September, therefore, whilst German troops in Bulgaria were still being disarmed, the Bulgarian cabinet decided to break off diplomatic relations with Berlin, though the war minister successfully argued for a delay of seventy-two hours to enable him to bring Bulgarian forces back from the occupied areas. At around 15.00 hours on 7 September the last German vehicles crossed the border and three hours later Bulgaria declared war on Germany with effect from 18.00 hours on 8 September. But by then the Soviet Union had declared war on Bulgaria which for a few chaotic hours was therefore at war with all the major belligerents of the second world war except Japan.

On the same day, 8 September, Soviet troops crossed the Danube and entered Bulgaria to a wildly enthusiastic welcome. Their arrival greatly encouraged the FF, whose partisan units had grown considerably in the chaotic summer months, as had their support amongst the population as a whole, particularly the intelligentsia. On 4 September a series of strikes had been staged to put pressure on Muraviev to break with Germany, and when he did so on the following day there were massive desertions from the army to the partisans. But, contrary to the post-1944 communist school of history, the action which brought the FF to power on 9 September

Plate 7.6   Sofia welcomes the Red Army in September 1944; the slogan in the lower picture reads, 'Eternal Glory to the Red Army'.

was not carried out by partisans but by units of the army loyal to the war minister Marinov. He it was who, with those practised coup-sters Georgiev and Velchev, arranged for the door of the war min-istry to be unlocked so that the rebels could take this key point in the city. With no resistance the Muraviev government was deposed within a few hours and a new administration formed by the FF.

The new cabinet, which was led by Kimon Georgiev, consisted of five zvenari, four agrarians, three social democrats and four communists. The communists held the key ministries of the interior and justice.

In October, after Marshal Tito had withdrawn his prohibition on Bulgarian troops entering Yugoslav territory, Bulgaria continued fighting, this time on the allied side. Its army joined with Marshal Tolbukhin's Third Ukrainian Front and fought with that army through Hungary and into Austria. Thirty-two thousand Bulgarians died in this campaign.

8

Bulgaria under communist rule, 1944–1989

THE COMMUNIST TAKEOVER, 1944–1947

Although the communists dominated the Fatherland Front government from the start, a monolithic, one-party system was not imposed until the end of 1947.

In their rise to power the communists, still operating as the Bulgarian Workers' Party (BWP), were helped by a number of factors. They were, initially at least, extremely popular, especially amongst the influential urban intelligentsia; that their membership grew from 15,000 in October 1944 to 250,000 a year later was not entirely due to careerism and opportunism on the part of the new members. Their close association with Russia also helped them; the traditional russophilia of the majority of the Bulgarians could not but be intensified in the months immediately after the expulsion of the Germans, months during which the full horrors of Nazi rule in Europe first became known. The fact that the war was to continue for eight months after September 1944 also helped the communists because the western allies had little time to spare for Bulgaria; the Soviets were given the permanent chairmanship of the Allied Control Commission (ACC) which was to oversee internal Bulgarian affairs until the conclusion of a peace treaty. And until then the Red Army was to remain in Bulgaria, another factor which certainly did not militate against the communists.

The communists had a sharp nose for political power. One of their first acts was to place political commissars alongside serving officers in the armies fighting with Tolbukhin. Some officers were considered too politically unreliable and eight hundred of them, including forty-two generals, were removed. In December 1944 Colonel Ivan Kinov, a Bulgarian who had served in the Red Army, was made chief of the general staff. Whilst most of the existing, trained army was engaged against the enemy, the former partisans formed the backbone of a new force, the People's Guard, which was kept in Bulgaria. It was entirely dominated by the communists.

The government controlled the radio and the distribution of newsprint, whilst the ACC, in effect the Soviets, had the right to sanction the import of foreign films and printed material; thus the FF had a virtual stranglehold over the media, but should a fail-safe be needed opposition newspapers could always be muzzled by the communist-dominated unions in the printing and distributing sectors.

The local FF committees were equally under the communist thumb. These sprang up immediately after 9 September and by November there were seven thousand of them. They conducted an implacable war against local representatives of the old order, policemen, teachers, and priests being prominent amongst them. Some of these were simply murdered; others went before the new people's courts to be sentenced to death or to long periods in labour camps. So energetically did some local committees conduct this campaign that they had to be restrained by the central BWP leadership in Sofia. The workers' councils, established in all industrial concerns, were another new feature of the Bulgarian social landscape and were also totally under communist domination. They had the power to scrutinise company accounts and were to report to the local FF committees who had had dealings with the Germans, the Italians or the Bulgarian 'fascists'.

At the central government level the communists' control of the ministry of the interior enabled them to establish an entirely new police force, the people's militia, as well as a covert political police to which the Soviets attached advisors, as they did to all central government bodies. At the same time the people's courts were controlled by the ministry of justice, which was also in communist hands. The new courts were required to punish 'collaborators and war criminals', but as Bulgaria had not been occupied by a foreign power and had not been engaged on the eastern front there were few

Bulgarians who fell into either category. Yet per capita more Bulgarians were accused of these crimes than any other East European nation. For the communists the problem was that the local intelligentsia and political establishment had not been decimated by the Gestapo or its local equivalent, and therefore the potential pool of opposition was greater than in other states; the Bulgarian intelligentsia and political classes were paying now for their relatively easy war.

A major payment was made in February 1945. A month before the police had arrested the former regents, royal advisors, all members of the last sûbranie, and all who had served in government since 1941. Most were found guilty and the prosecutor demanded death for fifty of them. Twice that number were taken out and executed in batches of twenty the night the verdicts were pronounced. The old right and centre of Bulgarian politics had been eliminated.

The left, however, was still an active force. Though still split the agrarians remained powerful. The faction which had joined the FF was led by G. M. Dimitrov, known as 'Gemeto' to distinguish him from the communist leader of the same name. Gemeto, however, did not join the government and was soon being attacked as a spy acting for the British, for whom he had acted as an advisor during the war. In April he fled to avoid arrest. His place was taken by Nikola Petkov who was a member of the cabinet. Petkov had long been a staunch opponent of association with Germany, had an impeccable war record, and had great oratorical and parliamentary skills. By 1945 he had become anxious at the actions of the local FF committees which he wanted freed from communist domination to ensure a return to full political liberties.

The agrarians were the major obstacle on the communists' road to power. The bulk of the peasantry, who still formed over four-fifths of the population, had always remained loyal to BANU despite the splits and the discreditable behaviour of its ministers between 1931 and 1934. After 9 September 1944 the peasants' allegiance to BANU was increased by their growing revulsion at communist brutality and by their suspicions of communist intentions with regard to collectivisation of the land. The communists were in a difficult position. They could not, as they had done in Hungary, Poland, Czechoslovakia, Romania and eastern Germany, win over the peasants by offering them confiscated aristocratic or *émigré* land; there were no aristocrats or *émigrés* and the vast majority of the peasants had enough land anyway. All the communists could do was launch a frontal assault on agrarian institutions and personalities.

In May 1945 communist intrigues forced another split in the agrarian party and the ministry of justice conveniently declared that all the party's property, including its newspaper and bank accounts, belonged to the anti-Petkov, pro-communist faction. Petkov resigned from the cabinet on 2 August, his group now becoming the Bulgarian Agrarian National Union – Nikola Petkov (BANU–NP). The communists engineered a similar split in the Social Democratic Party whose anti-communist group was led by Kosta Lulchev.

After splitting the agrarians the communists demanded a general election, but they wanted all parties within the FF to appear on a single list. Petkov, with the backing of the western powers, declared this to be anti-democratic. He succeeded in having the elections postponed until 18 November but when he failed to get his own way on the issue of the single list he told his supporters to boycott the poll. He believed the communists were losing support at home, which they were, and that the western powers were exercising more influence over the Soviets, which, in the long run, they were not. However, in the short term there was encouragement for Petkov; the USA refused to acknowledge the legitimacy of the new government which was headed by the BWP leader Georgi Dimitrov who had returned from the USSR on 7 November 1945, and at a meeting of the powers in Moscow the west persuaded the Kremlin to agree that two oppositionists should be included in the Bulgarian cabinet; but the matter went no further than that because Petkov and Lulchev insisted that the communists relinquish control of the ministries of the interior and of justice, dissolve the sûbranie and hold free elections; the communists, with full Soviet backing, refused all three demands.

In 1946 the battleground of Bulgarian politics widened. A concocted trial of a journalist was said to have disclosed another military conspiracy. This resulted first in another purge of the army which removed over two thousand officers from the active list, and secondly in a bill in July which passed control of the military

Plate 8.1   Nikola Petkov on trial, August 1947.

from the ministry of war to the cabinet as a whole. As the minister of
war was Velchev the move was clearly intended to diminish the
already declining influence of the zvenari. Shortly afterwards two
votes were announced: a referendum on the monarchy was to be
held in September, and in the following month elections for a Grand
National Assembly were to take place.

Both votes were meant to send signals to the Paris peace conference which in August began discussion of the Bulgarian peace
treaty. The referendum on the monarchy resulted in the declaration
of a republic, the simple, or simplistic message for the peacemakers
supposedly being that Bulgaria had rid itself of the dynasty which
had twice taken it to war on Germany's side. The convocation of a
GNA was intended to show the negotiators in Paris that Bulgaria
was keen to create a new form of government which could be relied
upon to behave in a mature and cooperative manner. These gestures
made little impact upon the basically anti-Bulgarian disposition
of the allies. Bulgaria, despite the sacrifices made in the campaigns
in Hungary and Austria after September 1944, was not recognised
as a co-belligerent, and the loss of all territories occupied during
the war was confirmed. The southern Dobrudja, however, was
retained.

The Paris debates indicated declining western interest in Bulgaria
and the opposition therefore combined resources to run on a single
ticket in the elections to the GNA on 27 October. The opposition
won 101 seats to the FF's 364; and of the latter the communists were
given the absurdly high number of 277. This was naked ambition
and a violent distortion of any notion that the number of seats taken
by the communists should represent their share of FF supporters or
of their share of votes cast for the FF list.

The battle was now moving to its final phase both at home and
abroad. At home the communists were clearly losing ground. The
holy synod rejected a plan put forward by the FF for the democrat-
isation of the church and even the old leftist party of the pre-
9 September era, the democrats, enjoyed something of a resurgence.
This was mainly because what remained of Bulgaria's bourgeoisie
was being pushed into oblivion. From September 1944 there had
been restrictions on profits and the property of alleged collaborators, war criminals and speculators had been confiscated.
Regulations on living space, grudgingly accepted at first in view of
the post-bombing housing shortage, limited the size of households,
and thereby decreased the already much diminished quality of life;
many of the intelligentsia, for example, were forced to dispose of
their personal libraries. In 1946 new tax laws required all arrears
from 1942 to be paid off in a very short time, but the heaviest blow

came with currency and banking reform in March 1947. The new currency was issued at rates which disadvantaged those with savings, in addition to which private accounts above a certain level were blocked and a once-and-for-all tax was levied on all savings. And this during one of Europe's worst ever winters.

Even the workers in the towns were showing signs of discontent. Unemployment was high and the winter affected them even more because food and fuel were especially short in urban areas. There were frequent strikes and many workers left the towns to cultivate their own or their relations' plots. The communists felt an increasing need to act before matters became any worse.

The same message came from abroad. In February 1947 the peace treaty had been signed and within ninety days of its final ratification the Red Army would be leaving Bulgaria. In March the Truman doctrine was promulgated threatening to resist further communist encroachment.

Meanwhile, in the GNA Petkov was castigating communist incompetence and arrogance, and lampooning these alleged friends of the people who were spending far more on the police and prisons than the so-called fascists had during the war. He demanded the restoration of the Tûrnovo constitution together with the return of full civil liberties. The communists decided to act. In June Petkov was arrested in the sûbranie and in August was subjected to a grotesque trial in which the defence was denied the rights to legal representation or to present evidence; this, it was decided would be 'of no use or importance'. Petkov was sentenced to death and hanged, being denied even the last rites and a Christian burial, despite the fact that he was one of Bulgaria's few genuinely religious public figures.

The death of Petkov broke the opposition. In October the founding meeting of Cominform enjoined all European communist parties in government to intensify the drive towards socialism. The BWP needed little encouragement. It rapidly mopped up what remained of political opposition and in December 1947 pushed through the GNA the 'Dimitrov constitution', so-called even though it had been drafted in the USSR.

The Dimitrov constitution declared Bulgaria a 'people's republic'. It was a typical Soviet-style system in which all freedoms were promised but where in reality power lay not with the official state organs but with those of the communist party. The means of production were to pass into public ownership and the higher ranks of the judiciary were to be subjected to parliamentary control; this in effect was communist control because local party organisations, acting through the local FF committees, had to sanction all parliamentary candidates. Within a few months all the parties within the FF had come to acknowledge the leading role of the communist party and accept that marxism-leninism was the ruling ideology. Untypically, however, rather than fuse all the elements of the coalition into one communist-dominated party, in Bulgaria there were to be two distinct parties in the ruling coalition. Because of the respect the peasants had for the agrarian tradition, that faction of BANU which had cooperated with the communists was to remain a separate party and was to join in a coalition government with them; it was to remain their coalition partner until 1990. The coalitionist agrarians, however, had little real power because they were represented only in state and not in communist party organisations.

In its fifth congress in December 1948 the BWP reverted to its former name, the Bulgarian Communist Party (BCP). Together with the other ruling parties in Eastern Europe the BCP adopted as its guiding, organisational principle that of 'democratic centralism'. This meant in effect that the chain of command was always vertical, from the centre down; there were to be no horizontal links because the centre could not tolerate the possibility of local conspiracies against it. The supreme body of the party was its congress which convened usually every five years; the congress elected the central committee which met in plenum at irregular intervals, and which could make important policy decisions. Those decisions, however, were usually to implement those already taken by the party's most powerful organism, the politburo, whose dozen or so members were chosen by the central committee.

Party control was exercised through a number of mechanisms. In all factories and other places of work and in government units at every level the local party cell, 'the primary party organisation', played a vital role in the running of the economic enterprise or government unit. Each primary party organisation kept two lists; one, the *nomenklatura* list, contained those posts in its area of responsibility which were important enough to be taken only by trustworthy individuals; the second, the cadre list, contained the names of trustworthy individuals; information on all individuals was kept up to date by the informers each primary party organisation recruited. The *nomenklatura* system ensured that anyone who wanted access to a decent job would keep his or her political nose clean; this was the base of the party's social power. For those within the party who carefully toed the party line there was the promise of rewarding jobs together with privileges such as access to better shops, holiday resorts, hospitals, schools, and other facilities.

Soon after December 1947 the trade unions, the youth organisations, the Soviet friendship societies, professional bodies, and women's groups were all brought under communist control, this control being exercised by the Fatherland Front.

Once its monolithic system was established the BCP hastened to the construction of a socialist economy and a society based on the Soviet model. The nationalisation of industry was quickly and easily accomplished, foreign trade was soon made a government monopoly, and Bulgaria was rapidly integrated into the system of alliances and agreements, economic and political, which Stalin's Soviet Union was building in Eastern Europe. In 1947 an emergency two-year plan for the economy had been introduced, but in 1949 the first five-year plan came into operation designed to shift the emphasis of the Bulgarian economy from the agricultural to the heavy industrial sector. In its plans for the collectivisation of the land, however, the BCP met with opposition. Historians do not yet know the full extent of this opposition but it seems that it was at its most obdurate in north-west Bulgaria where armed clashes are known to have taken place, but protest was by no means confined to that area and all over the country peasants committed acts of defiance such as burning their crops or killing their cattle rather than let them be taken into a collective farm. The resistance, however, had been critically weakened in February 1948 when farm machinery had to be handed over to the new machine tractor stations. By 1951 resistance had virtually ceased.

Even the setting up of the monolithic system did not mean the end of political persecution. The Orthodox church was amongst a number of organisations to be brought into line. The Exarch Stefan was packed off to a monastery and his clergy required to choose between joining the new Union of Bulgarian Priests or being sent to a labour camp. In February 1949 a new law on church organisation confirmed the subjugation of church to state. In 1951 the exarchate was raised to a patriarchate, further weakening the already tenuous links between the Bulgarian church and Istanbul. The non-Orthodox churches suffered a worse fate because their links with the non-communist world could not be dissolved, and links with the outside world were something which communist regimes greatly feared in these early days of the cold war. In 1949 the Sofia government had refused to allow the pope's newly appointed delegate to Bulgaria to take up his place and in the same year fifteen Protestant pastors had been put on trial, convicted and sentenced to long terms of imprisonment.

One of the organisations which was most heavily purged in the early years of communist rule was the communist party itself. In March 1949 a popular leading communist, Traicho Kostov, was sacked from his government posts and made director of the national library. In December he was put on trial and sentenced to death. His execution was the prelude to a savage purge in which at least 100,000 party members were expelled, many of them being sent to labour camps. Greater numbers from the civil service, the armed forces and all sections of society were purged at the same time. The purges were an East European phenomenon provoked by Stalin's paranoia. For justification of the purges the Soviet leader used the alleged danger of national communism as exemplified by Tito, whom he had expelled from the Cominform in the summer of 1948. But there were deeper reasons for the purges. The great social transformation caused by collectivisation and industrialisation would inevitably cause discontent which, equally inevitably, would seek some political vehicle for its expression. In Eastern Europe all political vehicles but one, the communist party, had been immobilised. The purges were therefore meant to warn the communist parties themselves not to have any dealings with the social discontent which their own policies were creating. There were also specifically Bulgarian factors in the Kostov case. In part the succession to the BCP leadership was at stake. Dimitrov had died in July 1949 and his nominated successor, Vasil Kolarov, was ill.

Kostov was a natural candidate but his pro-Soviet credentials were not good because he had criticised Soviet economic policies in the post-war years.

Also, in Bulgaria the Yugoslav dimension of the purges was especially large. Immediately after the war the BCP had agreed that those parts of Pirin Macedonia within Bulgaria should be ceded to Yugoslav Macedonia when a Balkan federation was established. In the meantime teachers were imported into Pirin to teach the locals how to read and write in the new Macedonian language recently defined by scholars in Yugoslav Macedonia. In Bulgaria this was an intensely unpopular policy and was abandoned the minute Tito and his Yugoslavia were ostracised. Kostov was not properly pro-Soviet so he could be accused of pro-Yugoslavism; and thus the BCP could try to shift onto Kostov some of the opprobrium for its Pirin policy. Also, the Kostov trial coincided almost exactly with the first elections under the Dimitrov constitution; it was a timely call for obedience to the official party line.

After the Kostov trial Vûlko Chervenkov, who had succeeded Dimitrov as head of the party and prime minister, was secure. Bulgaria's 'little Stalin' could continue the task of constructing socialism with a Soviet face. Every aspect of national life seemed to be refashioned on the Soviet model: education, culture, the economy, architecture and the military. To keep the Bulgarians on the correct line there were ever more Soviet advisors attached to every arm of government.

True to stalinist practice the purges also continued. Accusations that a Bulgarian translator at the US embassy had spied for the United States were used as the excuse for another round of repression against those who had any connection with the non-socialist world and especially America; the USA broke off diplomatic relations in protest. A victim of this purge was the Roman Catholic bishop of Nevrokop who was tried together with twenty-seven other priests and twelve members of the laity. On the other hand, Chervenkov did permit the emigration of almost all Bulgaria's surviving Jews, despite the fact that the Soviet Union had entered an extreme anti-Israeli phase. Chervenkov also encouraged the emigration of Turks. In fact he terrified Ankara in January 1950 by announcing that a quarter of a million Turks would be allowed to leave. After a good deal of negotiation the Turks admitted 162,000 before closing the border in 1952. Most of the *émigrés* came from the Dobrudja, the richest arable area of Bulgaria and the one Chervenkov wanted to collectivise fastest; the Turks were in fact displaced persons forced from their homes not by military events but by the social and economic change brought about by the application of stalinist dogma.

DESTALINISATION AND THE RISE OF TODOR ZHIVKOV, 1953–1965

Chervenkov sailed on in seemingly untroubled waters until 3 March 1953 when Stalin died. There was also a wave of industrial unrest in Eastern Europe, Bulgaria being one of the first countries to experience it when strikes broke out amongst the tobacco workers in Plovdiv. Within a few months Stalin's successors in the Kremlin had called for a 'new course' in Eastern Europe.

The regime in Sofia soon adapted itself to the revised Soviet attitudes. Bulgaria's new course was seen in improved relations with Greece, talk of repairing the breach with the USA, and the restoration of diplomatic relations with Yugoslavia. At home it was announced that more investment would be allocated to the consumer sector and to agriculture. More dramatically, the terror was relaxed. Police activity was reduced and thousands of detainees were released from prison and the labour camps. Other aspects of the new course included a decline in Soviet influence. Most advisors returned home and the joint stock companies which had given the Soviets great influence in certain sectors of the Bulgarian economy were disbanded. In March 1954 at the BCP's sixth congress Chervenkov announced that he would no longer hold the offices of prime minister and general secretary of the party, deciding to relinquish the latter. His successor was a young, efficient but self-effacing apparatchik named Todor Zhivkov.

The introduction of the new course was only the beginning of a series of events which were to convulse the USSR and Eastern Europe between 1953 and 1956. In 1955 Khrushchev began the rehabilitation of Tito; given that Chervenkov's eminence was a result of his defeat of Kostov on the grounds of the latter's titoism, this seriously undermined Chervenkov's legitimacy. When Khrushchev, speaking to the twentieth congress of the Communist Party of the Soviet Union in February 1956, criticised Stalin's mistakes he pulled another plank from Chervenkov's political platform. At the April plenum of the BCP central committee Chervenkov's cult of personality was denounced and he resigned. The new prime minister was Anton Yugov.

During the upheavals of 1956, which were to end with the Hungarian anti-Soviet revolution, Zhivkov remained steadfastly loyal to Khrushchev. The relaxations of 1956 had produced in Bulgaria a notable cultural thaw but after Hungary there was an equal and opposite reaction with the purge of the so-called 'anti-party group' in 1957 which was both a copy of events in Moscow and an assurance to the Soviet comrades that the Bulgarian party was in full control of events. The crack-down of 1957 enhanced Yugov's political stature. He was seen as the strong man of the party, a reputation he had earned between 1944 and 1949 when he had been minister of the interior. He had dropped out of favour after the Kostov trial but was back in the saddle as deputy prime minister in time to deal with the Plovdiv strikers in 1953. By 1957 he and Zhivkov were obvious contenders and probable competitors for supremacy within the party and therefore the country.

The late 1950s were dominated by economic policy. In 1958 Bulgaria announced it was the first state after the Soviet Union to have completed the collectivisation of agriculture. In the same year a drastic reform of the collective farms reduced their number from 3,450 to 932. Other reforms in the same year required all bureaucrats, both party and state, to work for a set number of days in a factory or on a farm to make sure they did not lose touch with the proletariat. In 1960 Zhivkov produced a fantastic, or phantasmagoric plan for economic expansion. The figures were absurd and were reduced in 1961 before being abandoned in 1963 after inflicting considerable damage on the economy, particularly agriculture. These 'Zhivkov Theses' of 1960 were sometimes referred to as Bulgaria's 'Great Leap Forward' but they were copied from Khrushchev not from Mao.

Both Yugov and Chervenkov were critical of the Zhivkov Theses, but Chervenkov himself was finally discredited in 1961 when

Khrushchev launched his second and much more vitriolic attack upon Stalin and stalinism. Chervenkov, after being denounced for not having learnt the lessons of 1956 and the April plenum, disappeared from public life.

Chervenkov's elimination intensified the duel between Zhivkov and Yugov. Zhivkov's strength was his backing from Moscow, and his position was bolstered in May 1962 when his patron, Khrushchev, paid a week-long visit to Bulgaria, touring the country with his protégé in the fashion of a Russian general of old. Zhivkov's weakness was the fast deteriorating agricultural situation which was producing shortages so severe that grain had to be imported from North America. Yugov capitalised on this, as he did on Khrushchev's mishandling of relations with China and his disastrous adventure in Cuba.

The final battle was due to be fought in the eighth congress of the BCP which had originally been scheduled for August 1962 but which was postponed until November because of the agricultural crisis. Shortly before the congress convened a plenum of the central committee met. Half-way through its proceedings Zhivkov flew to Moscow; when he returned a few days later he announced that Yugov had been removed from the politburo and relieved of his post as prime minister. Yugov retired into obscurity, to emerge as an old man in 1984 to receive the award of 'hero of socialist labour'.

Zhivkov's victory had clearly been engineered and confirmed by the Kremlin and henceforth Zhivkov was to be a byword for slavish obedience to the Moscow line. He did not rely on the Soviets alone, however. Soon after Yugov's ouster he brought his own supporters into the politburo and into other critical party posts at national and local level. By 1964 he was strong enough to survive the fall of his patron in Moscow and in the following year he defeated a military conspiracy aimed at lessening Bulgaria's subservience to the Soviet Union. Zhivkov was to remain virtually unchallenged for over twenty years.

THE *ZHIVKOVSHTINA*, 1965–1981

In 1965 the Bulgarian leadership introduced a series of reforms which were to bring in greater economic accountability and, under

the new system of 'planning from below', were to allow local enterprises and their managers greater responsibility. The upheavals in
Czechoslovakia three years later stopped the reform programme
dead in its tracks. Not only did the party return to economic orthodoxy, it actually tightened political controls. The Fatherland Front
took into its fold seemingly innocuous organisations such as the
temperance society and the slavic committee and a call went out to
make sure that all committees in urban residences and all those dealing
with the supply of water, food and other necessities were firmly within
the party's grasp. Inside the party itself there was to be 'iron discipline'.

Much of this renewed centralisation and ideological conformity
were reflected in two important innovations in 1971: a new constitution and a new party programme.

The 1971 constitution declared Bulgaria to be a socialist state
headed by its working class. The leading role of the BCP was
recognised, as was Bulgaria's membership of the socialist community. A new body was established, the state council, which was to
have legislative and executive powers, and whose chairperson was
to be head of state. That person was Zhivkov. The state council was
also to exercise certain supervisory functions over the administration, functions which in most other East European states were
the responsibility of party organs. The new party programme
announced that the guiding principles of the BCP were still those
laid down in the 'April Line' of 1956, but now that socialism had
been built a new strategy was needed to guide the party and the
nation through the process of constructing mature socialism in 'a
unified socialist society'. In the long term this process would involve
the homogenisation of Bulgaria; the emphasis at this stage was on
the amalgamation of urban and rural life, and of physical and
mental labour, but for those who chose to exploit it the idea of a
unified socialist society could also have ethnic connotations. The
move towards mature socialism would mean the transition from
extensive to intensive growth, a transition which was to be facilitated by the scientific-technological revolution which alone could
bring the required increase in productivity and therefore wealth.
Though the 1971 party programme was to be greatly modified in
the mid-1980s, the 1971 constitution remained in force until after
the collapse of the communist system.

The changes of 1971 did not greatly alter Zhivkov's regime. Its main feature remained an almost total obedience to the Soviet Union, especially in foreign policy; in September 1973 Zhivkov remarked that Bulgaria and the Soviet Union would 'act as single body, breathing with the same lungs and nourished by the same bloodstream'. On issues such as the Vietnam war, the third world, the Middle East, and Latin America there was not a hair's breadth of difference between Sofia and Moscow. So far did Zhivkov's devotion to the Soviet Union go that we now know that on two occasions he proposed that Bulgaria should be incorporated into the USSR. Khrushchev turned him down because he thought Zhivkov saw in such a union easy access to higher living standards; Brezhnev rejected the offer because he knew it to be impracticable in diplomatic terms.

Whilst he always followed the Soviet line in foreign affairs Zhivkov did develop more links with the west. In October 1966 he paid his first visit to the non-communist world when he was received in Paris by General de Gaulle, whose anti-American virtues were considered compensation enough for the vice of his conservatism. In December 1973 full diplomatic relations were established with the Federal Republic of Germany with whom Bulgaria had already developed considerable trading links. In June 1975 Zhivkov visited the Vatican and was received by Pope Paul VI. Later in the year the Bulgarian government sanctioned the nomination of Uniate bishops in Bulgaria and allowed a party of Bulgarian Catholics to make a pilgrimage to Rome; by 1979, for the first time since the 1940s, no Catholic see in Bulgaria was without a bishop.

Increasing links were also established with the third world. African students had been receiving university education in Bulgaria since the early 1960s, though life there was not always to their taste as demonstrations in April 1965 had proved. In the late 1960s and 1970s many trained Bulgarians went in the opposite direction to work as doctors, teachers, engineers, etc.; by 1981 there were over two thousand Bulgarian doctors working in Libya alone. In the 1970s and 1980s well-heeled, dollar-earning Bulgarians enjoying leave at home were a familiar feature of the country's somewhat exiguous fleshpots.

At home, the vast majority of the population were content or apathetic. Despite occasional rumblings of discontent there was no prospect of dissidence on the Polish scale; Bulgaria had no independent church to act as an alternative focus of loyalty, and when confronted with a political system which he disliked the Bulgarian tended to respond with apathy and withdrawal rather than with opposition and confrontation; the bogomil legacy lasted long. Zhivkov did not utter the word dissidence in public until 1977, and some years later when an acrostic reading 'Down With Todor Zhivkov' appeared in a literary journal he laughed it off, declaring that the regime would not be brought to its knees by a couple of poets.

Another, and more important reason for the relative stability of Bulgaria during the 1960s and 1970s was that for most of the population life was gradually becoming better. The political terror of the late 1940s and 1950s had given way to a reactive policing against the few who spoke out or caused the regime embarrassment. In December 1972 a central committee plenum had promised that in the new phase of economic and social development more attention would be paid to providing consumer goods and social facilities such as education and housing. Progress was always to be slow in these sectors, and there were periodic downturns, but anyone who had visited Bulgaria in the late 1960s and then returned in the late 1970s would have had no doubt that conditions had in general improved.

One reason for this gradual improvement was that Bulgaria benefited from Comecon schemes for economic specialisation introduced in the early 1960s. Under a 1965 agreement with the USSR Bulgaria was to assemble cars and lorries manufactured in the Soviet Union; Bulgaria also began to specialise in ship-building and in the production of railway rolling stock and fork-lift trucks; by 1975 one-third of its industrial output was for the transport sector. By then Bulgaria was beginning to produce magnetic discs and other computer parts for the East European market. Agreements such as these tied Bulgaria to the East European and even more to the Soviet customer, but on the other hand they provided Bulgaria with easy markets for its low-quality manufactured goods and they also allowed Bulgaria to import oil from the Soviet Union at low prices. In later years a good deal of this oil was sold profitably on the open market for hard currency.

Plate 8.2 Typical communist propaganda: party boss Todor Zhivkov with a group of children at the First Congress on Public Education, Sofia 1980.

In the early and mid-1970s food production was stimulated by another major reorganisation of the agricultural sector. In 1969 in the Vratsa area seven collective farms employing some 40,000 workers and covering 38,700 hectares were grouped into a loose federation or Agro-Industrial Complex (AIC). In 1970 the experiment was endorsed by a central committee plenum and applied nationally. The AICs employed at least 6,000 workers and were between 20,000 and 30,000 hectares in extent. They were intended to capitalise on the advantages of the local soil and climate by concentrating on two or three crops and one or two brands of livestock. In their early years the AICs gave encouraging returns and were another reason why most Bulgarians in the 1970s felt they had little reason to complain about their lot.

The placidity of the domestic political scene did not mean that Zhivkov was indifferent to potential opposition. One literary man who learned that to his cost was Georgi Markov, poisoned with a pellet shot from an umbrella on Waterloo Bridge, London, in September 1977. Markov had revealed too many details of the life style of Bulgaria's political élite; two weeks later a similar but this time unsuccessful attempt was made on the life of Vladimir Kostov in Paris, his sin being that he had exposed the workings of the Bulgarian secret police and the extent to which it, and much of the Bulgarian establishment, was subordinated to the Soviet Union.

Nor did Zhivkov tolerate any potential challenge to his leadership in the upper echelons of the party. Throughout his rule he conducted a game of musical chairs, moving ministers or senior party officials sideways if they seemed to be building up too strong a power base. Such changes seldom involved loss of office but occasionally more firm action was taken. In May 1977 Boris Velchev was removed from the politburo and extensive changes were made in a number of provincial party organisations. At the same time party membership cards were called in for examination; this was the standard method of carrying out a purge and in this one some 38,500 members were expelled from the party. This was the largest 'cleansing' of the party which took place whilst Zhivkov was in power, though there were further sackings of leading figures, particularly in the mid-1980s.

Like other Balkan communist regimes that in Bulgaria was not devoid of a nationalist tinge. This was useful because as ideological commitment declined the party needed greater legitimacy at home, particularly after the post-1968 tightening of the reins. There were, it seemed in the late 1960s, two easy roads to enhanced legitimacy: consumerism and a greater assertion of national identity. The Bulgarian economy was not yet developed enough to offer consumerism, but there were also problems with the second course. Because Bulgarian policy was so closely aligned with that of the Soviet Union national assertion was difficult in foreign affairs. The answer was more national, Bulgarian self-assertion at home; 1968 saw the end of all but one newspaper and one journal for the Turkish reader; Roma textbooks could henceforth be published in Bulgarian only; and Sofia's Roma theatre, which had flourished in the post-war years, became a thing of the past.

After the 1971 party programme had called for the creation of a unified socialist nation the assimilationist pressures on the Roma and on other minorities increased. In the early 1970s Pomaks who had become Turkified were required to adopt Slav names, and those who did not were punished; in 1974 five hundred of the thirteen hundred inmates of the notorious Belene labour camp were Pomaks who had resisted pressure to change their names. The Turks were not yet put under such pressure but increased emigration was encouraged. In 1968 Bulgaria and Turkey signed an agreement allowing for the reunification in Turkey of families separated by the exodus of the early 1950s. In the ten years during which the agreement remained in force some 130,000 Turks left Bulgaria.

The Macedonian question was also one where nationalist heart strings could be tweaked. After the break with Tito in 1948 the expression of Macedonian identity became more and more difficult. By the early 1960s severe penalties were being imposed on anyone who attempted such expression in public, and even though the 1963 edition of the shorter Bulgarian encyclopaedia still carried an article on the Macedonian language the 1965 census, which measured ethnicity by mother tongue, was the last in communist years to recognise Macedonian as an ethnic category. Any action on the Macedonian question inside Bulgaria inevitably affected and was affected by relations with Yugoslavia. If the Soviet Union's relations with Belgrade were bad the Bulgarians did not hesitate to take the offensive on Macedonia. In 1969, for example, the party circulated to its members a pamphlet claiming that two-thirds of the population of Yugoslav Macedonia were ethnic Bulgarians, an assertion to which Skopje naturally took great exception. Other disputes, most of them of an academic nature, were to break out periodically but Zhivkov never lost control of them and there was never any like-lihood under his rule that the Macedonian dispute would cause real international complications.

The most interesting and unusual aspect of Bulgarian nationalism
in the 1970s focuses not so much on Zhivkov as on his daughter,
Liudmila Zhivkova. Born in 1942 she was of the generation which
had grown up under socialism, albeit in its most privileged circles.
That privilege had been responsible for her being able to spend an
academic year in Oxford and in 1971 helped her to the post of
deputy chairperson of the committee for art and culture. She became
its head in 1975 and in the following year took over responsibility
for radio, television and the press. In 1980 she was given charge of
the politburo commission on science, culture and art. With the help
of established scholars she published a number of books and in
private she began to show an increasing and wholly unmarxist
interest in mysticism. In the small world of the Sofia intelligentsia
such private interests soon became public knowledge.

The intelligentsia were fascinated by the discussion of non-
materialist ideas and they could not help but be gratified by the
stress which Zhivkova placed on Bulgaria's long cultural traditions
and the individuality and separateness of those traditions. In 1981
she orchestrated a huge celebration of the 1,300th anniversary of the
founding of the first Bulgarian state. This was no doubt an exagge-
rated and an extremely expensive affair but it was part of the process
of emphasising that Bulgaria's history and culture were unique and
that therefore Bulgarians were culturally different from other peoples.
And of course this was immediately interpreted in private as
meaning different from the Russians. The 1981 celebrations highlighted the fact that the Bulgarians had had an organised state long
before the Russians. Later the Bulgarians were to mark their conversion to Christianity where, once again, the Bulgarians preceded
the Russians. But by then Zhivkova was dead. She died in July 1981
aged only thirty-nine. There were immediately rumours that the
Russians had murdered her, but there is no evidence to cast doubt
on the official cause of death, cerebral haemorrhage, perhaps
induced by the effects of a serious motor accident a few years before.
Zhivkova's nationalism had been cultural not ethnic and was a call
to celebrate Bulgarian achievements not to discriminate against
indigenous minorities; even if she lived a privileged and extremely
self-indulgent life, Zhivkova was probably more mourned at her
death than any public figure since King Boris.

GEORGI CHALUKOV

Plate 8.3   A critical cartoon of Liudmila Zhivkova as patron of the arts.
Those in line are mostly caricatures of leading Bulgarian academics and men
of letters.

THE DECLINE AND FALL OF TODOR ZHIVKOV, 1981–1989

The death of Liudmila Zhivkova was a symbolic turning point after which hope seemed to turn increasingly to despair amongst Bulgaria's ruling élite, no matter what contortions of organisation and policy it imposed.

In the first place the gloss of Zhivkova's cultural self-congratulation was tarnished by a series of international scandals. These had begun with the Markov and Kostov affairs in 1977 but they showed no signs of ending. There were accusations that Bulgaria was involved in the production of counterfeit whisky; that the state trading agency, Kintex, was involved in a complex operation which smuggled drugs into the west and used the money so gained to send arms to subversive groups in countries such as Turkey which the communists wished to destabilise; in 1981 came the accusation that Bulgarian secret service agents had been involved in the attempted assassination of Pope John Paul II in Rome; and in July 1982 the United States branded Bulgaria as a country engaged in 'state-sponsored' terrorism. Since the fall of the communists Bulgaria has acknowledged its guilt in the Markov affair but continues strenuously to deny any implication in the attempt on the pope's life.

By 1981 a more general problem was becoming clear in Bulgaria as it was in other East European states. The transfer from extensive to intensive economic growth was not being accomplished as easily or as rapidly as planned. The scientific-technological revolution in which so much hope had been placed proved disappointing, not least because planned economies could not keep pace with the increasingly rapid changes in computer sciences and fibre optics. The import of western technology, upon which some reliance had been placed, became more difficult partly because of the trading restrictions President Reagan imposed, but much more so because the oil-price hikes of the mid-1970s had made western goods so much more expensive. At the same time efforts to expand trade with central and western Europe were doomed to frustration because all that Bulgaria could offer in the way of high-quality exports were agricultural goods, the very ones which the EEC was determined to exclude. Bulgaria did find some alternative markets in Scandinavia, North America and the Far East but it was becoming more difficult to meet foreign debt obligations; much more difficult, indeed, than the fabricated figures published in the 1980s indicated. By 1981 growth rates were slowing and expectations becoming correspondingly more sober; the eighth five-year plan introduced in that year anticipated an increase in national income of 20 per cent as opposed to the 45 per cent of the seventh plan in 1976.

The regime's answer was the New Economic Mechanism (NEM) outlined in a plenum of March 1979 and applied to the entire economy by 1982. The purpose of the NEM was to raise productivity, to improve the quality of Bulgarian goods and services, and thereby secure the exports needed to eliminate existing trading deficits and hard currency debts. To achieve this the NEM was to provide 'a new approach to the management of the economy in the scientific-technological revolution'. The new approach was based on five principles. First, decentralisation was to mean greater freedom for all enterprises which would now receive from the central planning agencies not detailed production quotas but general guidelines. Second, democracy was to be implemented by the election of brigade leaders and other officials in a new system of 'mobilisation from below'. Third, competition was to be extended and would determine investment allowances as well as wages. Fourth, market forces were to be allowed into the economy with enterprises being left to find their own resources and outlets for their products. And fifth, self-sufficiency was to be applied to all plants which could no longer automatically count on government subsidies.

These were grandiose schemes but they had little real impact. The quality of production showed no sign of improvement. In 1983 Zhivkov gave a lecture, which was broadcast live on radio and television, in which he savagely denounced the quality of Bulgarian goods, even alleging that foreign products assembled under licence had been 'bulgarised' by sloppy workmanship and poor labour discipline. In March 1984 a special party conference met to discuss the problem. It produced yet more exhortations and suggestions for industrial reorganisation but once again these had little effect.

The NEM, the attempt to improve quality, and the efforts to increase the supply of consumer goods to the home market, faced a number of obstacles. In the first place the need to tackle the foreign debt had to take priority over other needs if future imports of technology were to be assured and export markets secured. This meant that foreign currency had to be diverted to debt payments rather than to importing foreign consumer goods or the machinery to manufacture them at home. It also meant that much of the best of domestic production had to be diverted into the export trade. The Bulgarians did not have to suffer the privations Ceauşescu's manic determination to overcome Romania's foreign debt inflicted on his country, but the Bulgarian home buyer was denied enjoyment of the best his country had to offer, not least in wine. It made life in Bulgaria grey and uniform just at a time when foreign travel was becoming easier and when more western films, TV programmes and videos were being seen, thus making an increasing number of Bulgarians more conscious of that greyness.

Energy was another problem facing the Bulgarian economy. The country has little in the way of indigenous fossil fuels and is forced therefore to rely heavily on imports. In the 1980s the Soviets, facing economic problems of their own, were forcing up their prices and in the second half of the decade were to switch to world prices. Bulgaria had developed a nuclear power capability at Kozlodui on the Danube and was constructing a second facility further down the river at Belene. But construction work at the latter and repairs at the former were way behind schedule by the mid-1980s, and as Kozlodui produced in the region of 30 per cent of the nation's electricity, not having it at full capacity was an extra economic problem. So too were the severe droughts of 1984 and 1985 which reduced hydro-electric power generation.

The most important obstacle in the path of economic advance, however, was that Bulgaria's managerial cadres were not trained for operating in a system which called for self-reliance, responsibility and the making of decisions on purely economic grounds. Managers feared buying western machines if similar Soviet ones were available because they feared they might be suspected of political disloyalty; plant managers who had for decades been used to having their production routines settled for them by central organisations often did not know how to find their own raw materials or their own markets; and producers accustomed to sacrifice everything to achieving plan totals were deaf to calls to improve the quality of their goods, particularly if that meant reducing the quantity of production. By the mid-1980s the NEM was seen not to be working. For the first time in twenty years there was no perceptible improvement in living standards, nor any expectation of one. This was a quiet but profoundly important shift in public attitudes.

From 1985 economic difficulties combined with two other factors to wreck the Zhivkov regime. Those two factors were the attempted assimilation of Bulgaria's ethnic Turks and the advent of Gorbachev.

The decision to enforce the assimilation of the Turks, beginning with the requirement that they should take Bulgarian or Slav names, was taken in the highest echelons of the party late in 1984. In the 1940s when the southern Dobrudja had been reincorporated into Bulgaria place names had been changed but it had been considered too draconian to change personal ones. The experience with the Pomaks in the 1970s suggested that the more extreme step was possible. But it was soon to be apparent that it was not easy. In 1985 Bulgarian Turks were told to choose from a list of Slav names that which they wished to adopt; and if they delayed or refused one was chosen for them. In many cases they resisted and troops had to be called in, with even tanks and the élitist paratroop red beret units being deployed. It was the largest military operation undertaken by the Bulgarian army since the end of the second world war. Nor was the new policy confined to making Turks change their names. Turkish newspapers were closed and radio broadcasts in Turkish ceased; it was even declared unlawful to speak Turkish in public. The official government line was that the Turkish speakers were not in fact Turks but the descendants of Bulgarians who had been forcibly converted to Islam and turkified after the Ottoman conquest. The new 'regenerative process' would allow these lost Bulgarians to return to the bosom of their mother nation.

The attack was not merely against the Turks. The taking of an Islamic name is an integral part of the maturation of a Muslim and the new prohibition on taking Islamic names was a continuation of a quiet assault begun some years previously on Islam itself. The washing of the dead had already been prohibited as a danger to public health; circumcision had been outlawed; and for years it had been all but impossible to make the pilgrimage to Mecca or the other holy places, whilst inside Bulgaria itself many treasures of Islamic architecture had been destroyed.

The regenerative process produced a world-wide storm of protest. Bulgaria was condemned by the United Nations, the Islamic Conference Organisation, the European Court of Justice and other international organisations. Given the weight of such disapproval and the small apparent internal gains it is difficult to understand why such a policy was adopted. It has been suggested that there was a belief that Islam was fundamentally conservative and could never coexist with the modern mentality demanded by the scientific-technological revolution. But if this were so, why attack the Turkish language as well as Islam?

It is also possible that the regime was frightened of the long-term demographic trends which were apparent by the mid-1980s. By then the Turks formed approximately 10 per cent of the population but differential birth rates meant that this proportion would grow rapidly. This could easily create difficulties in a conscript army, or if Turks in any one area demanded autonomy. That could be the prelude to an Eastern Rumelia in reverse, and if such a notion seemed fanciful those who feared it pointed to the example of northern Cyprus. These dangers would be decreased if the difference between Bulgarian and Turk were made to disappear. This argument is strengthened by the fact that a census was to be held in December 1985.

A more likely explanation is the simple one that the regime believed that beating the nationalist drum would increase popular support or at least mask some of the economic difficulties which were being encountered. The lack of progress on the economic front and the bad image of Bulgaria abroad had depressed the population to some degree. What later became known as 'civil society' was spreading in the form of martial arts clubs, wild-life protection associations and others which were operating outside the control of local party officials and often outside the law. More sinister was the reappearance of terrorism. On one day in 1984 bombs exploded in Plovdiv railway station and at Varna airport; on that day Zhivkov was to visit both cities, and shortly after the explosions leaflets appeared in the street proclaiming, 'Forty Years, Forty Bombs'.

If the regenerative process were meant to produce political stability in Bulgaria it failed miserably and it greatly reduced Bulgaria's standing in the world, even in Moscow. And it was in Moscow that the second great change of 1985 took place. When Mikhail Gorbachev became first secretary of the Communist Party of the Soviet Union Todor Zhivkov was seventy-four years of age and was the longest serving communist leader in Eastern Europe. In 1981 the central committee of the BCP had an average age of 57.5 years, and only 27 per cent of its members were under 50. The contrast between the new broom in the Kremlin and Zhivkov, to whom still clung the odour of Brezhnevite corruption and stagnation, was enormous. When Zhivkov paid his first visit to Gorbachev's Moscow he was kept waiting till the second day before meeting the Soviet leader, an unprecedented snub. What Zhivkov found hard to realise in subsequent years was that the Kremlin, so long the ultimate bastion of his power, had now become indifferent to his fate; Gorbachev was content to leave each East European party and state to conduct its own affairs.

In 1985 the Bulgarian party's main preoccupation was with the economy. Party plena in February 1985 and in January 1986 heralded more changes. The move was being made, said the propagandists, from bureaucratic to economic planning. In December 1986

Plate 8.4   The Imaret Mosque, Plovdiv, also known as the Sehabüddin Pasha Mosque, built in 1444; during the 'regenerative process' the grounds of the mosque were turned into a rubbish tip; this photograph was taken in 1987.

another plenum, called to draw up the ninth five-year plan, having faced uncomfortable facts about the recent performance of the economy, moved the engine of reform into a higher gear, emphasising now the idea of self-management.

These events were but the overture to the restructuring which was put on stage at the plenum of 28–29 July 1987. Zhivkov admitted to

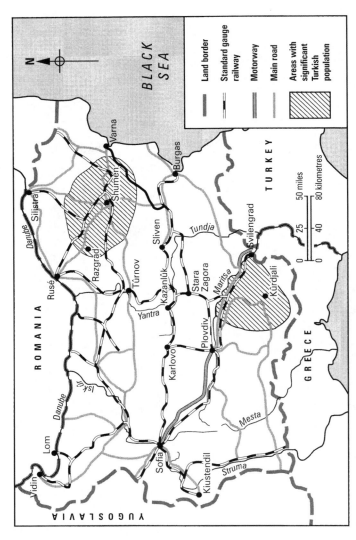

Map 8.1   Bulgaria in the 1980s.

the many failings of socialism and launched a massive attack on the middle bureaucracy; this was now to be made self-managing and was to be much more accountable to popular feeling. So great was the reordering of party priorities that the 'July concept' was to replace the 'April Line' of 1956 as its guiding principle. In August 1987 the sûbranie enacted a raft of reforms meant to give legislative substance to the ideas expressed in the July plenum. A number of ministries were abolished, local government was extensively reformed, and a commission was established to consider constitutional changes. In economic terms the welter of reforms in the 1980s brought little beyond massively destructive dislocation in economic administration, but Zhivkov did try to put the reforms to some political purpose.

In his speech to the July plenum the Bulgarian leader had admitted that the party had reached a turning point at which, he said, it should remember Levski's words, 'Either we shall live up to our times, or they will destroy us'. One danger which faced Zhivkov himself was that since the advent of Gorbachev, Moscow, previously the fount of all wisdom for the BCP leadership, had become the centre of dangerously subversive ideas. With one channel of Bulgarian TV regularly relaying Soviet programmes, those subversive ideas were available to all. Zhivkov responded by arguing that the purpose of glasnost in the USSR was to expose the need for perestroika in the economy, but since Bulgaria had already introduced economic perestroika it had no need for glasnost.

This convinced few outside the party or even within it. And the ranks of the unconvinced and discontented were growing rapidly in number. The ethnic Turks were still angry at the regenerative process but they had no established intelligentsia of their own to orchestrate their campaign. The Bulgarian intelligentsia, however, was becoming more and more active. It also found a means by which it could form positive links with the mass of the population: environmental degradation. The Chernobyl disaster of April 1986 had given rise to ugly rumours of contaminated food being placed on the open market for public use whilst the party élite enjoyed safe products imported at great cost from outside the affected zone. A problem which the authorities were prepared to acknowledge was that in Rusé where poisoning from a chemical plant across the Danube in

Romania was having devastating effects. The party allowed an exhibition in which one item was a plain notice showing the local incidence of lung disease which had risen from 969 per 100,000 in 1975 to 17,386 per 100,000 in 1985. Throughout 1988 there was constant agitation on this and on other issues, and despite hamfisted efforts by the police to silence poets or philosophers, oppositionists even began to form groups. By the spring of 1989 these included: The Discussion Club for the Support of Perestroika and Glasnost; the Independent Association for Human Rights in Bulgaria; Ecoglasnost; an independent trade union, Podkrepa (Support); and the Committee for the Defence of Religious Rights.

Zhivkov's regime was facing unprecedented challenges and they were made much more serious by the continuing legacy of the regenerative process which was to dominate the fateful spring and summer of 1989 in Bulgaria. By the late spring the oppressed Turkish minority had found its champions amongst the Bulgarian intelligentsia. In late May, shortly before the Paris meeting of the CSCE, a number of leading Turks began a hunger strike. Within days there was a confrontation and when Zhivkov on 28 May called a meeting of the politburo on a Sunday it was clear that the leadership was seriously concerned. They had every reason to be. The Turkish areas of the north-east were in a state of virtual revolt. Zhivkov's response was to go on TV and announce that if they really preferred capitalist Turkey to socialist Bulgaria the ethnic Turks were free to leave. Zhivkov seems to have believed that this would call the Turks' bluff and that few would emigrate. He was wrong. By August, when the despairing authorities in Turkey itself closed their borders, some 344,000 ethnic Turks had left Bulgaria.

Emigration on such a massive scale clearly created difficulties with the Turkish republic. President Bush promised backing to Ankara but Moscow informed Sofia that it did not wish to become involved in Bulgaria's national question. Zhivkov was isolated internationally.

He was virtually isolated at home too. Within the party leadership Petûr Mladenov, a member of the politburo and minister for foreign affairs, was more aware than anyone how damaging the regenerative process had been to Bulgaria's standing abroad. He it was who led the cabal against Zhivkov. By the end of October the two were in bitter conflict and Mladenov's hand was much strengthened when on 26 October, in full view of foreign journalists, police manhandled demonstrators during an ecological protest. It was a most convenient occurrence for Mladenov who was soon to leave for China. On his return journey he stopped in Moscow to talk with Gorbachev. Immediately upon his return the cabal swung into action and on 10 November, the day after the Berlin Wall was breached, Zhivkov resigned.

9

Post-communist Bulgaria

*Dismantling the apparatus of totalitarianism, November
1989–December 1990*

Zhivkov's fall was the work of the party hierarchy; it was a
palace coup rather than a revolution, and 'people power' in
Bulgaria was to be more the consequence than the cause of the
change of leadership.

Soon after 10 November a number of new political organisations
appeared. Some of these had lived a shadowy, semi-legal half-life in
the final years or months of the old regime and were now assuming
a full and open existence; some were entirely new creations; and
others were reborn versions of historic parties, amongst which
were the social democrats, and the agrarians who, to distinguish
themselves from the collaborators of the post-1947 years, reverted
to the name of Petkov's agrarians: the Bulgarian Agrarian National
Union – Nikola Petkov (BANU–NP). On 14 November fourteen of
the non-communist political groups came together in a federation
which called itself the Union of Democratic Forces (UDF). As its
leader the UDF chose Zheliu Zhelev, an academic philosopher who
had incurred the displeasure of the old regime.

Meanwhile the new leader of the BCP, Mladenov, had arranged
for a central committee plenum to meet from 11 to 13 December. It
expressed contrition for the mistakes of the past and promised that

in future there would be more party democracy, and that there would be real parliamentary life rather than the stage-managed show it had been since 1947.

By now the anti-communist forces were demanding more than contrition or promises of change from the ruling party: they wanted real change. This was made manifest on 14 December when the UDF organised a huge demonstration in Sofia calling for the abolition of article one of the constitution which guaranteed the communist party a leading role in the state and in society. With communist rule crumbling all round them the Bulgarian comrades could not be deaf to such calls, the more so as the demonstrations had shown the UDF was able to command and control massive public support. The BCP leaders agreed to begin discussions with the opposition. The way was open to the creation of a Bulgarian 'round table' on the Polish and Hungarian models.

Before the round table convened there were further large-scale protests in Sofia. Even before the meeting of the BCP plenum in mid-December Mladenov had apologised for and repudiated the regenerative process which was formally abandoned in a decree of 29 December. This provoked a fierce reaction. On 7 January thousands of protesters arrived in Sofia from all over Bulgaria, obviously with the connivance of local party officials who alone could have sanctioned use of so much rationed petrol. People power, it was clear, could be on the side of reaction as well as revolution. Counter-demonstrations in favour of the decree were held a week later. The demonstrations, together with the mayhem across the border in Romania, emphasised the need for the round table and encouraged a constructive attitude by both the BCP and the UDF which, it had been agreed, were to be represented equally at the discussions.

Almost everyone agreed that the apparatus of totalitarianism had to be destroyed. It was the round table's function to determine how this should be done. It had to decide how to circumvent the contentious article one of the constitution and to secure the withdrawal of the party from its position of political and social dominance, and to separate the party from the social and political bodies it had penetrated and subdued for over forty years. In the event, it was eventually agreed to amend article one substantially, but here the round table was following as much as it was leading events. Many institutions had taken their own action and abolished the primary party organisations in the workplace; the Union of Journalists banned them in its ranks at the end of January, and on 24 January the politburo dissolved those in the military and in places of work. Other changes followed rapidly. In February the old trades' union central council was abolished and the unions entirely separated from any political organisation, a new body, the Confederation of Independent Trade Unions in Bulgaria (CITUB), being established. A few days later another prominent landmark of communist Bulgaria disappeared when the communist youth organisation dissolved itself. At the end of March the Fatherland Front underwent its dose of restructuring to emerge as the Fatherland Union.

At the end of January the BCP had called its fourteenth congress. It enacted a drastic restructuring of the party. Both the politburo and the central committee were replaced by larger bodies which were to be more responsible to the membership; the old regime, said Mladenov, had been a dictatorship over the party as well as over the people, and to underline his point it was announced that Zhivkov was to be arrested on charges which included embezzlement, the misuse of power, and incitement to racial hatred. Mladenov also declared that the economy was to be restructured on the basis of privatisation, decentralisation, and demonopolisation; that a multi-party democracy was to be introduced; and that there was to be complete separation of party and state, in conformity with which he relinquished his post of party chief which went to Aleksandûr Lilov, Mladenov remaining head of state. At the same time a new government was formed with Andrei Lukanov as prime minister. The agrarians, embarrassed at their collaborationist record, did not join the new administration; ironically, the collapse of totalitarianism had produced the first purely communist government in Bulgaria's history. It was communist only in name, and not even that for long because at the beginning of April the BCP changed its name to the Bulgarian Socialist Party (BSP).

The attempt to separate the party from the state and from society involved the further extension of individual liberties and fundamental social and economic reform. The most significant move to extend individual liberties was the abolition of the sixth department of the ministry of the interior, the old secret police. Between February and

April private agriculture was legalised and there were decrees lifting restrictions on the employment of labour and allowing free enterprise in retailing, the service industries, and tourism. On 6 March strikes were legalised, after compulsory arbitration and mediation, though they were not to be permitted in the army, the police, the ports, the medical services and the power industry. There were also further concessions to the ethnic minorities; on 5 March the sûbranie accepted a bill allowing free choice of names for all citizens.

The fourteenth congress of the BCP and discussion on issues such as ethnic minorities had delayed movement towards full constitutional revision. So too had a number of disagreements between the BCP and the UDF in the round table, but these were resolved at the end of March when it was agreed that a Grand National Assembly should be called to redesign Bulgaria's political system. Concessions had to be made by both sides before it was finally agreed that half the GNA's four hundred deputies would be elected by proportional representation and half by the first past the post system.

The elections were held on 10 and 17 June 1990 and gave the BSP 211 seats, the UDF 144, the predominantly Turkish Movement for Rights and Freedom (MRF) 23, and the agrarians 16. Lukanov remained prime minister.

The meeting of the GNA should have marked the beginning of the phase of constitutional construction, but it did not. The ceremonial opening in Tûrnovo was accompanied by noisy demonstrations by anti-Turks angered by the presence of the MRF, and when the assembly moved to Sofia students and others staged protests against the failure to investigate alleged electoral irregularities. Early in July the protesters revealed a video tape which, they said, showed Mladenov urging the use of tanks against demonstrators in December 1989; Mladenov resigned and Zhelev succeeded him as president with Petûr Beron, a zoologist, becoming leader of the UDF. Mladenov's fall was not the end of the protests. Calls which had been heard for months for the ending of communist domination over the media and other aspects of national life continued and at the end of August led to the burning of a section of the party's headquarters in the centre of Sofia.

The fire induced a more sober mood but real progress towards change was still not possible. There had to be an emergency packet of

Plate 9.1   The fire in the Bulgarian Socialist Party (former Communist Party) headquarters, August 1990.

economic reforms but Lukanov wanted these to be passed by a coalition government because that would give the appearance of full national backing for them. The UDF refused to be drawn. By November the political impasse and a deteriorating economic situation was producing social unrest. Demonstrations had been a constant feature of Bulgarian political life since 1989 and once more the streets filled with protesters, many of them students. Towards the end of the month both CITUB and its rival trade union organisation, Podkrepa, declared strikes and on 29 November Lukanov resigned, chased from office by public action on the streets rather than by due parliamentary process. On 20 December a new administration took office under the premiership of Dimitûr Popov, a non-party lawyer.

Constructing the apparatus of democracy, December 1990–October 1991

Between November 1989 and December 1990 most of the apparatus of totalitarianism had been dismantled and in foreign relations Bulgaria was presenting a new face to the world; the close links with the USSR were gone and diplomatic relations had been established with Israel, Chile and South Africa. But if the mechanisms of totalitarianism had been dismantled those of democracy had not yet been constructed. This was in part because no workable consensus could be found within the GNA or perhaps within the nation.

It was the task of the Popov government to find that consensus. It called itself 'a government to guarantee the peaceful transition to a democratic society', and as a condition of its taking office insisted that the major parties must agree to a peaceful and orderly transition. Given this consensus the Popov government could set about rescuing the political process from the streets and returning it to constitutional channels; having accomplished this it could allow the GNA to redesign those channels. It would also have to draw up and impose economic reforms.

Initially the latter took precedence. There was no pretence that the task would be easy but help came from the trade unions and the managers/employers who on 8 January 1991 signed, with the government, a tripartite agreement on social peace. The trade unions accepted a 200-day moratorium on strikes in return for which government and the managers agreed to handle the economic transition with as much sensitivity as possible. The social peace was soon to be tested when Popov's government in effect introduced a Polish-style 'big bang' economic reform which began with the deregulation of the prices of many goods, a measure which caused much social distress.

In addition to the dislocating effects of economic reforms there were also ethnic tensions. In February the minister of education had announced that in Turkish areas there was to be four hours of teaching per week in Turkish if that was what the local population desired. There was a swift reaction. Teachers in the affected areas, especially Razgrad, Kûrdjali and Shumen, went on strike whilst Bulgarian parents demonstrated and withheld their children from school. The UDF claimed that those opposing the reform were those who had been responsible for the regenerative process in the 1980s but whether this were the case or not, the government deemed it prudent to postpone the introduction of the plan until the beginning of the new academic year in September.

When the GNA was not discussing economic or ethnic issues it found other problems to divert its attention from the constitutional debate. There were stormy scenes when the question of police files and the relationship of GNA members to the former political police were discussed. One casualty of this conflict was Beron who resigned after admitting to having played a minor role as an informant on foreign academic visitors; his successor as leader of the UDF was Filip Dimitrov. When the constitutional debate did at last begin there were still a series of distractions. A number of UDF deputies argued that a constitution drawn up by a communist-dominated assembly could not be trusted, and in June thirty-nine of them staged a hunger strike on this issue. There was also a delay when it was decided to hold a national referendum on the future nature of the Bulgarian state, a euphemism for asking whether or not the monarchy should be restored. After the question had taken up almost two weeks of GNA time the referendum was cancelled.

Eventually, however, the GNA did address itself to the political structure it was meant to define and on 12 July the new constitution was approved. Bulgaria was to be a democratic state subject to the rule of law with complete separation of powers. The head of state was to be a president elected by direct vote for a five-year term of office, and all candidates for the presidency had to have been resident in Bulgaria for five years, this restriction being introduced to prevent King Simeon presenting himself for election as president. A constitutional court was to be established, and the legislature was to be a sûbranie of 240 members elected by proportional representation with an electoral threshold of 4 per cent of the national vote for parties to achieve representation in the assembly.

The first elections under the new system were held on 13 October 1991, but only after the right of the MRF to stand had been challenged, unsuccessfully, on the grounds that it contravened a law of 1990 stating that no party might be formed on the basis of ethnic or religious affiliation. Thirty-eight parties eventually entered the contest, but only three managed to cross the 4 per cent hurdle and the result produced was agonisingly close. The UDF had the most votes, but only just, their share of the poll being a mere 1 per cent greater than that of the BSP. The UDF emerged with 110 seats, the BSP with 106, and the MRF held the balance with 24. The agrarians, true to tradition, had damaged themselves by splitting. More than one in five of the votes cast had been for parties which had failed to cross the 4 per cent threshold.

The UDF government, October 1991–October 1992

After the election a new government was formed by the leader of the UDF, Filip Dimitrov. His cabinet consisted mainly of UDF members but the MRF, on whom he relied for his parliamentary majority, declined to enter a coalition lest this alienate public opinion from the new administration. Also, outside the cabinet the MRF would enjoy greater freedom of action.

Lilov resigned as leader of the BSP at the end 1991 to be replaced by the thirty-two-year-old Zhan Videnov. At the beginning of 1992 presidential elections reaffirmed Zhelev as head of state though he was surprisingly taken to a second round of voting.

The Dimitrov government was to stay in office for just under a year. It achieved little. It spent a great deal of energy, to little effect, in trying to enforce the repatriation of land confiscated by the communists and it indulged in lustration, or the punishment of officials from the former regime. Seven hundred and fifty officers, including ten generals, were pensioned off by Dimitûr Ludjev, Bulgaria's first civilian minister of defence since 1934. Lustration was also evident in September with the sentencing of Zhivkov to seven years in prison; Zhivkov was the first of Eastern Europe's former leaders to be tried and convicted but he was to be allowed to serve his time under house arrest rather than in gaol. Tough attitudes towards former communists were also reflected in the Panev law which banned from administrative posts in the universities or academies anyone who had held party office under the old regime.

The effect of the lustration process on the Bulgarian Orthodox church produced a drama which was both tragedy and farce. On 9 March 1992 Patriarch Maxim was sacked; a report by the parliamentary commission on religious faiths said that his election in 1971 had been improper and there was gossip that he had been a 'collaborator'. In May his opponents elected Metropolitan Pimen as acting chairman of the holy synod. In June, however, the constitutional court declared that it was the removal of Maxim which had been wrong because this was an unlawful intrusion of the government into ecclesiastical affairs. The supporters of Pimen refused to accept the judgement or to vacate the holy synod building, and the

Plate 9.2   Cartoon by Georgi Chaushov on the ineffectiveness of the
Bulgarian Orthodox church; the drawing appeared in December 1992;
the church had split disastrously earlier in the year.

Orthodox church, the founding father of the nation, was reduced to
the degrading spectacle of its priests fighting on the steps of the
Aleksandûr Nevski cathedral. Not even a visit by the Oecumenical
Patriarch from Istanbul could mend the breach. The sacking of
Maxim was seen by many as the right thing done in the wrong
way, a proper end achieved by improper means. Many, including
even the president, held the Dimitrov government responsible for
the tragedy.

The few successes which the Dimitrov government could set
against its failures were to be found mainly in foreign affairs. One
was the admission of Bulgaria to the Council of Europe in May 1992.
There were also significant improvements in official relations with
Turkey. This was in part because the two countries held similar views
on how to react to and contain the crises caused by the collapse of
Yugoslavia. But there were other reasons. With the dissolution of the
Warsaw Treaty Organisation, Bulgaria believed it had to seek new
forms of protection against its neighbours, the largest and most

powerful of which was Turkey. An approach to NATO in 1990 received scant sympathy and the Bulgarians were advised to seek an accommodation with Ankara. Bulgaria had little choice but to comply and in May 1992 a treaty of friendship was signed.

One foreign issue which could never be far from Bulgarian politics was Macedonia. Soon after 10 November 1989 those in Bulgaria who regarded themselves as Macedonian had attempted to establish a Macedonian party in Bulgaria, to be called 'Ilinden', but this was refused recognition. The collapse of the Yugoslav state and the proclamation of independence by the Skopje government posed considerable difficulties for Sofia but on 16 January 1992 Bulgaria became the first country to recognise the Macedonian state. The decision was an improvised one, with not even the Bulgarian minister for foreign affairs being told of it beforehand. It was also a controversial decision. It greatly angered Greece which rejected recognition of any state bearing the name 'Macedonia'. Bulgaria could ill afford to alienate Greece who was both an increasingly important trading partner and source of inward investment and who could also be an advocate of the Bulgarian cause in the European Community's tortuous corridors of power. In an attempt to assuage Greece, and also nationalist opinion at home, a sizeable portion of which continued to regard the Macedonians as part of the Bulgarian nation, the Bulgarian government therefore recognised the Macedonian state but refused to recognise the existence of a separate Macedonian nation. This failed to mollify the Greeks, it did little to placate offended nationalist feelings in Bulgaria, and it made for fearful complications in Bulgarian–Macedonian relations, not least because the Bulgarians refused to recognise the separate Macedonian language which, the Macedonians insisted, had to be used in official agreements and exchanges between the two states. The impasse was not to be solved for eight years. On the other hand, an accommodation between Bulgaria and Macedonia, however flawed, could not but be an element of stability and order in an increasingly unstable and disorderly south-eastern Europe, particularly when other parties in the region were seriously considering the forcible partition of the country.

President Zhelev had made the running over the recognition of Macedonia and the government, despite its misgivings, had not in

Plate 9.3   President Zheliu Zhelev.

the end frustrated him. But relations between the two were bad. There had been intermittent skirmishing over issues such as the control of the intelligence services but in the late summer of 1992 the president launched an outright attack on the government. Gratuitous aggression on its part, said Zhelev, had not only caused social deprivation but had alienated the trade unions, the press, the non-parliamentary parties, and even the Church. The UDF fought back with equal vigour but it now had an added cause for concern because Ahmed Dogan, the leader of the MRF, upon which the government depended for its majority in the assembly, sided with the president.

The MRF itself faced grave difficulties. The government's economic reforms had hit the Turkish areas even harder than the rest of the country, and many ethnic Turks believed the land privatisation programme was discriminating against them; they responded by emigrating. If this second wave of emigration were to continue the Turkish population might be so depleted as to deprive the MRF of the 4 per cent of the national vote it needed for representation in the sûbranie. In September the MRF, to prove its muscle, drove the chairman of the sûbranie from office.

In October relations between Dimitrov and Zhelev deteriorated even further when it was alleged that one of the prime minister's advisors had been involved in attempts to sell arms illegally to Macedonia. Dimitrov denounced the rumours as a smear spread by the chief of the intelligence services acting in concert with some of the president's close associates. This was yet another round in the dispute over control of the intelligence services and it was also the final nail in Dimitrov's prime-ministerial coffin. On 28 October he resigned after losing a vote of confidence in the sûbranie.

The Dimitrov government had entered and departed from office in due constitutional manner. But it had failed to live up to the expectations of many of its supporters. This was to some degree a result of its lack of a dependable sûbranie majority, but there were also faults closer to home. The elevation of Zhelev to the presidency in 1990 had removed the strongest moderating element in the UDF and thereafter the committed, anti-communist ideologues enjoyed greater influence. The differences of emphasis between Zhelev and the members of the Dimitrov cabinet therefore highlighted the main unsolved question of Bulgaria's constitutional reforms: the relative powers of the presidency and the government.

The anti-communist drive in the UDF was intensified by the continuing economic and social crisis which imposed immense hardship on most Bulgarians and which forced the leading parties within the alliance into ever more confrontational attitudes. Dimitrov and his cabinet dared not alienate these groups. Therefore, instead of seeking or preserving consensus the government bowed to pressure from its own more extreme supporters. As a result too much time and energy were spent on acts of lustration against individuals such as Zhivkov and Patriarch Maxim and on ill-prepared legislation on such issues as the decollectivisation of agriculture, and too little devoted to considered, effective economic reform not least with regard to the problems of the loss-making state enterprises. This chicken was to come home to roost in dramatic fashion half a decade later.

The Berov government, December 1992–September 1994

The vacuum left by the collapse of the Dimitrov government could not be filled by the BSP. It could not command sufficient support in the assembly and its new leader had not yet established himself fully either in his own party or in the public eye. The president and the MRF alone remained as effective forces but the latter could not form an administration. It did, however, agree to sponsor one which consisted largely of non-party, technical experts. The new prime minister was to be Liuben Berov, a distinguished professor of economic history and a former economic advisor to the president.

Shortly before the Berov government was formed the European Union announced that it would sign an interim trade agreement with Bulgaria. If this created hopes of a new dawn for Bulgaria such hopes were soon dashed. Wrangling within the EU prevented implementation of the agreement until December 1993. It was symbolic of the disappointments that were to characterise the Berov administration.

Under Berov Bulgaria trod water. His attempts to revitalise the economic reform process failed and he angered many who thought his administration was not merely treading water but swimming backwards. There were complaints that many in the media who opposed the government were being replaced but the fiercest criticism was directed against the judiciary bill of October 1993 which meant that the highest echelons of the legal profession would be confined to those who had held such office under the communists. The bill was submitted to the constitutional court. The judiciary bill was one of the few occasions on which the Berov government showed any resolution.

A major problem for the cabinet was its lack of clear support in the sûbranie. By the summer of 1993 the cohesion of the MRF, upon which the government depended in parliament, was weakening, whilst the UDF and the BSP also suffered defections. This intensified the politicking which seemed by the summer of 1993 to have replaced government in Bulgaria. And there was little improvement in 1994, partly because in the spring of that year Berov himself was incapacitated and had to undergo heart surgery.

The lack of firm government made itself felt most notably in the continued inability to enact proper economic reform and to contain the mounting wave of crime. Both problems were intensified by the imposition of sanctions on Yugoslavia.

The Berov government, undermined by popular disillusion over economic stagnation and rising crime, finally collapsed in September 1994 and a caretaker administration under Reneta Indjova, Bulgaria's first woman prime minister, was appointed. When elections were held in December the BSP secured an outright victory. The previous administration's failure to combat economic drift and rising crime were important reasons for this victory but they were not the only ones. The previous five years had been perceived as years dominated by the UDF, and even though the UDF had been in office for only one of those five years it was that group's ideology which was believed to have dominated the period. The UDF was in effect held responsible for the failure to produce proper economic reform, for the social crisis which the transition from totalitarianism had produced, for rising crime and corruption, and for the general lack of morale which affected the whole country.

The failure of economic reform, 1989–1994

In his address to the central committee plenum of 11–13 December 1989 Mladenov had admitted that Bulgaria's foreign debt stood not at $3 billion, as Zhivkov had stated, but at $12 billion. It was only the first of many indications of the depth of Bulgaria's economic difficulties, but despite this in the Bulgarian transition economic reform always seemed to rank second behind political reconstruction and party wrangling. The round table discussions of 1990, for example, paid relatively little attention to the problems of the economy.

Bulgaria faced a number of particular economic difficulties not experienced by other members of the former Soviet bloc. In the first place, the Bulgarian economy had been tied far more closely than that of any other East European state to Comecon and the collapse of that organisation meant that Bulgaria had to construct new patterns of trade with the prime objective of establishing much more developed trading relations with the EU and the dollar area. This was complicated by a number of factors. Bulgarian manufactured goods were of such poor quality that they could be exported only to controlled markets such as those Comecon had offered; western Europe and the Americans would not buy them. Primary produce was equally difficult to sell abroad, principally because what Bulgaria could best provide were those products, such as fruit and wine, of which the EU already had a surfeit. There was also soon to be a problem with domestic production levels. A further problem unique to Bulgaria was that just as Comecon was collapsing it was felt advisable to decrease exchanges with two other important previous trading partners, Libya and Iraq. The need to create and retain a favourable image in the west persuaded Sofia to follow rigorously the UN sanctions imposed on both those countries. But this was done at considerable cost; Iraq was Bulgaria's largest debtor and agreement had only recently been reached that its debt should be repaid in oil, 600,000 tons of which were due for delivery in 1990. A further complicating factor was that in March prime minister Lukanov had suspended capital repayment of Bulgaria's foreign debt, and in June he did the same to interest payments. This made hard-currency loans much more difficult to secure.

Despite this setback the west, and in particular the USA, was still prepared to assist, and American advisors helped Lukanov draft the emergency reform programme which he knew was essential if

Bulgaria were to regain economic stability. But here he faced political difficulties when the UDF refused to join a coalition with him, insisting that as the communists/socialists alone had created the mess they alone must take the political consequences for clearing it up. And mess it was. The harvest of 1989 had been poor, not least because of the disruptive effects of the exodus of the Turks, many of whom worked on the land or in the distributive processes; in September food rationing was extended from the provinces to Sofia. In the first seven months of 1990 production was 10 per cent below the poor levels of 1989; inflation in May and June alone had reached 108 per cent and unemployment was rising. When he left office in November Lukanov had been able to do nothing to remedy the situation.

The Popov government tried to do this by introducing Bulgaria's 'big bang' on 1 February 1991. February also saw a bitter sûbranie battle in which the government finally prevailed in its efforts to enact laws paving the way for the eventual decollectivisation of agriculture and the privatisation of small businesses. In the summer there was a second stage of economic reforms which included further price deregulation and which also made the Bulgarian National Bank accountable to parliament rather than to the government.

Both sets of reforms had been painful but they did prove Bulgaria's reforming intent and this reassured some western politicians and bankers. Early in March Bulgaria was one of the beneficiaries of aid released by the European Community for reconstruction in Eastern Europe, and in August a major loan of $250 million was granted by the World Bank.

The Dimitrov government continued the process. In February 1992 foreign ownership of Bulgarian enterprises and the export of profits were legalised. More banking reform was enacted and after considerable delay a privatisation law was passed in April. In the same month the sûbranie, despite opposition from the BSP, gave its consent to a law restoring to its former owners property confiscated by the authorities during the years 1947 to 1962. In the previous month a land privatisation law had decreed that all agrarian collectives must be dissolved by 1 November 1992. This was a flagship bill but it had been poorly prepared and was to lead to enormous problems over defining individual claims and adjudicating between them in the many cases where they clashed. Furthermore, without help from either the government or the cooperative system of old, many of the new individual proprietors retreated into subsistence farming with serious consequences for the supply of food to the domestic and export markets.

The lack of foresight in the decollectivisation legislation was one of the many indications that the Dimitrov government was less interested in economic reconstruction than in pursuing political vendettas. It did continue with economic reforms but no longer enjoyed the cushion of the social consensus created under Popov whose tripartite agreement collapsed in April 1992. By mid-summer social and industrial unrest were widespread with strikes by civil servants, on Sofia's transport network and, despite the provisions of the 1990 law, in the ports, and in the medical services. The government was forced to grant a 26 per cent wage increase to all state employees, an act which weakened its attempts to control the budget deficit and inflation and which did little to impress the international financial organisations (IFIs).

Shortly after coming to office Liuben Berov produced an economic 'plan of action'. It had little effect. Inward investment was extremely disappointing whilst privatisation, particularly of land, was way behind schedule. Berov's plan was based on the assumption that the current economic recession could be cured by more government investment; reflation, it was argued, would stimulate growth. This alarmed not only the UDF. The powerful International Monetary Fund (IMF), which had already expressed concern at the lack of economic reform, criticised Berov's plan for allowing too high a government spending deficit. Meanwhile, the foreign debt problem had become even worse. In March at a meeting in Frankfurt, the London Club of Bankers, who held most of the credits, had offered a remission of 38 per cent of the total debt, but this the Berov government had refused, holding out instead for 50 per cent. In this it was eventually successful, though agreement on the amount of debt to be repaid also meant that repayments had soon to begin. This would be made more difficult by another economic setback: the decline in the value of the lev. One of the few economic successes of the Bulgarian big-bang had been to stabilise the national currency which for three years had moved gently between 25 and 30 leva to the US dollar. In the summer of 1994 it began to decline and though its value was bolstered by intervention by the BNB, that intervention inevitably encouraged inflation. Had not VAT, introduced by the Berov administration, produced 40 per cent more revenue than anticipated, the government deficit and therefore inflation would have been an even greater problem.

To make matters much worse Bulgaria, for political reasons, had agreed to observe the sanctions applied on Serbia and Montenegro in 1992 and severely tightened in the spring of 1993. Bulgaria held fast to the UN line but, as with the sanctions against Iraq, the cost was horrendous. The rail and road routes through the former Yugoslavia had been one of the chief arteries for Bulgarian trade, particularly for the export of perishable products, and the only available alternatives, through Romania or by sea, were slow and congested; the Romanian route was even partially closed by a rail strike in August 1993. By September the cost of sanctions was calculated at $2.71 billion, and one estimate put the total cost of all sanctions, i.e. those against Iraq and Libya as well as against Yugoslavia, at $13 billion or the equivalent of Bulgaria's total foreign debt. At the end of 1993 the UN had approved a transit arrangement for Bulgarian goods but it was limited in extent and so beset with bureaucratic regulations that it was almost useless.

Five years after the fall of Zhivkov the Bulgarian economy clearly had not been effectively reconstructed. The most serious disappointments were in the privatisation process. It was soon to become apparent, however, that the entire economy and the reform of it were subject to new and sinister forces.

The Videnov government and the catastrophe of 1996

As a result of the December 1994 elections the BSP was the first party since 1989 to enjoy an overall majority in the sûbranie. It won 52.08 per cent of the votes and 125 seats; the UDF had 28.65 per cent of the votes and 69 seats; the MRF took 6.25 per cent of the votes giving it 15 seats. Also represented were the Popular Union (PU) which took 7.5 per cent of the votes and had 18 seats, and the Bulgarian Business Bloc (BBB) which had 5.42 per cent of the vote and 13 seats. The main constituent elements of the PU were the Democratic Party and BANU–NP, both of which had left the UDF in September. The BBB, as its name implies, represented commercial interests and its electoral image was enhanced by its exotic leader, Georgi Ganchev, a former fencing star who had taught at Eton.

The return of a party which had an absolute majority in the sûbranie gave rise to the hope, in even many a non-BSP breast, that at last firm government and effective restructuring would be possible; that, at last, government would replace politicking in post-totalitarian Bulgaria. Initially Videnov did nothing to belie such hopes. He appointed a cabinet which included some members of the Bulgarian Agrarian National Union and a representative of the environmental pressure group, Ecoglasnost. Within his own party he had broken from his former sponsor, the conservative Lilov, and had surrounded himself with ex-Komsomol colleagues who were young and gave the impression of efficiency and modernisation. Videnov confirmed the newly raised hopes in his inaugural speech as prime minister when he asserted that his aims were to reverse the economic decline, to further Bulgaria's integration into European institutions, and to combat crime. In May 1995 he introduced an action programme in which he reaffirmed these commitments and his belief in the benefits of the 'social market economy'. Videnov also made it plain that he intended to repair and improve Bulgaria's relations with Russia.

Not only did Videnov fail in all four of his main stated aims; he also brought the country to the verge of starvation and economic and social collapse.

The early months of the new regime gave no indication of the calamities that were to come. Relations with Russia, already improved by the Berov government which in April 1993 had signed a long-term agreement in Moscow for the supply of Russian gas to Bulgaria, appeared even warmer in May 1995 with the conclusion of further agreements on cooperation in trade, defence and the building of pipelines to carry Russian oil and gas from the Bulgarian port of Burgas to Alexandroupolis in Greece and to other points in the Balkans. A new Russo-Bulgarian joint company, Top-Energy, was created to implement the agreement and the former prime minister, Lukanov, was appointed its head.

In the economy, too, there appeared to be a fresh dawn. GDP increased by 3 per cent in 1995 and the first half of that year produced a trade surplus of $106.3 million. Even inflation seemed to be coming under control, the overall rate for the first half of the year being 15.2 per cent compared to 59.4 per cent for the same period in 1994. In the circumstances the Bulgarian National Bank felt confident enough to lower interest rates no fewer than seven times in 1995.

The dawn proved false. Even relations with Russia soon began to sour. In the long negotiations over the construction of pipelines the Russians proved such difficult partners that the Bulgarians accused them of unfair dealing. The Russians even insisted, without any compensating concession on their part, that Bulgaria give a pledge not to join NATO. Videnov had no intention of joining NATO but he could not give such a pledge at the behest of a foreign government. In April 1996 Russia's president Yeltsin gravely embarrassed the Sofia administration and infuriated many Bulgarians by stating that Bulgaria, like Belarus, might sign an integration agreement with Russia and other former Soviet republics. By the end of 1996 relations between Bulgaria and Russia were worse than when Videnov took office.

The critical failings of the Videnov government, however, were in domestic rather than foreign affairs. One problem was food. Videnov could not be blamed for the many shortcomings of the UDF's land privatisation policies but where the new administration could be held accountable was in allowing the export of grain. The selling of grain abroad in times of shortage at home was of questionable legality and the exporting agencies included a number of the large conglomerates which were soon to play a baleful role in Bulgarian affairs, and with which a number of ministers, including Videnov himself, were said to have close connections.

On the wider economic front the end of 1995 brought the first indications that the recovery was illusory. The privatisation programme which the government had promised was making little progress. The Videnov administration favoured the voucher scheme which had been used in the Czech Republic and which was more acceptable to left-wing parties than the alternatives because it passed ownership to the population at large not to wealthy sections of it. Voucher privatisation, however, does not ensure that ownership and control of the enterprises passes to those best qualified to run them, nor does it create a great deal in the way of foreign currency earnings, the more so when, as in the Bulgarian case, firms were not privatised unless they were in desperate straits. In fact, the heart of the Videnov government was not in privatisation and when it did at last offer some 1,500 enterprises, some 20 per cent of the state's assets, for privatisation the economic and political climate had changed beyond recognition.

The first storm cone was hoisted in December 1995 when the minister of finance announced that the budget deficit for the year would be 17 per cent greater than predicted. This put pressure on the lev on the foreign exchanges, to counteract which interest rates were raised in February 1996 from 8 to 42 per cent. The critical event came in the same month. Early in the year the Bank for Agricultural Credit 'Vitosha' had found itself in difficulties and in January had received $33 million dollars from the BNB. But not even this could keep it afloat and it therefore attempted to call in a number of non-performing loans. The money was not forthcoming and at end of February the BNB took it over; in effect the Vitosha Bank had failed.

The Vitosha affair laid bare the weaknesses of Bulgaria's transition from communism, in the political as well as the economic sphere, and it highlighted the nexus between corruption, the political system, and the economy. In the early years of the transition many industrial managers had come to agreements with private entrepreneurs to buy raw materials from the latter at inflated prices and to sell the finished product, often with state subsidies, at reduced levels. The managers then took a slice of the profits made by the entrepreneurs whilst the industrial workforce was kept happy by unrealistic pay increases. When the government attempted to discipline the enterprises by imposing credit restrictions the enterprises escaped control by failing to pay for their supplies or by taking loans from the banks. The banks knew that there was little or no prospect of these loans being repaid. The state enterprises and the banks were in effect beyond the control of the state. It was widely believed they were under the control of the conglomerates or, in popular parlance, 'the mafia'.

The origins of the Bulgarian mafia are obscure. In the last years of communist rule many in the higher ranks of the party in Bulgaria, as elsewhere in Eastern Europe, realised what was happening and were reported to have used their powerful positions within the system to shift money into safe havens in Switzerland or elsewhere. After 1989 this money was sometimes used to establish companies which traded domestically and internationally, a number of companies merging into loose confederations or conglomerates. The wealth and influence of the conglomerates were increased by sanctions on Yugoslavia; huge sums were earned in smuggling illicit goods and much was spent in bribing officials at all levels to keep silent. The conglomerates were also involved in the mulcting of the state enterprises. Any organisation making profits from these activities would not wish to see effective economic restructuring or the privatisation of the enterprises from which they were making their profits; and many such organisations had money enough to buy both votes in the assembly and influence within the ruling party. It was also feared that they would not refrain from extreme methods to protect their interests and the murder of former prime minister, Andrei Lukanov, in October 1996 was attributed to criminal gangs associated with the conglomerates. The muscle of the conglomerates could also ensure that the banks continued to be compliant when hopelessly insolvent enterprises came forward with requests for yet more loans. It was with this in mind that President Zhelev declared in March 1996 that the banks were 'plundering' the nation.

Despite the president's words the crisis deepened. The lev fell constantly and on 16 May came 'Black Friday' when two more banks had to be placed under the supervision of the BNB; depositors, fearing their savings would be destroyed, rushed to withdraw their leva and turn them into goods or dependable currencies. The government was forced to act and Videnov announced that sixty-four of the largest loss-making enterprises would be closed and a further seventy would be 'isolated', that is they would be denied further state subsidies or loans. At the same time the budget deficit was to be eased through a series of drastic measures which included raising VAT from 18 to 22 per cent, a levy on imports, and large increases in fuel and public utility prices. It was not enough. The lev continued to fall and the IMF announced that it would offer no more help unless Bulgaria allowed it some say in running the BNB and also introduced a currency board which, independent of all government control, would regulate the money in circulation. The government's refusal to accept these terms provoked a further loss of confidence in the banks, a further nine of which had to be placed under BNB control in September, and precipitated yet another crisis in the foreign exchange market, notwithstanding another hike in interest rates which now stood at a staggering 300 per cent. Inflation remained unchecked and by the end of the year had reached an annual level of 578.6 per cent. The latter inevitably devalued salaries, a problem which was made much worse by delays of up to three months in payment.

Public reaction to the growing crisis had not been absent. There had been large demonstrations in Sofia, one on 7 June involving an estimated million people, but it was in the presidential elections in October–November that popular anger was most tellingly expressed. In the summer President Zhelev had been forced by the UDF into a primary campaign which he had lost, the party taking its revenge for the disagreements between him and premier Dimitrov. The UDF candidate was an anti-communist lawyer, Petûr Stoyanov, who easily won the second round of the contest, scoring 60 per cent of the poll to the BSP candidate's 40 per cent; the BSP polled a million fewer votes than in the parliamentary contest two years before.

Anger at the government's performance was also expressed within the BSP. In November nineteen leading party figures signed an open letter calling for the formation of a new administration under a different leader. On 21 December Videnov resigned both as prime minister and leader of the party. The protesters' anger was not assuaged, the more so when Nikolai Dobrev was named as BSP leader. He was considered little different from Videnov.

At the end of 1996 Bulgaria was in a dangerous condition. The economy was in tatters and social deprivation was intensifying and spreading. Any hope that the country would be included in the list of applicant states to the EU had evaporated and with it Videnov's proclaimed policy of bringing Bulgaria closer to Europe. The public, in the presidential elections, had passed a vote of no confidence in the ruling party which was generally believed to be too close to a number of dubious organisations. At the end of the year the outgoing president apologised to the nation and admitted that he was 'ashamed of the Bulgarian political class'. But with the next parliamentary elections not due until 1998 there seemed no way out of the impasse.

In January 1997 the scene began to change. The UDF, led since its 1994 electoral defeat by Dimitrov's minister of finance, Ivan Kostov, announced that, unlike the BSP, it was prepared to follow IMF orders and introduce a currency board. At the same time it demanded that elections be held immediately because such a drastic measure could only be imposed by a government enjoying the nation's confidence. The UDF statement galvanised the population. Peaceful demonstrations began, and were much inspired by those in Belgrade where gentle but massive popular pressure was soon to force Slobodan Milošević to accept opposition victories in the Serbian local elections. On 10 January, however, the mood turned sour when opposition deputies walked out of parliament and in the evening protesters invaded the sûbranie building to be met with tough action by the police; over a hundred were injured, among them Filip Dimitrov. Tension rose further on 22 January when constitutional convention forced the incoming president Stoyanov to invite Dobrev, as leader of the largest group in the assembly, to form a government. Strikes and demonstrations raged across the country and Bulgaria stood nearer to open revolution and perhaps civil war than at any other time since 1989. The situation was saved by Dobrev who announced on 4 February that he would resign and that a general election should be held in April, a caretaker ministry under the UDF mayor of Sofia, Stefan Sofiyanski, being formed until then.

Before the elections some party realignment took place. The UDF joined with the smaller right-of-centre PU to form the United Democratic Forces (UtDF), though the UDF remained by far the dominant partner. The leadership of the MRF meanwhile joined with a number of other small parties, including some monarchists, to form the Alliance for National Salvation (ANS); this caused some discontent in party ranks and in the north of the country some MRF local organisations broke ranks and formed electoral alliances with the UtDF. The BSP suffered a number of defections, the defectors forming a new party, the Euro-Left.

These realignments had little effect upon the outcome of the election. The UtDF secured an absolute majority of 52.36 per cent of the votes and took 137 seats in the sûbranie. The BSP had 22.07 per cent of the votes and 58 seats. The ANS emerged with 19 seats and the Euro-Left 14, whilst 12 seats went to the Bulgarian Business Bloc.

The Videnov government had transformed the nature of Bulgarian politics, albeit in a fashion it had not intended. Its attempt to restore closer relations with Russia had brought rebuff bordering on humiliation. The widespread belief that the BSP, up to the very highest levels, was closely associated with the conglomerates greatly decreased the party's moral standing. And the utter failure of its economic policy alienated large sections of the Bulgarian nation. The cumulative effect of these shortcomings, particularly the economic failures, meant that Bulgaria now had no alternative but to seek shelter, safety and salvation within the Euro-Atlantic structures, primarily the EU and NATO. That meant that real reform and restructuring had to begin.

PART II. REAL TRANSITION, 1997–2004

The Kostov government and the attainment of stability,
April 1997–June 2001

The government of Ivan Kostov achieved a notable record in becoming Bulgaria's first post-communist administration to run its full constitutional term of four years. Kostov's period in office also served to strengthen the position of the prime minister against the presidency, thus doing much to ease, if not resolve this major constitutional problem. The Kostov government could claim another notable success when, in December 1999, the Helsinki meeting of the EU agreed that Bulgaria should be included in the list of states with which negotiations for accession would be held. In March 2000 Bulgaria was allowed to begin negotiations on eight of the thirty-one chapters of the *acquis communautaire*.

Closer integration into the Euro-Atlantic system was the fundamental aim of the administration. It was never an easy and was frequently a contentious policy. The EU consistently took a tough line, so much so that in March 1999 a frustrated Kostov announced that there was no point setting long-term goals because people were not interested in objectives fifteen or twenty years distant; if membership talks did not start soon, he threatened, Bulgaria would have to postpone the issue indefinitely. Yet there seemed no alternative to the EU and Bulgaria continued to negotiate, whatever the terms dictated in Brussels.

Progress towards accession depended first upon economic stabilisation, recovery and reform, then upon compliance with other demands made by the EU and NATO, and thirdly upon the containment of crime and corruption at home. It would obviously be aided by EU- and NATO-friendly attitudes in foreign affairs.

Economic stabilisation was relatively easily and rapidly achieved. True to his pre-election promise, Kostov introduced a currency board in June 1997. The lev was pegged to the Deutschmark – and after 1999 to the euro – and the BNB was forbidden to increase the money supply unless the national reserves had risen by an equivalent amount. The medicine was nasty but effective. Inflation, which in February 1997 alone had been 242.7 per cent, had fallen to 1.7 per cent by July 1999. Bank interest rates moved in the same direction, dropping from the high of 300 per cent in September 1996 to 4.42 per cent in August 1999. Foreign debt also fell, shrinking by almost a billion US dollars in the first quarter of 2000. Financial stability helped wage levels recover from the inflation-hit troughs of 1996 and 1997; the average monthly wage in the public sector in February 1997 had been a mere $25 but by May 1999 it had risen to $124.

Recovery made renewed reform possible. Prices were once again deregulated, the Videnov government having reimposed central control on the prices of some 52 per cent of goods and services. In January 1999 a second wave of privatisation was launched with thirty-one companies being put on the market and by the end of 2000 seven-tenths of Bulgaria's enterprises were in private hands. Some privatisations were of large enterprises such as the country's major oil refinery, Neftochim, which was sold to the Russian LUKoil concern, though the Bulgarian government retained a 'golden share' to allow it a veto on decisions which might involve a substantial decrease in production. Another economic advance was the selling off of most loss-making state enterprises. In July 1999 the minister of finance announced that Bulgaria had met the IMF's deadline for closing or selling forty-one large loss-making enterprises. The massive metallurgical complex at Kremikovtsi outside Sofia was amongst those sold; the price was one dollar. These efforts earned the country plaudits from the international financial institutions. In May 1999 a senior official of the IMF described Bulgaria's economic behaviour as 'exemplary' and good conduct brought more tangible rewards, especially in the form of grants and loans, including $125.5 million from the EU and a general loan of $200 million from the World Bank.

Other economic reforms were adopted as a result of direct pressure from Brussels, even though they occasioned considerable pain. In 2000 Bulgaria shut down 311 meat-producing concerns and 230 dairy farms because they failed to meet EU standards, and at the same time Bulgaria abolished import duties on 470 agricultural products from the EU. It received little in return. By April 2001 the EU had refused to license any of the remaining 570 meat-producing farms in Bulgaria and had recognised only four of the country's 280 dairy farms. By March 2004 there were twenty dairies, twelve slaughterhouses, four meat-processing and four fish-product plants with EU export certificates. The restriction of food-processing plants resulted in upward pressures on food prices.

The demands made by the EU were never confined to the economic sector and other reforms introduced by the Kostov government reflected what Brussels wanted or was assumed to want. In 1998 legislation was introduced providing for state-sponsored programmes in languages other than Bulgarian aimed at 'Bulgarian citizens whose mother tongue is not Bulgarian', which made possible the introduction in May 2000 of Turkish-language broadcasting on state radio and television. The government also aimed to impress the EU by founding educational institutions which provided at least some teaching in Turkish. That not as much provision for broadcasting or teaching in Turkish was made available as was expected, or demanded by a number of external agencies, was not entirely the fault of the Bulgarian authorities. There was a lack of trained personnel, both broadcasters and teachers, whilst in the educational sector many Turkish parents, and children too, preferred not to take classes in Turkish if doing so meant, as it frequently did, sacrificing the opportunity to study another foreign language such as English or German. An educational reform more overtly designed to enhance Bulgaria's prospects in Europe was the introduction in January 2001 of EU-integration courses in high schools. The classes were to provide knowledge of contemporary Europe through lessons in geography, history, economics and philosophy. Subconsciously, perhaps, the educationalists were leading the Bulgarians to European national consciousness as they had led them a century and a half before to consciousness of their own, Bulgarian nationality, and the intelligentsia which a century and half before had led the peasant population to national consciousness was now leading the nation towards European integration.

Greater transparency in national life was a valid goal in itself but it was also one which would further enhance Bulgaria's image in the EU. In autumn 1997 police files were made open for inspection and the ministry of the interior for the first time released the names of some politicians and state officials, there were twenty-three of them, who had worked for the communist intelligence agencies; a report published in May 2001 revealed that 129 or nearly one in ten of the members of the Bulgarian parliaments since 1990 had worked for the former security services and a number of distinguished non-political figures such as Bulgaria's first astronaut, Georgi Ivanov, were also named as one-time informers. The revelations embarrassed some politicians but the publication of the names, and the greater access to these sensitive files granted by a law of February 2001, did much to stop the damaging innuendoes which had previously been a prominent feature of Bulgarian public life. The revelations also made much more difficult the unpleasant practice of 'file blackmail'.

Another important archival finding, though one resulting from private research rather than government policy, came in January 2001 when an investigative journalist discovered and published material on the regenerative process of the 1980s. This showed that in January 1985 Georgi Atanasov, shortly before he was nominated as Zhivkov's prime minister, had ordered the assimilation of the Turks in northern Bulgaria. The findings also showed that although there was no direct proof that Zhivkov ordered the assimilationist process or the violent measures which accompanied it, there was clear evidence that he knew of and did not object to those policies.

If economic reform, the widening of education in minority languages, and greater transparency in national life had been introduced voluntarily because it was believed this would enhance

Bulgaria's chances of progress towards EU accession, there were direct demands from Brussels which were much more difficult to accept and implement. There were three in particular which were to plague both the Kostov government and its successor. The first was the closure of parts of the nuclear power complex at Kozlodui; the second was the reform of the judiciary; and the third was the elimination of corruption.

The EU considered four of Kozlodui's six reactors unsafe and demanded that they be closed. As the plant produced at least a third of Bulgaria's energy and the country had no alternative indigenous source of power this was a tough demand. It was this demand which had sparked Kostov's rage in March 1999 and he added that the closure of Kozlodui would destroy what little international competitiveness Bulgaria enjoyed. Eventually, however, the Kostov government bowed to Brussels' demands and in November 1999 agreed to close the two oldest reactors by 2002 and another two by 2006; the EU in return promised $200 million in aid to help alleviate the effects of the closure. The problem of judicial reform was not seriously tackled until after Kostov had left office. The problem was closely linked with that of corruption on which the EU also made rigorous demands which the Kostov government found impossible to fulfil.

The Kostov cabinet had few difficulties in settling upon foreign policies approved by the Euro-Atlantic communities, though these policies did not always meet with widespread approval at home. Kostov had declared on coming into office that it was his government's objective to join NATO and parliament had supported him. Even the BSP, once so hostile to NATO, had for some years recognised that there was no alternative security umbrella. It was not surprising, therefore, that the government gave full diplomatic support to the NATO action over Kosovo and allowed NATO planes use of Bulgarian airspace, a privilege it denied to the Russians when they wanted to fly supplies to the troops they had rushed from Bosnia to Prishtina airport in June 1999. Though intensely unpopular at home Bulgaria's stance over Kosovo was recognised and rewarded in November of the same year by a visit to Sofia by President Clinton, this being the first time that a ruling US head of state had set foot in the country.

If Bulgaria were to progress towards NATO a compliant foreign policy would have to be complemented by a restructuring of the Bulgarian armed forces which in many respects still bore the imprint of the Warsaw pact. In September 1999, therefore, the government introduced 'Plan 2004' to slim down and streamline the military establishment. The link between Balkan instability and the desire for closer relations with NATO was clearly illustrated in the early months of 2001 when it seemed that Macedonia might become destabilised by Albanian insurgents. The Kostov government immediately concluded an agreement allowing NATO to use Bulgarian territory to transit and deploy troops. It was the first government to sign such an agreement and it did so without parliamentary approval, though this was easily and rapidly secured.

Another development, warmly approved by NATO, was the creation of a Balkan regional peacekeeping force. Meeting in Skopje in September 1998 the defence ministers of Italy, Albania, Bulgaria, Greece, Macedonia, Romania and Turkey agreed to establish a joint three-thousand-strong force whose headquarters were to be in Plovdiv for the first four years and were thereafter to rotate amongst member states. The headquarters were opened in September 1999.

The fact that NATO will not admit any state which has border disputes with a neighbour no doubt lay behind the agreement of February 1999 concluded between Bulgaria and Macedonia. Both sides denied any territorial claim upon the other and at long last the problem of the language or languages to be used in the text of agreements between the two states was resolved; they were to be 'the official languages of the two countries'. In effect, Bulgaria had recognised the existence of a Macedonian language without explicitly saying so which meant that around twenty accords, some of which had been pending for years, could be made effective. Thereafter Bulgarian–Macedonian relations were generally friendly.

Another bilateral Balkan development of significance in the Kostov years was the conclusion of an agreement with Romania on the construction of a second bridge across the Danube. This had been under spasmodic discussion for a decade or more. It was desperately needed. The one existing bridge, between Rusé and Giurgevo, was hopelessly inadequate with lorries frequently having to wait as long as ten days to cross the river. The Romanians had resisted Bulgarian

Plate 9.4   Nadezhda Mihailova, then the minister for foreign affairs, accompanied by her daughter, presents her passport at the border with Greece in April 2001. More importantly, the passport does not have a visa as Bulgaria had secured visa-free entry into the Schengen zone for its citizens.

arguments that the bridge should be built in the westernmost parts of the common frontier, the Romanians preferring a more easterly route which would be nearer Bucharest and which, because transit distances in Romania would be greater, would bring more revenue. Two factors changed attitudes in Bucharest. The first was pressure from the EU, which wanted the bridge built as part of its Pan-European Transport Corridor Four, a projected route linking Greece and western Europe via Bulgaria, Romania, and Hungary. The second was the 1999 Kosovo crisis which showed how inadequate communications were once the routes through Yugoslavia were closed. The EU agreed to provide some financial help.

During the negotiations with Brussels on accession Bulgaria was generally coupled with Romania, a fact which many Bulgarians resented because they believed that Bulgaria's reforms were more advanced and effective than those of their larger, northern neighbour. It was a considerable encouragement to Bulgarians, therefore, when, at the end of 2000, it was announced that Bulgarian citizens, though not those of Romania, would be allowed to enter the Schengen area without visas. The agreement was to become effective in April 2001 and meant that Bulgarians wishing to travel to most of the EU were released from the demeaning, time-consuming, and expensive procedures for securing visas.

By the end of 2000 the Kostov cabinet was in desperate need of good news such as the concession on the Schengen area. The government's popularity was plummeting and a public opinion poll in February 2001, the beginning of an election year, revealed that support for the UtDF was 30 per cent lower than before the last election in 1997. The reasons for the government's unpopularity were many.

In the first place the economic recovery was slowing down just as the painful impact of the new reforms was beginning to be felt on a wide scale. Growth had been a robust 18.9 per cent in the first quarter of 1998 but that had been against the depressed levels of 1997; for 1998 as a whole the rate of growth in GDP was only 3.5 per cent and in the first quarter of 1999 it was down to 0.7 per cent. It did not rise greatly from these levels. The trade deficit had also increased mainly because of a decline in exports rather than an increase in imported raw materials. This was in part a result of the Russian economic crisis of 1998 but a much more important contributory factor was the interruption to Bulgarian trade caused by sanctions on Yugoslavia. This intensified the general public's anger over the government's support for the NATO campaign. Whatever its causes, the sluggish rate of economic growth discouraged vital inward investment. Inflation, too, was moving in the wrong direction. It had risen to over 6 per cent in 1999 and was to exceed 7 per cent in 2000. This was largely responsible for a worrying fall in the average monthly wage which by November 2000 had fallen back to $110. Early in 2001 the government was further embarrassed by the collapse of the privatised national airline whose planes had to be grounded in the early months of the year.

The impact of the economic reforms was most painful for those on fixed incomes, notably pensioners and single parents. But the most widespread problem was a rise in unemployment which by February 2000 had reached 18.4 per cent; in some depressed areas, especially those populated mainly by Roma, it could be as high as 80 per cent. A further worrisome aspect of the problem was unemployment amongst the young, and not least among the most educated of the young. One young unemployed man took the extraordinary step of hacking into the presidential website; he did not destroy anything but left a message complaining of the difficulties of finding work. President Stoyanov promptly offered him a job but for the vast majority of able and enterprising young Bulgarians there was no such escape and they joined the depressingly large number of talented young people who were lost to the country by emigration.

An even more disturbing fact was that many of the hard-hit suspected that the newly acquired riches of the few had not been legitimately acquired. Crime was rampant and seemingly unchecked. Early in 2001 there were six murders in Sofia within ten days and although the minister of the interior denied there was a crime wave he did have to admit that the crime rate had risen with an average of 380 offences being committed per day. Even the former king had been a victim, thieves depriving him of a cellular phone and some jewellery belonging to his daughter when he visited Sofia in 1999. The rise in crime, and the proliferation of firearms caused widespread fear and resentment amongst the population.

Even greater resentment was felt over corruption at high levels and this resentment was to be the major cause for the decline and fall of the Kostov government. Corruption and economic crime were hard to disentangle. In May 2000 it was estimated that the black economy accounted for over a third of the country's GDP and that in 1998 illegal trade across the borders had been worth $850 million, a sum equal to the entire defence budget. It was suspected that the smugglers were using channels once operated by the communist-era secret services and that many of the smugglers themselves were former secret service officers who had become businessmen by privatising their former secret police networks. When he came into office Kostov had made it clear that there would be no tolerance or indulgence of ministers who used their new office to become corrupt; not only was this morally unacceptable and socially destructive but the EU and other international agencies insisted that the elimination of the evil of corruption was essential. But the evil would not go away and with the dawning of the new millennium it became the dominant feature of Bulgarian politics.

In the summer of 2000 a number of Russian businessmen accused of illegal activities were expelled and in March 2001 three Russian diplomats were ejected for spying. This was the first time Bulgaria had ever expelled Russian diplomats and was reminiscent of the action taken against the Russian generals in the 1880s. Kostov's administration was not unduly concerned at a decline in relations with Moscow and when the Russians asked for intelligence material on the businessmen expelled they were reminded by the Bulgarian minister for foreign affairs, Nadezhda Mihailova, that the Warsaw pact no longer existed and that Bulgaria was now a fully sovereign, independent state. But if state sovereignty could be emphasised over the expulsion of the Russian diplomats, the last word had not yet been said on the question of the businessmen.

The expulsion of corrupt foreigners brought the Sofia administration some credit but not enough to outbalance the deficit caused by corruption at home. In April 2000 government spokesman Mihail Mihailov was forced to resign after being accused of accepting a $10,000 bribe from a businessman, a charge which Mihailov denied. In June came an even more embarrassing case when the government's chief negotiator with the EU, Aleksandûr Bozhkov, was also forced to resign after the prosecutor-general's office had sent a report on his activities to Kostov; Bozhkov had previously been minister with responsibility for privatisation where he earned himself the nickname 'Mr 10 per cent'. The most damaging blow, however, came in September when the opposition daily *Trud* revealed that the Russian mafia had given $80,000 to a charitable foundation run by the prime minister's wife, Yelena Kostova. She made no attempt to deny the allegation, even arguing that there was nothing wrong in putting bad money to good use. But the scandal intensified when the Russian businessman who had transferred the money to Kostova's foundation told *Trud* that he had been giving nearly half a million US dollars a month to the UtDF. It was in the wake of these allegations that the Russian businessmen were expelled from Bulgaria.

Kostov admitted in April that he had been at fault in not pursuing corruption with greater vigour and he pushed through legislation requiring government officials to declare their wealth at the beginning and the end of their period in office. But the damage had been done, the government's reputation was sullied and few people believed that in this respect the administration was any better than its predecessors.

The UtDF therefore entered the election year of 2001 beset by possible economic restagnation, static or declining standards of living for many people, rising crime, and all-pervading corruption by which a few became hugely rich at the expense of the many. The party was further weakened by defections from and dissent within its ranks. As the political world began to prepare for the coming electoral battle the UtDF was scarcely more popular than its main rival, the BSP which had now joined with a motley group of parties to form the Coalition for Bulgaria, an alliance between the BSP and the MRF being impossible after the recent revelations of Atanasov's responsibility for the regenerative process.

All seemed set for a close struggle at the forthcoming polls. But then the situation was drastically changed. Early in 2001 there had been rumours that the former king, Simeon II, might return from exile to contest the presidential elections due later in the year. This was impossible because of the constitutional requirement that a presidential candidate be resident in the country for five years preceding an election. But Simeon did return in April, announcing that he would form a new organisation, the National Movement Simeon II (NMSS), to contest the parliamentary elections.

The NMSS's programme was unashamedly populist. It set itself three essential objectives. One was to end political partisanship, another was to eliminate corruption, but the most striking was the promise of immediate and qualitative reform which would produce a real market economy in line with EU criteria; 'I am ready', the former king told the voters, 'to propose a system of economic measures and partnerships which, within eight hundred days and based on the well-known Bulgarian work ethic and entrepreneurial skills, will change your life.' He asked the public for its trust in restructuring the ethical as well as the material bases of the state and society. The new movement appealed particularly to the young and to women. Simeon promised to include more of both groups in the party's list of candidates, and his entourage included many young men and women with varying types of expertise including some television presenters and one pop star, but the most prominent were the successful financiers and economists with western experience who prepared the movement's economic programme. This, though still imprecise, promised to foster small business and to stimulate general economic growth by providing incentives for reinvesting profits and promoting the development of capital and stock markets. The NMSS also promised immediate increases in pensions, child benefit payments, and teachers' salaries. The NMSS's populism was inclusive rather than exclusive. It was not racist and appealed to all ethnic groups and to all sections of society. It had no bogeymen apart from the racketeers who had corrupted society and the political process whilst enriching themselves.

The movement's programme was vague, simple and stunningly successful. The NMSS rapidly established a commanding lead in the polls and this was confirmed in the elections of 17 June. It took 42.47 per cent of the vote and emerged with 120 seats in parliament, precisely half the total number. The UtDF had 51, the Coalition for Bulgaria 48, and the MRF 21. The 2001 elections returned the highest number of women deputies ever in Bulgarian history; they now formed over a quarter of the total, as opposed to a maximum of 10 per cent in previous years, and most of them sat for the NMSS, 40 per cent of whose deputies were women. The movement had won support in all sections of the electorate, urban as well rural, intelligentsia and professional as well as working class, old as well as

Plate 9.5   A first for Bulgaria, for Europe, and the world. A former king casts his ballot in the elections which will make him prime minister of the country he was once forced to flee. The party of Simeon Coburggotski, or 'the King' as he is usually called, won the largest number of seats.

young. It also galvanised the votes of the Bulgarian Turks, both in Bulgaria itself and amongst those who had emigrated to Turkey. In 1994 only 2,000 of the latter had chosen to vote; in 2001 55,000 did so, many of them voting for the NMSS in line with the traditional support Bulgarian Muslims gave to the throne.

The NMSS had been helped by the weakness of its opponents, particularly the UtDF which was discredited by its four years in office and further impaired by the negative campaign it conducted, choosing to concentrate on the shortcomings of its main opponent's programme rather than the presumed superiority of its own. But despite this the success of the NMSS was largely due to its own strengths and popularity. Also there was no doubt that the former king was a hugely powerful electoral magnet. He had personal charm, proven ability and connections with the outside world which many hoped might help Bulgaria. More importantly, unlike all previous political leaders in post-totalitarian Bulgaria, he had never been part of the pre-1989 system, and had no associations with either of the two main groups which had dominated political affairs since the fall of Zhivkov. But his greatest electoral asset was that he was absolutely free from any suspicion of personal corruption.

The government of 'the king'; the road to the EU and NATO

It was a remarkable turn of events for a former king to return to his native ex-communist country as a head of government. It was even more remarkable that that government, despite considerable difficulties on the domestic front, was able to bring Bulgaria into NATO and to the threshold of membership of the EU.

After his return to Bulgaria Simeon adopted the official surname Saxecoburggotski, though he continued to be known universally as 'tsarya', the king. There were still some who suspected that his aim was a restoration of the monarchy but Simeon was far too astute a reader of the political runes to harbour any hopes of an early restoration. His preoccupations were, he insisted, not with long-term constitutional designs but with the immediate task of bringing about economic regeneration and social renewal. His cabinet contained not only members of the NMSS but also two members of the MRF and two others who were from the BSP. His minister for foreign affairs, Solomon Pasi, was from the small Jewish community in Bulgaria and had long been an active proponent of Bulgaria's joining NATO, but the most prominent figures were the two young financial technocrats fresh from success in the west, the 31-year-old Nikolai Vasilev who became minister for the economy and a deputy prime minister, and Milen Velchev, aged 35, who became finance minister.

The fundamental policy objectives espoused by the new administration were little different from those of the Kostov government: progress towards admission to the EU; membership of NATO; accelerated economic reform; an increase in living standards; a decrease in crime; and the elimination of corruption.

The first task, however, was to begin the economic reform programme, the prime minister having insisted that the 800 days would begin as soon as his government had been formed. On 2 August Vasilev promised that the energy market would be liberalised and that privatisation of major assets such as power stations would be accelerated. On 19 August the prime minister announced a series of technical fiscal reforms to encourage investment and in October a 20 million leva fund was created to provide micro-credits to small businesses. Saxecoburggotski also promised to reform the customs service whose officers were to work 'for the state and not for themselves' and there were to be measures to eliminate corruption from the privatisation process. On the social front a minimum monthly salary of 100 leva, approximately $50, was announced for 1 October when wages in the public sector in general were to rise by 17 per cent, and as from 1 January 2002 child benefit payments were to be doubled. Less welcome was the announcement that electricity and central heating costs would have to rise by 10 per cent on 1 October 2001.

The liberalisation of the energy market and the efforts to eliminate corruption were part of the government's campaign to secure accession to the EU. This was to be a complex and at times frustrating process with Brussels blowing hot and cold and domestic factors at times complicating the process. A cold douche from Brussels came in October 2001 when it was decided that although Bulgaria had concluded twelve of the thirty-one chapters of the *acquis communautaire* the country did not yet have that *sine qua non* for EU admission, 'a functioning market economy'. In the following month Brussels widened its criticism, insisting that more had to be done to eliminate corruption, that the judicial system must be restructured, and that discrimination against the Roma must be diminished. That the Laeken meeting of the EU in December 2001 excluded Bulgaria from the states to be included in the first round of enlargement therefore came as no surprise. The Bulgarian government had little choice but to intensify its efforts to meet Brussels' requirements and later in December parliament approved a series of measures designed to move the country more rapidly in the required direction.

The Saxecoburggotski regime faced increasing resistance in its efforts to tailor Bulgaria to Brussels' cloth. In November 2001 the presidential elections produced a surprising result with the victory of Georgi Pûrvanov, the leader of the BSP. Pûrvanov's victory was mainly due to the fact that the incumbent president, Stoyanov, was deserted by his own UDF supporters. Pûrvanov made it clear that he would defend those who were hard hit by the economic reform programme and that he wanted to improve relations with Russia. This was unwelcome news to the government, as was the fact that Pûrvanov's assertiveness could reopen the constitutional struggle between president and prime minister.

The latter also faced difficulties with his own party. From the outset the NMSS had been a heterogeneous body which was one reason why, from the beginning, the former king had established a firm control, insisting personally, for example, on deciding on the suitability of each candidate on the movement's electoral list. The responsibilities of government meant that the leader could not always exercise so tight a control and rifts began to appear in the movement. There were also signs of indecision on the part of the prime minister, one such occasion being over whether the NMSS should transform itself into a political party. This it did in April 2002 but the divisions remained and in the early months of 2004 a series of defections from the party deprived it of its sûbranie majority, though the defectors declared that they would continue to support the king's government.

A further obstacle on the path towards EU accession was the toughness of the terms insisted upon by Brussels. This was most apparent over the question of Kozlodui. The Saxecoburggotski cabinet came under increasing pressure from the BSP, the president, and a considerable proportion of public opinion to demand a renegotiation of the terms of this part of the *acquis*. And in March 2003 the Supreme Administrative Court ruled that the closure of reactors three and four was unconstitutional.

This was only one of a number of issues at dispute between the government and the judiciary. At the end of 2002 major privatisation agreements were concluded for the sale of Bulgartabak and BTK, the state telecommunications monopoly. The courts declared both privatisations irregular and invalid. The government's response was to limit the power of the courts in this area, but this only provoked a trench war between the executive and the judiciary which in effect froze the two privatisations for a year. Brussels made it clear that this validated its own concerns over the state of the judiciary and in response the government pushed through reforms which limited the power of the judiciary, the necessary amendments being enacted in September 2003.

Of the other concerns voiced by Brussels in the autumn of 2001 the question of the Roma had been addressed and a number of concessions had been made. Action was taken to speed up the implementation of a framework programme for the integration of Roma into Bulgarian society, adopted by the Kostov government in 1999, the action including in 2003 a government scheme to help illiterate Roma aged over sixteen, special courses in the universities of Tûrnovo and Stara Zagora to train those who would teach Roma children, and a general anti-discrimination law enacted in September. The latter won the approval of the Budapest-based European Roma Rights Center.

To these advances could be added significant progress on the macro-economic level. Real GDP growth of over 4 per cent was recorded in the five consecutive years up to 2002. In that year Bulgaria's credit rating was upgraded five times and Milen Velchev was given the Euromoney Finance Minister of the Year award; state revenues were $157 million greater than forecast, and customs revenues were 92 per cent above expectations thanks to the reforms implemented since 2001. Even unemployment rates, though still high, showed signs of sinking, the level for April 2003 being 14.9 per cent compared with 17.85 per cent twelve months before. Inflation, too, declined. In November 2003 the yearly rate was down to 2.5 per cent and Velchev even spoke of its reaching zero by the summer of 2003, though this did not happen. In the vital area of privatisation the embarrassments over Bulgartabak and BTK were to some extent offset in August 2003 by the privatisation of the last remaining state bank, the State Savings Bank, the second largest in the country. By then 82.3 per cent of the state assets earmarked for privatisation had in fact been privatised.

Though not always popular the government's efforts to man-oeuvre Bulgaria into a position where it could be considered for admission to the EU were effective. In December 2002 the Copenhagen conference of the EU decided that serious accession negotiations with Bulgaria and Romania should begin with a target entry date of 2007. A second huge stride forward came in November 2003 when the EU announced that Bulgaria, unlike Romania, had achieved the status of a functioning market economy. By then twenty-six of the chapters of the *acquis* had been closed and the prospects for Bulgarian accession to the EU at the planned date of 2007 looked better than at any other time. There was further advance in February 2004 when the European parliament also gave Bulgaria a very encouraging message whilst at the same time casting doubt on the credentials of Romania for entry into the EU. This decoupling was greeted with relief by many in Bulgaria. Finally, on 14 June 2004, negotiations for Bulgaria's accession were concluded in Luxembourg with the expectation that the country would join the EU on 1 January 2007. The only slight cloud on the horizon was that the European Commission might decide to postpone the accession date for twelve months if there were a 'serious risk' that Bulgaria might not be able to implement the remaining necessary reforms on time. This was an explicit exhortation not to slacken in the reforming process and an implicit warning not to reopen the Kozlodui issue.

The path to accession to NATO was easier than that to the EU. The use of a Bulgarian base by US KC-135 Stratotankers during the war in Afghanistan in 2001 raised Bulgaria's profile but in February 2002 the secretary general of NATO said in Sofia that although Bulgaria had made significant strides towards NATO membership 'there is still much to be done'. One area in which Bulgaria had made, and was continuing to make progress was in slimming down the military establishment and turning the Bulgarian army from a conscript into a professional force. By November enough had been done for NATO, at its conference in Prague, to issue an invitation to Bulgaria to join the alliance and in March 2003 the sûbranie accepted the necessary protocols of accession.

At the time when this act was passed Bulgaria was enjoying an international significance unequalled since the second and perhaps the first world war. The fact that it was a member of the UN Security Council when the debate over Iraq was at its most intense gave it a higher than usual diplomatic profile. But the major enhancement came when the fighting began. Both Romania and Bulgaria gave

Plate 9.6   A female member of the US Air National Guard's 150th Fighter Wing usually based in New Mexico working with a Bulgarian policeman to patrol Camp Sarafovo, near Burgas. In a striking declaration of Bulgaria's new alignment with the west, the camp was used by US aircraft for refuelling operations during Operation Iraqi Freedom. The facilities offered to the coalition during the Iraq war no doubt helped Bulgaria secure admission to NATO in 2004.

permission for coalition planes to use their territory, in Bulgaria's case the base at Sarafovo near Burgas, but these facilities became much more important when Ankara refused to allow US troops the right of passage through Turkey. After the war Bulgaria agreed to send troops to Iraq and five hundred were deployed under Polish command in Kerbala. In December 2003 five were killed and sixty injured in a terrorist attack. At the beginning of April 2004 Bulgaria was admitted as a member of the NATO alliance.

Support for the coalition in Iraq occasioned some friction with France and Germany but Bulgaria moved swiftly to repair such rifts lest they endangered its progress towards EU accession. Bulgaria therefore refused American pressure to conclude an agreement exempting each other's citizens from prosecution by the International Criminal Court, a decision which led to the temporary suspension of US military aid to Bulgaria.

Other possible impediments to Bulgaria's EU accession were the related issues of corruption and organised crime. The king's government took energetic action on both fronts. A national anti-corruption strategy was adopted in October 2001 and in the following February a national action plan, which included the setting up of a national service for combating organised crime, was introduced, whilst Scotland Yard was invited to help tackle corruption in the ministry of the interior and the police. This bore some fruit and in September 2003 alone two hundred officials were sacked whilst eighteen hundred were being investigated, seven hundred of the latter being from the ministry of the interior. In March 2004 the Corruption Transparency Index ranked Bulgaria 54th out of 113, more or less equal to the Czech Republic and better than Slovakia; Romania was 83rd.

Such figures indicate that corruption is not a purely Bulgarian phenomenon. What is distinctive about Bulgaria, however, is the linkage between the criminal groups and corrupt elements in business and the administration, especially at the local level. One NMSS member of parliament declared that Bulgaria was unique amongst small countries in the high profile enjoyed by heavily armed criminal gangs. These gangs were generally believed to be responsible for the series of violent gang-land crimes seen in the first half-decade of the new millennium, crimes which included the shooting dead in March

2003 of Iliya Pavlov, one of Bulgaria's richest businessmen and a boss of the Multigroup conglomerate, and the death of four people when a bomb exploded in a Sofia lift in January 2004. Pavlov was killed one day after testifying in the trial of those accused of murdering Lukanov in October 1996.

The murder of Pavlov was one of a number of incidents which cast the judiciary in a poor light. Another was when the deputy prosecutor general made accusations of corruption and criminality against his boss, the prosecutor general. Yet another was the murder in December 2002 of a high ranking prosecutor, Nikolai Kolev. There were suspicions that his death was the result of feuding and personality clashes within the prosecution service, and whether such rumours were true or not the very fact that they could circulate harmed the image of the judiciary. More damage was done in January 2003 when general Boiko Borisov, the chief secretary of the ministry of the interior and the head of the nation's police services, accused the country's leadership and the judiciary of not supporting him in his efforts to combat organised crime. In April, after the attempted murder of another businessman, his ministry prepared a report which, Borisov told the media, contained photographs of meetings between former and current politicians, magistrates, and members of the underworld. Rumours, revelations, and accusations such as these added yet more pressure on the beleaguered judiciary but at the same time made it easier for the government to push ahead with its plans for judicial reform.

There is no doubt that the twin problems of crime and corruption adversely affected public morale in Bulgaria where by 2003 there was a distinct feeling that 'the mafia' had reappeared. What was important was the *re*appearance. Initially it was hoped that the problems of crime and corruption had been contained and the depression arose from the feeling that they had staged a comeback.

Public morale was also depressed by economic factors because, as is usually the case, macro-economic gain meant micro-economic pain. For most people the gains which impressed the external agencies and the EU were imperceptible. The USAID Annual Report for 2003 declared that the average Bulgarian 'is plagued by poverty, unemployment, and low living standards'. The average working salary was only $134 per month and the average pension $50 per month whilst GDP per capita was still only a quarter of the EU average. And if unemployment was falling slightly in 2002, long-term unemployment was depressingly high at 11.9 per cent; in the same year, whilst the overall unemployment rate was 18.1 per cent, the rate for the under-25s was 35.6 per cent. The bleak prospects for future employment and the much wider opportunities, to say nothing of the higher salaries, to be found abroad meant that many educated young people continued to emigrate. In 2001 it had been reported that since the fall of communism an estimated 700,000 people had left the country, many of them young, whilst an opinion poll in 2002 revealed that between 12 and 15 per cent of those under twenty-nine intended to emigrate in the near future. Emigration of the young, together with, in the mid-1990s, the lowest birth-rate in Europe, has brought about an alarming shift in the age pyramid. Whereas in 1976 16.0 per cent of the population had been over 60, in 1999 the figure was 19.1 per cent. The implications for pension provision are alarming. The immediate loss to the country could be made up if a significant number of these young people return later with enhanced skills and personal wealth to invest in the country. What cannot be made up, however, is the impact on families and friends; parents will no doubt understand and rejoice in the fact that their children have greater chances for self-advancement, but most will nevertheless be depressed by the break-up of the nuclear family, the more so in the Balkan context where family ties have historically been so strong and so important.

The sense of national depression was also increased by the fact that whilst the majority of the population felt little, if any, improvement in their circumstances a very small minority was becoming extremely wealthy. For a nation with a long and deeply ingrained egalitarian tradition this was difficult medicine to swallow.

There are few observers, either in Bulgaria or in the wider world, who would argue that Bulgaria had any alternative but to pursue a policy of further integration into the Euro-Atlantic structures. Nor would many seriously doubt that admission to NATO and the closure of negotiations with the EU were major achievements for the king's government. There are fewer who would recognise the importance of potential conflicts between the values championed by the Euro-Atlantic community and the social and psychological values nurtured by Balkan nations such as the Bulgarians. The conflict between the enrichment of the few and the poverty of the many is but one of the many problems which will have to be resolved when Bulgaria has settled into its new position as a full member of the European Union.

CONCLUSION

At the time of writing, almost a decade and a half has passed since the fall of communism in Eastern Europe. The 'post-totalitarian' era has seen its own brand of cynicism and disillusion as the hopes for rapid material advance were disappointed and economic reform exacted a heavy social price. But in Bulgaria there is an extra dimension to the puzzlement and disillusion of post-totalitarianism.

It is significant that for more than half a decade after 1989 the Bulgarians were not able to agree upon a new state emblem. There was, it seemed, a sense of doubt as to their national identity and their place in the contemporary world. There have been many articles and books dealing with this issue. An excellent example is Ivan Elenkov and Rumen Daskalov's compilation, *Zashto nie sme takiva; v tûrsene na bûlgarskata kulturna identichnost*, published in Sofia in 1994. The title means 'Why are we like we are? In search of Bulgaria's cultural identity', and the book is a collection of fifty articles written by nineteen authors and published in Bulgarian journals between 1898 and 1943. All the articles try and define what it means to be Bulgarian, what is specific about 'Bulgarianness'. At a time when the future contains many challenges as well as many possible rewards it is to the past that many present-day Bulgarians look for clues as to their true identity, for grid references to plot their position in an increasingly unstable and unsure world. What, then, can their own history tell the Bulgarians of their national identity and their place in the contemporary world as they are about to enter the European Union?

One of the themes in Bulgarian history is the dichotomy between an eastward and a westward orientation. This we can see in the great debates over whether to align with the western or the eastern branch of Christendom. In later centuries early nationalists debated the merits of relying on Russian or central/west European assistance, and this debate was continued in intensified form in the fierce and frequently violent political struggles between the russophobes and russophiles of the Bulgarian state after 1878.

Inevitably the debate over external orientation was linked, consciously or subconsciously, with the process of modernisation. Somewhat paradoxically, both traditionalists and extreme radicals could find role models in Russia, the former primarily in the church and the latter in revolutionary movements from the narodniks to the bolsheviks. For the newly emerging bourgeoisie and intelligentsia, however, the west had more to offer. Economic and trading ties with Russia were weak. Russia and Bulgaria exported similar commodities and therefore there was little trade between them; both also looked to central and western Europe for capital to rebuild and modernise their economies. But it was not only for economic help that the Bulgarians looked westward. Before the first world war Bulgarians knew that they had to adapt to western manners and customs if they were to integrate into that world. One of the most famous of Bulgarian literary creations is Aleko Konstantinov's Bai Ganiu, a peasant who visits the wider world, an encounter which produces bemusement and puzzlement on both sides but in which Bai Ganiu's raw, peasant cunning serves him well. It was in order to distance themselves from the unsophisticated Bai Ganiu image that those few Bulgarians who could afford to do so sent their children to be educated abroad; but very few of those children went to Russia and most went to Germany, Austria or France. Of the nineteen authors in Elenkov and Daskalov's compilation, one did not go to university at all, three did so in Bulgaria, one studied in both Russia and the west, one in Russia alone, and thirteen in the west.

In the political arena decisions on whether to align with Russia or its adversaries could and did prove critical. In 1913 and 1915 and again in 1941 Bulgaria chose to defy Russian interests with ultimately catastrophic consequences for Bulgarian aspirations towards full national unification. After 1944 Bulgaria's rulers opted for close relations with Russia at enormous cost to the political liberty of the Bulgarian citizen, as well as to the long-term economic and environmental well-being of the country. In the immediate aftermath of the changes of 1989, Bulgarian foreign policy swung around full circle. Close association with the EU became the ultimate goal of Bulgaria's foreign policy-makers and there was a wave of intense pro-American feeling. A malign fate meant that shortly before Bulgaria began to make its most concerted effort ever to integrate with the states of central and western Europe, it was cut off from those states by economic sanctions against Serbia and Montenegro; a new curtain descended over the Balkans and as far as many western Europeans were concerned Bulgaria seemed to have dropped off the edge of the map. Bulgaria was reintegrated into the western world during the Afghan and Iraqi wars and the politicians of Sofia showed considerable skill in ensuring that their commitment to helping the US-led wars did not seriously or lastingly impair their standing in the EU. By the summer of 2004 Bulgaria was experiencing a new form of integration with central and western Europe as citizens from the EU poured into the country not only as holiday-makers and tourists but as prospective property purchasers; the British and the Italians were prominent in this process.

The crassness of modern mass tourism and frustration with the exacting conditions laid down in Brussels and, at times, with the seemingly arrogant and insensitive attitude of negotiators led a few Bulgarians to feel Bulgaria might be better off developing links with the middle east, north Africa and the states of the Black Sea littoral. There was a historical precedent for this, though few Bulgarians would welcome it. The economic revival of the Bulgarian communities in the nineteenth century was based mainly on the expansion of trading relations not with central and western Europe but with the rest of the Ottoman empire, that is with European Turkey and Anatolia. Liberation in 1878 meant exposure to what the Bulgarians of the day would have called 'European' competition, bringing widespread economic dislocation and the destruction of much of the existing manufacturing system: and here is another obvious parallel with the post-1989 situation.

The dichotomy between an eastern and a western orientation has been an inevitable consequence of Bulgaria's geographic position and her historical development. These two factors have dictated that Bulgaria, occupying a nodal position between Europe and Asia, will always be on the edge of both the east and the west. In the present world that could be a distinct advantage. If land transportation between Asia and Europe is to continue developing as the planners seem to intend – witness the building of the second Bosphorus bridge and the plans for a rail connection between European and Asiatic Turkey – then Bulgaria will be a crucial link in the European–Asiatic transportation chain. Three other projects will reinforce Bulgaria's importance in the world's trading and transportation structure. The first is the plan to build a highway from Durres on the Adriatic through Macedonia and Bulgaria to Istanbul, which will provide the first new east–west route across the Balkans since the Romans built the Via Ignatia. The second is the intended new road leading from the Greek frontier northwards through Bulgaria to the new bridge to be built over the Danube to Romania. And the third is the pipeline which will take Russian oil and gas from Burgas to the Greek port of Alexandroupolis. In these circumstances neither Russia nor the other European states, nor indeed the nations of the middle east, could afford an isolated or an unstable Bulgaria. Europe will then need Bulgaria just as much as Bulgaria will need Europe.

If Bulgaria is to be integrated into Europe it will have to continue to conform to the democratic practices established in the post-totalitarian years. Does an examination of Bulgarian history give reason to believe that this will be the case? Is the capacity to build and sustain a democracy part of Bulgaria's cultural identity?

In the first place it must be recorded that since 1989 Bulgaria has had five general and three presidential elections. It has experienced minority government by the BSP, government by the UDF, government by two non-party technocratic cabinets, government by the BSP with a majority in parliament, by a UDF government with the same advantage, and by a government of the former king. Changes between governments have twice been precipitated by widespread extra-parliamentary action but incumbent cabinets have seen that bowing to popular pressure is a wise policy in such circumstances. That indicates a respect for the popular will which can be an important safeguard in a functioning democracy. At the same time individual liberties have largely been respected and efforts have been made to improve the well-being of the ethnic minorities. The press and the electronic media have at times been subjected to governmental influence but in the majority of cases this has been resisted and the press, together with the trade unions and other institutions has remained free.

If a healthy respect for education is a qualification for democracy then Bulgaria is strongly placed. The national revival of the nineteenth century would have been impossible without the development of a network of schools both at primary and more advanced levels. Any westerner reading the memoirs of Bulgarians who attended schools in centres such as Constantinople, Salonika, Sofia, Plovdiv and Varna cannot but be impressed both by the range of subjects taught and by the dedication of teachers and pupils alike. To judge from the quality of students coming from Bulgaria to western universities in recent years that tradition has certainly survived, in no small measure thanks to the specialist gymnasia which have for generations been a prominent feature of Bulgarian secondary education.

Crime and corruption remain serious problems. These are not purely Bulgarian phenomena and at present organised crime has not yet seriously threatened the political process as it did before the first world war and in the inter-war period. Murders have been largely the result of turf wars between rival gangs. Corruption, the close ally of crime, is still a danger which saps public morale, frustrates the political process, and damages the country's image abroad. But the will to tackle the problem has been demonstrated. The Kostov administration tilted ineffectively at this windmill but the popular reaction to its failure, as seen in the June 2001 elections, surely proved that the Bulgarian nation as a whole detested this poisoning of its body politic. And the government of 'the king', however burdensome its reforms were for many Bulgarians, has shown application and some success in tackling this age-old curse, not least in the judicial reforms of September 2003.

Bulgaria's past reveals a strong social base for egalitarianism and democracy. When the modern Bulgarian nation emerged from Ottoman rule in the final quarter of the nineteenth century, Bulgarian society was largely homogeneous. The pre-conquest aristocracy had been destroyed and differentiations of wealth had been slow to reappear. On the land, in the late nineteenth century, even the most prosperous, with few exceptions, tilled their own plots; their work was not qualitatively different from that of their poorer co-nationals and fellow-villagers. In the towns and the manufacturing communities production, before and for many years after the liberation of 1878, was almost entirely based on traditional processes organised along traditional lines. Here the guilds played a major role. The guilds, of course, with their hierarchical structures, did see differentiations of wealth and influence, but they also retained a sense of collective responsibility in which the wealthy had obligations to the less fortunate. This lack of social and occupational division created a system and a mentality in which there was equality of opportunity for all and education provided the medium through which that opportunity could be realised. This mentality still persists and it is puzzled by the sharp differences in wealth which have appeared since 1989. Disillusion with this product of western values could clash with the historic disposition for equality and thereby create problems for the integration of Bulgaria into the Euro-Atlantic system.

In 1879 the Bulgarian state was given a political system which reflected its egalitarian society. How effectively did that society manage its new democracy? The record is not entirely reassuring, though it is probably no worse than other states of similar age which emerged from similar backgrounds. It is true that political life in Bulgaria soon contracted the disease of corruption and clientalism; but so, too, did the political life of Greece, Serbia, Romania and, dare one suggest it, the trading of political support for contracts or other favours was not entirely unknown in the United States at the end of the nineteenth century. In the early years of the state the executive established an increasing control over the legislature, a process which weakened democratic impulses and smoothed the way for royal authoritarian rule and, after it, the totalitarianism of the communists. The post-totalitarian era has seen few signs that this undesirable phenomenon might manifest itself anew. In 1990 the reformers defeated the ex-communists' proposal that the sûbranie should elect the president; separate elections for parliament and president should help maintain the separation of powers. Nor is the legislature and government likely totally to dominate the presidency. President Zhelev showed a robust determination not to be dominated by the assembly and if Kostov seemed to establish supremacy over the presidency, Pûrvanov has asserted his powers *vis-à-vis* the king's cabinet in confident, almost confrontational manner.

Another dispiriting feature of Bulgaria's political past which has, mercifully, failed to reappear is the propensity towards political violence. Three prime ministers or ex-prime ministers were assassinated between 1895 and 1923 and there were a number of other killings; in the 1920s and 1930s violence was widely practised by the government, the various Macedonian factions, and the communists, whilst after 1944 the latter indulged in an orgy of retributive and prophylactic murder, official and unofficial. The violence which has reappeared in Sofia and elsewhere in the 2000s is extremely unsavoury but, so far, it has not been political violence.

In modern Bulgarian history the military have played a major role. One faction within the army was responsible for the initial deposition of Alexander Battenberg in 1886; his short-lived return to Bulgaria would have been impossible without another group of soldiers. Prince Ferdinand, that master craftsman of political calculation, made sure of his control of the ministry of war and the officer corps before he moved against Stambolov in 1894. In 1923 and 1934 the army was the instrument of major political upheaval; the overthrow of the old regime on 9 September 1944 was also a military coup but this time against the background of enormous international and domestic upheaval. At present, however, there seems little likelihood of military action against the civilian power. Despite demoralisation engendered by the collapse of the Warsaw pact and by fierce budgetary restraint, the army has remained loyal, allowing its grievances to be given occasional public utterance through the new officers' organisation, the Rakovski Legion. A propensity for military coups may not be the most desirable of historical traditions but it has not prevented Greece, Spain, or Portugal from gaining full membership of the European Union.

Since the signature of the treaty of Berlin in 1878 the national question has never been far from the surface of Bulgarian politics. The loss of much of San Stefano Bulgaria, and above all of Macedonia, burnt deep into the Bulgarian national psyche. Most of the great decisions over external policy since 1878 have hinged on the Macedonian issue. In 1912 an alliance was concluded with Serbia to redeem much of lost Macedonia and in the following year the disastrous second Balkan war was fought and lost in an effort to prevent Serbia and Greece from taking too much of the coveted land. In 1915 it was the hope of retrieving lost Macedonia which, above all, persuaded King Ferdinand and his prime minister to commit Bulgaria to the German cause; in 1941, when King Boris came to the conclusion that Bulgaria could no longer remain neutral, he sweetened the bitter pill by swallowing most of Macedonia. Internally, for the fifty years from the mid-1880s to the mid-1930s, the Macedonian sore itched and aggravated almost without cessation, and it made a fearful contribution to the growth of political violence in the country. But if a longing for national reunion was a constant feature of Bulgarian history between 1878 and 1944 there is as yet little sign of it re-emerging as a powerful factor in the political life of post-totalitarian Bulgaria. The recognition of the Macedonian state disappointed many Bulgarians but reassured other governments. And with the weight of immediate social, economic, and environmental problems pressing upon them, the majority of the Bulgarian people have shown few signs of wishing to relaunch the drive for territorial expansion, though it is impossible to predict what would happen if the Macedonian state were to be destabilised or to collapse.

There is another trend in Bulgarian history which looks neither to the east or the west and which shows no interest in territorial expansion. This is the tradition of introspection, an introspection at times so intense that it engendered disdain for or even rejection of the entire world of politics. The patron saint of the Bulgarians, Ivan Rilski, was a hermit, and the tradition of hermitism was strong in mediaeval Bulgaria. The bogomils, of course, took this much further and rejected not merely external alignments but the entire structure of the temporal state. During the long centuries of Ottoman rule Bulgarian culture survived primarily in the small, often self-sufficient villages and in the monasteries which were by definition distanced if not divorced from society and the official apparatus of the state.

Some observers believe that this tendency towards withdrawal into the inner self was in part responsible for the apparent lack of

Bulgarian involvement in the struggle for political independence from Ottoman rule and against later examples of political oppression. We have seen how few Bulgarians responded to the call to arms in 1876, nor should it go unnoticed that when the delegates of the powers met in Berlin to devise the treaty which was so harmful and hurtful to Bulgarian aspirations and sensibilities, there were no Bulgarians in the German capital to lobby the ambassadors or influence the press; the Bulgarians, it seemed, hoped or even assumed that the Russians could be relied upon to do the job for them. In the early years of the life of the reborn Bulgaria no family could ignore the state because it insisted on extracting taxes from them, educating their children, and conscripting their sons; yet there was a massive political apathy reflected particularly in very low turn-outs at elections. In the second world war there was little in the way of resistance to the regime until allied bombing began to make an impact and the prospect of a Soviet advance into the Balkans became a reality.

Under the communists Bulgaria became a byword for acquiescence and conformity with the Soviet model. There was no Bulgarian equivalent of the independent policies pursued by the other communist regimes in the Balkans, nor of Berlin 1953, Budapest 1956, Czechoslovakia 1968, or Poland 1980–1; the word dissident was not uttered in public in Bulgaria until 1978. We now know that there was more opposition to communist power, particularly in the early years and amongst the peasantry, than was previously believed, whilst both the attempted military coup of 1965 and Liudmila Zhivkova's assertion of Bulgarian cultural identity showed that not all Bulgarians were content with complete subjugation to Moscow. Nevertheless, it was the case that Bulgaria's reputation for conformity and quietude was, at least on a comparative basis, justified.

There are some obvious explanations for this. Under the communists the party's grip on the state and on society was strong and, at least in the years up to about 1970, the regime, quite literally, delivered the goods. But perhaps the placidity of Bulgaria was not simply the result of police power and increasing material well-being. Perhaps it was also to some degree a modern resonance on the string of disassociation from worldly affairs, a contemporary reassertion of the long cultural tradition which rejects the temporal world as tainted, transitory and tawdry. If this is the case what seems like compliance with existing authority is just conformity with that national tradition which rejects political authority as irrelevant.

It would, however, be dangerous for Bulgarians to dwell too fondly on this theme. Rejection of the state was possible for a mediaeval monk, for the inhabitants of a small, self-sufficient mountain village in the days of Ottoman rule, or even for a disaffected intellectual under German or Soviet domination; it is scarcely a wise prescription for the creation of a functioning, modern, representative democracy.

Apathy towards or withdrawal from political affairs contains another danger for post-totalitarian Bulgaria. A major factor in Germany's success since the second world war has been *Bewältigung der Vergangenheit*, the ability to come to terms with and to overcome the past. Bulgaria's past contains nothing to compare with the horrors of the final solution. The saving of the Jews from Bulgaria proper during the second world war was an achievement of almost the entire nation in which the entire nation takes justifiable pride. In the past Bulgaria had also provided a safe refuge for Armenians threatened with persecution and worse in Turkey; in recognition of this the Armenians in Bulgaria formed their own military detachment to fight with the Bulgarians in the Balkan wars. On the other hand, the Bulgarian national state did place some pressure on its Turkish minority. In the early years after liberation that pressure was cultural and perhaps unintentional to the extent that what the Bulgarians regarded as natural celebration of national independence and cultural liberation, the Turks saw as an intolerable alteration to their traditional way of life. There could be no compromise in such circumstances, but for the most part the Turks who left Bulgaria after 1878 did so voluntarily. So too did the majority of those who left in the late 1980s but there was no denying that extreme cultural and political pressures had been put upon them.

The post-1989 governments rapidly rectified the errors of the regenerative process and if the Bulgarians now have a problem in overcoming their past it is less in the way that they have treated other peoples than in the way they believe foreign domination has affected them. There is still a tendency amongst many Bulgarians, particularly when an outsider points out a shortcoming, to relapse into a regressive fatalism, a fatalism expressed most often in phrases such as 'Five hundred years of Ottoman rule ...' This is an unhelpful attitude. It is using the past to escape from the present and more so from the future. Furthermore, the Bulgarians are not alone in having suffered long centuries of foreign domination. That domination was without doubt at times extremely repressive but the Bulgarian nation, the Bulgarian church, and the Bulgarian language survived. When the Ottomans departed from Bulgaria the Bulgarians still spoke Bulgarian and Bulgarian manufacturing had flourished as a supplier to the Ottoman army; when British rule ended in southern Ireland the Irish language was almost dead and Irish industry had been stifled to prevent competition with British manufacturers. Past oppression is inevitably a part of national consciousness and respect for those who suffered is a proper sentiment, but that oppression should not be used as an excuse for present failings or for a lack of commitment to rectifying them.

Bulgarian history has better things to offer the Bulgarian nation than a lack of confidence in their own ability to adapt and survive.

Bulgarian monarchs

KHANS

Asparukh	681–700
Tervel	700–721
Kormisosh	721–738
Sevar	738–753/4
Vinekh	753/4–760
Telets	760–763
Sabin	763–766
Umor	August–September 766
Toktu	766–767
Pagan	767–768
Telerig	768–777
Kardam	777–803
Krum	803–814
Omurtag	814–831
Malmir	831–836
Pressian	836–852

KINGS OR TSARS: FIRST KINGDOM

Boris I	852–888
Vladimir	888–893
Simeon 'the Great'	893–927
Petûr I	927–970
Boris II	970–971

Roman	971–997
Samuil	997–1014
Gavril-Radomir	1014–1015
Ivan-Vladislav	1015–1018

KINGS OR TSARS: SECOND KINGDOM

Petûr II	1185–1187
Ivan Asen I	1187–1196
Petûr II (restored)	1196–1197
Kaloyan	1197–1207
Boril	1207–1218
Ivan Asen II	1218–1241
Kaliman I	1241–1246
Mihail II Asen	1246–1256
Kaliman II	1256–1257
Konstantin Asen	1257–1277
Ivailo	1277–1279
Ivan Asen III	1279
Georgi Terter I	1279–1292
Smilets	1292–1298
Chaka	1298–1300
Todor Svetoslav	1300–1321
Georgi Terter II	1321–1323
Mihail Shishman	1323–1330
Ivan Stefan	1330–1331
Ivan Alexander	1331–1371
Ivan Shishman	1371–1395
Ivan Stratsimir	1395–1396

PRINCES AND KINGS OF MODERN BULGARIA

Alexander of Battenberg	1879–1886
Ferdinand	1887–1918
Boris III	1918–1943
Simeon II	1943–1946 *

* King Simeon II left Bulgaria after a referendum in September 1946. The legality of the referendum has been questioned.

Prime ministers of Bulgaria, 1879–2004

Todor Burmov	July–November 1879
Metropolitan Kliment (Vasil Drumev)	November 1879–March 1880
Dragan Tsankov	March–November 1880
Petko Karavelov	November 1880–April 1881
Johan Kazimir Ehrenrot (Russian)	April–July 1881
No prime minister	July 1881–June 1882
Leonid Sobolev (Russian)	June 1882–September 1883
Dragan Tsankov	September 1883–June 1884
Petko Karavelov	June 1884–August 1886
Metropolitan Kliment (provisonal government)	9–12 August 1886
Petko Karavelov (provisional government)	12–16 August 1886
Vasil Radoslavov	August 1886–June 1887
Konstantin Stoilov	June–August 1887
Stefan Stambolov	August 1887–May 1894
Konstantin Stoilov	May 1894–January 1899
Dimitûr Grekov	January–October 1899
Todor Ivanchov	October 1899-January 1901
Racho Petrov	January–February 1901
Petko Karavelov	February–December 1901
Stoyan Danev	December 1901–May 1903
Racho Petrov	May 1903–October 1906
Dimitûr Petkov	October 1906–February 1907
Dimitri Stanciov	February–March 1907
Petûr Gudev	March 1907–January 1908

Aleksandûr Malinov	January 1908–March 1911
Ivan Geshov	March 1911–June 1913
Stoyan Danev	June–July 1913
Vasil Radoslavov	July 1913–June 1918
Aleksandûr Malinov	June–November 1918
Teodor Teodorov	November 1918–October 1919
Aleksandûr Stamboliiski	October 1919–June 1923
Aleksandûr Tsankov	June 1923–January 1926
Andrei Lyapchev	January 1926–June 1931
Aleksandûr Malinov	June–October 1931
Nikola Mushanov	October 1931–May 1934
Kimon Georgiev	May 1934–January 1935
Pencho Zlatev	January–April 1935
Andrei Toshev	April–November 1935
Georgi Kioseivanov	November 1935–February 1940
Bogdan Filov	February 1940–September 1943
Dobri Bozhilov	September 1943–June 1944
Ivan Bagryanov	June–September 1944
Konstantin Muraviev	2–9 September 1944
Kimon Georgiev	September 1944–November 1946
Georgi Dimitrov	November 1946–July 1949
Vasil Kolarov	July 1949–January 1950
Vûlko Chervenkov	January 1950–April 1956
Anton Yugov	April 1956–November 1962
Todor Zhivkov	November 1962–July 1971
Stanko Todorov	July 1971–June 1981
Grisha Filipov	June 1981–March 1986
Georgi Atanasov	March 1986–February 1990
Andrei Lukanov	February–November 1990
Dimitûr Popov	December 1990–November 1991
Filip Dimitrov	November 1991–December 1992
Liuben Berov	December 1992–September 1994
Reneta Indjova	October 1994–January 1995
Zhan Videnov	January 1995–December 1996
Nikolai Dobrev	January–February 1997
Stefan Sofiyanski	February–April 1997
Ivan Kostov	April 1997–June 2001
Simeon Saxecoburggotski	July 2001–

SUGGESTIONS FOR FURTHER READING

Adanir, Fikret. *Die Makedonische Frage: Ihre Entstehung und Entwicklung bis 1908* (Wiesbaden, 1979)

Bar-Zohar, Michael. *Beyond Hitler's Grasp: the Heroic Rescue of Bulgaria's Jews* (Holbrook, MA, 1998)

Barker, Elizabeth. *Macedonia: Its Place in Balkan Power Politics* (London, 1950)

Beaman, A. Hulme. *Stambuloff* (London, 1895)

Bell, John D. *Peasants in Power: Alexandûr Stamboliski and the Bulgarian Agrarian National Union, 1899–1923* (Princeton, NJ, 1977)

The Communist Party of Bulgaria from Blagoev to Zhivkov (Stanford, CA, 1986)

Black, C. E. *The Establishment of Constitutional Government in Bulgaria* (Princeton Studies in History, I, Princeton, NJ, 1943)

Boll, Michael M. (ed.). *The American Military Mission in the Allied Control Commission for Bulgaria, 1944–1947: History and Transcripts* (Boulder, CO, and New York, 1985)

The Cold War in the Balkans: American Foreign Policy and the Emergence of Communist Bulgaria, 1943–1947 (Lexington, KY, 1984)

Brailsford, H. N. *Macedonia, its Races and their Future* (London, 1906)

Bristow, J. A. *The Bulgarian Economy in Transition* (Cheltenham, 1996)

Brown, J. F. *Bulgaria under Communist Rule* (London, 1970)

Browning, Robert. *Byzantium and Bulgaria: A Comparative Study across the Early Medieval Frontier* (London, 1975)

Chary, Frederick B. *The Bulgarian Jews and the Final Solution, 1940–1944* (Pittsburgh, 1972)

Clarke, James F. *Bible Societies, American Missionaries and the National Revival of Bulgaria* (New York, 1971, reprint of Harvard Ph.D., 1937)

Constant, Stephen. *Foxy Ferdinand, Tsar of Bulgaria* (London, 1979)

Corti, Egon. *Alexander of Bulgaria* (London, 1954)
Crampton, Richard J. *Bulgaria 1878–1918: A History* (Boulder, CO, and New York, 1983)
'Bulgarian Society in the Early Nineteenth Century', in Richard Clogg (ed.), *Balkan Society in the Age of Greek Independence* (London, 1981)
A Short History of Modern Bulgaria (Cambridge, 1987)
The Balkans since the Second World War (London, 2002)
Dimitroff, Pashanko. *Boris III of Bulgaria (1894–1943): Toiler, Citizen, King* (Lewes, Sussex, 1986)
Dimitrov, Vesselin. *Bulgaria: the Uneven Transition* (London, 2001)
Dimitrova, Ekaterina. *The Gospels of Tsar Ivan Alexander* (London, 1994)
Feiwel, George R. *Growth and Reforms in Centrally Planned Economies: The Lessons of the Bulgarian Experience* (New York, 1977)
Friedrich, Wolfgang-Uwe. *Bulgarien und die Mächte 1913–1915* (Stuttgart, 1985)
Genchev, Nikolai. *The Bulgarian National Revival Period* (Sofia, 1977)
Giatzidis, Emil. *An Introduction to Post-Communist Bulgaria* (Manchester, 2002)
Groueff, Stephane. *Crown of Thorns: the Reign of King Boris III of Bulgaria, 1918–1943* (Lanham, Maryland, New York, and London, 1987)
Hatschikjan, Magarditsch A. *Tradition und Neuorientierung in der bulgarischen Aussenpolitik, 1944–1948* (Munich, 1988)
Hoddinott, R. F. *Bulgaria in Antiquity; An Archaeological Introduction* (London and Tonbridge, 1975)
Hoppe, Hans-Joachim. *Bulgarien-Hitlers eigenwilliger Verbündeter* (Stuttgart, 1979)
Hupchik, Dennis P. *The Bulgarians in the Seventeenth Century: Slavic Orthodox Society and Culture under Ottoman Rule* (Jefferson, NC, and London, 1993)
Hupchik, Dennis P. (ed.). *The Pen and the Sword: Studies in Bulgarian History by James F Clarke* (Boulder, CO, and New York, 1988)
Isusov, Mito (ed.). *Problems of Transition from Capitalism to Socialism* (Sofia, 1975)
Jelavich, Charles. *Russian Policy in Bulgaria and Serbia, 1881–1897* (Berkeley, CA, 1950)
Tsarist Russia and Balkan Nationalism: Russian Influence in the Internal Affairs of Bulgaria and Serbia, 1876–1886 (Berkeley, CA, 1958)
Karpat, K. H. (ed.). *The Turks of Bulgaria: The History, Culture and Political Fate of a Minority* (Istanbul, 1990)
Kiel, Machiel. *Art and Society of Bulgaria in the Turkish Period* (Maastricht, 1985)

Kostov, Vladimir. *The Bulgarian Umbrella: The Soviet Direction and Operation of the Bulgarian Secret Service in Europe* (London and New York, 1988)

Kuhne, Victor. *Bulgaria Self-Revealed* (London, 1919)

Lampe, John R. *The Bulgarian Economy in the Twentieth Century* (London, 1986)

Lang, David Marshall. *The Bulgarians from Pagan Times to the Ottoman Conquest* (London, 1976)

Lory, Bernard. *Le Sort de l'Héritage Ottoman en Bulgarie: L'Exemple des Villes Bulgares 1878–1900* (Istanbul, 1985)

Macdermott, Mercia. *The Apostle of Freedom: A Portrait of Vasil Levski against a Background of Nineteenth-Century Bulgaria* (London, 1967)

Freedom or Death: The Life of Gotse Delchev (London, 1978)

Markov, Georgi. *The Truth that Killed* (transl. Liliana Brisby with an introduction by Annabel Markov, London, 1983)

McIntyre, Robert J. *Bulgaria: Politics, Economics and Society* (London and New York, 1988)

Meininger, Thomas A. *Ignatiev and the Establishment of the Bulgarian Exarchate, 1864–1872: A Study in Personal Diplomacy* (Madison, WI, 1970)

Miller, Jeffrey B. and Derek C. Jones (eds.). *The Bulgarian Economy: Lessons from Reform during Early Transition* (Aldershot, 1997)

Miller, Marshall Lee. *Bulgaria during the Second World War* (Stanford, CA, 1975)

Mocsy, A. *Pannonia and Upper Moesia* (London, 1974)

Moser, Charles A. *Dimitrov of Bulgaria: A Political Biography of Dr Georgi D. Dimitrov* (Ottawa, IL, 1979)

A History of Bulgarian Literature, 863–1844 (The Hague, 1972)

Muir, Nadejda. *Dmitri Stancioff: Patriot and Cosmopolitan, 1864–1940* (London, 1957)

Nestorova, Tatyana. *American Missionaries among the Bulgarians (1858–1912)* (Boulder, CO, and New York, 1987)

Neuburger, Mary. *The Orient Within: Muslim Minorities and the Negotiation of Nationhood in Modern Bulgaria* (Ithaca and London, 2004)

Nicoloff, Assen. *The Bulgarian Resurgence* (Cleveland, OH, 1987)

Obolensky, Dmitri. *The Bogomils: A Study in Balkan Neo-Manichaeism* (Cambridge, 1948; repr. New York, 1979)

The Byzantine Commonwealth: Eastern Europe 500–1453 (London, 1971)

Oren, Nisssan. *Bulgarian Communism: The Road to Power, 1934–1944* (New York, 1971)

Revolution Administered: Agrarianism and Communism in Bulgaria (Baltimore and London, 1973)

Padev, Michael. *Dimitroff Wastes No Bullets: the Inside Story of the Trial and Murder of Nikola Petkov* (London, 1948)

Perry, Duncan. *The Politics of Terror: The Macedonian Revolutionary Movements, 1893–1903* (Durham, NC, and London, 1988)

Stefan Stambolov and the Emergence of Modern Bulgaria, 1870–1895 (Durham, NC, and London, 1993)

Rachev, Stoyan. *Anglo-Bulgarian Relations during the Second World War (1939–1944)* (transl. Stefan Kostov, Sofia, 1981)

Rothschild, Joseph. *The Communist Party of Bulgaria: Origins and Development, 1883–1936* (New York, 1959)

Runciman, Steven. *A History of the First Bulgarian Empire* (London, 1930)

Sanders, Irwin T. *Balkan Village* (Lexington, KY, 1949)

Simsir, Bilal N. *The Turks of Bulgaria (1878–1985)* (London, 1988)

Slavov, Atanas. *The 'Thaw' in Bulgarian Literature* (Boulder, CO, and New York, 1981)

With the Precision of Bats (Washington, DC, 1986)

Stephenson, Paul. *The Legend of Basil the Bulgar-Slayer* (Cambridge, 2003)

Stoyanoff, Zachary. *Pages from the Autobiography of a Bulgarian Insurgent* (transl. M. W. Potter, London, 1913)

Sumner, B. H. *Russia and the Balkans, 1870–1880* (Oxford, 1937)

Swire, Joseph. *Bulgarian Conspiracy* (London, 1939)

Thracian Treasures from Bulgaria: A Special Exhibition Held at the British Museum January–March 1976 (London, 1976)

Todorov, Kosta. *Balkan Firebrand: the Autobiography of a Rebel, Soldier and Statesman* (Chicago, 1943)

Todorov, Nikolai. *The Balkan Town, 15th–19th Centuries* (Seattle, Washington, 1983)

Troebst, Stefan. *Mussolini, Makedonien und die Mächte 1922–1930* (Cologne and Vienna, 1987)

Vazov, Ivan. *Under the Yoke: A Novel* (transl. Marguerite Alexieva and Theodora Atanassova, Sofia, 1976)

Velkov, A. *Cities in Thrace and Dacia in Late Antiquity* (Amsterdam, 1977)

Velkov A. (ed.). *Roman Cities in Bulgaria: Collected Studies* (Amsterdam, 1980)

Todor Zhivkov: Statesman and Builder of the New Bulgaria (Oxford, 1982). In the second edition (Oxford, 1985) references to the Turkish minority and its rights have been excised.

Ludmila Zhivkova, Her Many Worlds (Oxford, 1982).

INDEX

aba 55, 56, 65
Academy of Sciences 151
ACC (Allied Control Commission) 180,
181
Adrianople (Edirne) 24, 27, 53, 55, 83,
106, 114, 128, 133, 135
Adriatic 16, 22, 25, 262
Aegean coast 26, 83, 135, 169
Aegean Sea 4, 16, 25, 135
Aegean Sea, Bulgarian access to 144,
164, 166
Afghanistan 253, 261
agrarians 145–7, 156, 161, 162, 174,
175, 179, 182–3, 212, 214, 215
see also BANU *and* BANU–NP
AICs (Agro-Industrial Complexes)
197–8
Albania (Albanians) 11, 20, 22, 71, 131,
133, 241
Aleksandûr Nevski cathedral 220
Alexander II, Tsar of Russia 90
Alexander III, Tsar of Russia 90, 101, 110
Alexander of Battenberg, Prince of
Bulgaria 89–93, 94, 97, 97–9,
100–1, 102, 105, 108, 119, 121,
265
Alexander the Great 4
Alexandroupolis 230, 262
alphabet (Cyrillic and Bulgarian) 15,
15–16, 96, 151
Anhialo (Pomorie) 126
animal rearing 55, 56
ANS (Alliance for National Salvation) 235
Antim, Exarch 74, 87
anti-semitism 166
April uprising 78–81, 267
Aprilov, Vasil 60, 65
Armenians in Ottoman empire 36, 110,
126
army 88, 90, 92, 96, 97, 98–9, 100, 101,
102, 105, 108, 112, 114, 119, 125,

129, 133, 137, 139–40, 142, 143,
144, 145, 147, 152, 158, 159,
160–1, 166, 168–71, 175, 179, 189,
190, 193, 214, 215, 219, 241, 253,
265
and communists 180, 183
Asenov, Hadji Dimitûr 76
Asia Minor 10, 11, 20, 56
Asparukh, Khan 8
Atanasov, Georgi 239
Athens 73, 75, 157, 161
Athos, Mount 39, 45
Austria-Hungary 17, 83, 126, 127, 128,
130, 131
see also Habsburg monarchy
ayans 51, 52, 53, 55

Bagryanov, Ivan 176–7
Balchik 133
Balkan alliance 73, 131–2
entente 157, 165, 235
federation 76, 77, 125, 126, 190
mountains 4, 9, 13, 53, 72, 77, 83, 99,
113, 115
peacekeeping force 241
Balkan war, first 132–3
second 134–5, 158, 266
banks and banking 118, 122, 148, 159,
186, 227, 232, 233, 234, 252
see also BNB
banks, German 122, 137
BANU (Bulgarian Agrarian National
Union) 123–5, 145–53
see also agrarians
BANU (coalitionist) 187
BANU–NP (Bulgarian Agrarian
National Union – Nikola Petkov)
183, 212, 230
bashibazouks 80–1, 84
Batak 80
BBB (Bulgarian Business Bloc) 229, 236

BCP (Bulgarian Communist Party)
145, 153, 172, 180, 187, 189–90,
194, 199, 207–9, 212–13,
214
leading role of 187–8, 194, 213, 214
Beckerle, Adolf-Heinz 171, 188–90
Belassitsa 20
Belene 199, 204
Belgrade 10, 55, 75, 76, 77, 99, 104,
127, 151, 235
Benkovski, Georgi 78, 80
Berlin 237, 267
Berlin, treaty of (1878) 83–4, 92, 94, 95,
96, 105, 112, 114, 265, 267
Beron, Petûr (zoologist) 215, 218
Beron, Petûr 61
Berov, Liuben 224–5, 228–9, 230
Bitola 83, 106, 139
Black Sea 10, 25, 51, 166, 168, 261
Blagoev, Dimitûr 142
BNB (Bulgarian National Bank) 92, 94,
97, 227, 229, 231, 232, 233, 234,
237
Bobov Dol mines 137
bogomilism 18–19, 21, 22, 24, 196,
266
Bogoridi, Stefan 67
Bogorov, Ivan 62, 63
bombing, by Bulgaria 133
of Bulgaria by allies 174, 175, 267
Boris I (Khan and King of Bulgaria) 11,
110–11
Boris III (King of the Bulgarians,
1918–43) 108, 143, 153, 154, 160,
164, 168–71, 172, 173, 175, 200,
266
Bosnia and Hercegovina 78, 130,
131
Botev, Hristo 64, 76, 78, 80
Boyana church frescoes 25
Bozhilov, Dobri 174–6
Bozveli, Neofit 60, 67
Braila 54, 63, 64, 75
Braşov 54, 61
Bratsigovo 80
Brezhnev, Leonid 195, 206
brigandage 90, 114
broad socialists 125
see also SDP

BSP (Bulgarian Socialist Party) 214, 215,
218, 224, 225, 227, 229, 234, 235,
236, 246, 249, 251, 262
BTK (state telecommunications concern)
251
Bucharest 54, 62, 63, 67, 76, 78, 243
treaty of (1886) 99, 122
treaty of (1913) 135
treaty of (1918) 143
Budapest 48, 54
Bulgaria, and Austria-Hungary 99, 105,
140–2, 143, 260
and Belgium 105, 117
and France 105, 137, 160, 195, 255,
260
and Germany 105, 115, 137–8,
140–2, 143, 165, 166–7, 168–74,
176–7, 195, 255, 260, 266
and Great Britain 101, 105, 115, 154,
160
and Greece 99, 132, 133, 134–5, 139,
154, 164, 191, 221–3, 230, 266
and Israel 190, 217
and Italy 105, 159, 164, 165–7
and League of Nations 150
and Libya 195
and North Africa 261
and Ottoman empire 106, 111
and Republic of Macedonia 221–3,
241, 266
and Romania 133, 135, 241–3
and Russia 124, 131, 230, 231, 236,
237, 245, 246, 251, 260–1, 262,
267
and Serbia 99, 129, 131, 132, 134–5,
154, 266
and South Africa 217
and Switzerland 105
and third world 195
and Turkey 201, 210, 220–1
and USA 167, 186, 190, 191, 201,
210, 226, 240, 255, 261
and USSR 150, 160, 164, 165–7, 169,
171, 175–9, 181–3, 188, 189–90,
191–2, 193, 195, 196, 198, 200,
203, 204, 206, 209, 210, 216,
267
and Vatican 195
and west 260, 261, 263

Bulgaria, and Austria-Hungary (cont.)
  and western allies, second world war
    175, 180, 183–5
  and Yugoslavia 150–1, 156, 160, 164,
    190, 191, 199
Bulgarian Academy of Sciences 64
Bulgarian church 14, 16, 17, 21–2, 24,
    25, 38, 46, 58, 64–75, 84, 88, 106,
    125, 219–20, 223, 269
  and state 106–7, 108, 151, 168, 172,
    185, 188–9
  Patriarchate 14, 21–2, 25, 28, 38, 40,
    46, 65, 168, 189, 219–20, 224
Bulgarian diaspora 54, 63–4
Bulgarian language 11, 15, 16, 21, 35,
    37–8, 39, 40, 46, 48, 60, 61–2, 63,
    64, 65, 67, 74, 122, 269
Bulgarian Legion 75, 76, 77
Bulgarian Literary Society 64
Bulgarian literature 15, 16, 37–8, 40,
    45–6, 62, 63, 77
Bulgarian Revolutionary Central
    Committee (BRCC) 77, 78
Bulgarian Secret Central Committee
    (BSCC) 76
Bulgarian Secret Central Revolutionary
    Committee (BSCRC) 97
Bulgarians and Greeks 14–15, 16, 22, 25,
    36, 38, 46, 60, 61, 65–6, 129, 167
Bulgartabak 251
Burgas 53, 115, 118, 176, 230, 262
BWP,
  see BCP
Byzantium, Bulgarian relations with
    9–11, 14–15, 16, 17, 19–20, 21, 24
Byzantium,
  see Constantinople

calendar, Gregorian xvi
  Julian xvi
Capitulations 84, 102
Catholic church 24, 42, 72, 107, 108,
    110, 189, 190, 195, 201
Ceauşescu, Nicolae 203
Chernobyl 209
Chervenkov, Vûlko 190–2, 193
Chintulov, Dobri 64
Chiprovets 42
chitalishta 62

Christianity 4
  in Bulgaria 260
  conversion of Bulgarians to 11–15, 16
Christians in Ottoman empire 29–33,
    33–8
Clementine, Princess 107
Clinton, William 240
CLS (Compulsory Labour Service)
    150, 166
Coalition for Bulgaria 246, 247
collectivisation of land 182, 188, 189,
    191, 192
Comecon 196, 226
Cominform 186, 189
Comintern 161
communists 145–7, 150, 151, 153, 154,
    155, 156, 157, 158, 161–2, 166,
    171, 174, 175, 179, 180, 225, 227,
    265, 267
  see also narrow socialists
conglomerates 256
  see also corruption
conscription 22, 30, 112, 114, 131, 267
conservatives 87–8, 90, 92, 93, 94, 96,
    108
Constantinople 5, 9, 16, 24, 25, 30, 34,
    51, 55, 56, 58, 63, 64, 67, 72, 74,
    75, 89, 104, 106, 107, 114, 115,
    130, 138, 263
  Bulgarian church in 67, 69, 74
  Bulgarians in 68, 69, 72, 74
  treaty of (1913) 135
constituent assembly, Tûrnovo (1879)
    84, 85–9
constitution (1971) 194
  (1991) 218
  Dimitrov 186
  Tûrnovo 88–9, 90–1, 93, 94, 108,
    162, 186
Constitutional Bloc 152, 153
constitutional court 218, 219, 225
cooperatives 124, 147, 148, 228
corruption 17, 56, 66, 140, 148, 151,
    152, 174, 206, 225, 231, 232–3,
    234, 236, 240, 244–6, 247, 249,
    250, 255–6, 263, 264
  see also partisanstvo
cotton 51, 54
coup (1881) 90–1, 96, 119, 121

(1886) 101, 102
(1923) 153, 175
(1934) 158
(1944) 178
(1965) attempted 193, 267
(1989) 212
Constantinople (1908) 130
Plovdiv (1885) 97–9
Craiova, treaty of 165, 166
Crete 73, 126
crime, problem of in post-communist
  Bulgaria 225, 244, 246, 249, 255–6,
  263
Crimean war 68, 72, 75
Crusades 24, 25
Cuba 193
currency 90, 140, 186, 228–9
currency board 233, 235, 237
Czech Republic 231, 255
Czechoslovakia 164, 194, 267

Dalmatia 60, 138
Danev, Stoyan 124, 127, 134, 135
Danube 4, 8, 9, 16, 19, 40, 51, 54, 76,
  80, 83, 92, 101, 139, 167, 177, 203,
  209, 241, 262
Daran Kulak 124
Dardanelles 166
debt, foreign (and loans) 84, 118, 122,
  127, 137, 154, 202, 203, 225, 228,
  229, 237
decollectivisation of land 215, 219, 224,
  227–8
Dedeagach 135, 138
defence of the nation act (1940) 166
defence of the realm act (1923) 153
Delchev, Gotse 128
Democratic Alliance 153, 156
Democratic Party 94, 124, 130, 143,
  145, 153, 155, 157, 162, 185,
  230
demographic change 53–4, 111–13
depression (1930s) 156, 157
devetnaiseti 158–60
  see also Zveno
devshirme 33, 35
Dimitrov, Filip 218, 219–24, 228, 234,
  235
Dimitrov, Georgi 161, 183, 189, 190

directorate for social renewal 158, 161
Dobrev, Nikolai 234, 235
Dobrudja 55, 114, 124, 142, 165, 177
  northern 143
  southern 133, 134, 135, 139, 165,
    185, 191, 204
Dogan, Ahmed 223
Dondukov-Korsakov, Prince 87
Drama 139
Dresden 54
Dubrovnik 40

Eastern Rumelia 83, 84, 89, 91, 95–9,
  111, 121, 122, 126, 130, 205
Ecoglasnost 210, 230
education 15, 39, 58–62, 63, 66, 74, 77,
  96, 107, 108, 150, 151, 152, 162,
  168, 190, 196, 217, 238–9, 252,
  260, 263, 264, 267
EEC (European Economic Community),
  see also EU 202
emigration, of Bulgarians 54, 244, 257
  of Jews 190
  of Turks 113, 190–1, 199, 210, 223,
    227, 268
encouragement of industry act (1894)
  117, 122
energy, gas 230, 231, 262
  market 250
  nuclear
  see Kozlodui
  oil 230, 237, 262
  problem of 203
Enos 134, 138
environment, problems and protests
  209–10, 211
Epirus 22
EU, and Bulgaria 221, 224, 226,
  227, 234, 236–7, 238–9, 240,
  243, 245, 247, 249, 250, 251,
  252–3, 255, 257, 258, 259,
  261, 265
Euro-Left 235
Exarchate,
  see Bulgarian church

factories 57, 115, 117, 118
fascism 156, 157, 158, 159, 161, 172,
  175, 186

Ferdinand of Saxe-Coburg-Gotha,
    Prince of Bulgaria 1887–1908, and
    King of the Bulgarians 1908–1918
    103–7, 108–11, 119–21, 125, 127,
    129, 131, 132, 133, 135, 137,
    138–9, 143, 265, 266
    marriage of 107–8
    recognition of 103, 105, 108, 110–11,
        118, 119
FF (Fatherland Front) 154, 174–5,
    177–9, 180–7, 194, 214
Filov, Bogdan 164–74, 175
France 51, 72
French Revolution 48, 60
FYROM (Former Yugoslav Republic of
    Macedonia),
    see Macedonia, Republic of

Gabrovo 62, 114, 115, 142
    school in 60, 65
gaitan 56
Gallipoli 138
Ganchev, Georgi 230
Gemeto (agrarian leader, G. M.
    Dimitrov) 182
Georgiev, Colonel Kimon 158, 160, 175,
    178
Germans 15, 42
Germany 98, 100, 122, 164
Geshov, Ivan 131, 134
GNA (Grand National Assembly) 88,
    90–1, 101–2, 103, 108, 131, 173,
    184, 185, 186, 215, 217–18
Gorbachev, Mikhail 204, 206, 209,
    210, 211
Göring, Hermann 158, 161
Gorna Djumaya (Blagoevgrad) 127
Great Britain 51, 58, 63, 67, 81, 83
Greece (Greeks) 3–4, 11, 22, 32, 48
Greece, autocephalous church in
    67, 68
    independent state of 60, 144, 157,
        161, 164, 166, 167, 230, 241,
        243, 264, 265
Greek church (Patriarchate) 15, 16,
    21, 32, 38, 43–4, 65, 66–74, 75,
    94, 106, 126, 128, 220
Greek war of independence 55, 60, 75
Greeks, Phanariot 43, 44, 65

Greek-Turkish war (1897) 126, 128
Gregory VI, Patriarch 72
Gudev, Petûr 129
guilds (*esnafs*) 37, 55, 58, 61, 65, 114,
    264

Habsburg monarchy 40, 42, 51, 72, 76,
    77, 85
    see also Austria-Hungary
haiduks 40
Haskovo 25, 114
heresies 18–19, 25
Hitler, Adolf 162, 166, 169, 173
Hitov, Panaiot 76, 77
Hristo Botev radio station 175
Hungary 75, 176, 179, 243
    (1956) 192, 267

Ilinden rising 128
IMF (International Monetary Fund) 228,
    233, 235, 237, 238
IMRO (Internal Macedonian
    Revolutionary Organisation) 126,
    127–8
Indjova, Reneta 225
inflation 140, 151, 174, 227, 228, 229,
    231, 234, 237, 244, 252
intelligentsia 40, 64, 74, 92, 120, 124,
    156, 177, 180, 182, 185, 200, 209,
    210, 239, 247, 260
Iraq 226, 229, 253–5, 261
Istanbul 262
Italo-Turkish war 132
Italy 69, 138, 241
    second world war 169, 174
Ivan Rilski 18, 39, 266

Janissary corps 33, 42, 51, 56
Jewish question, second world war
    171–3, 177, 268
Jews 36, 249
John Paul II, Pope 201
judiciary 88, 90, 181, 187, 225, 240,
    250, 251–2, 256, 263

Kaimakchalan 139
Kalofer 55
Karadja, Stefan 76
Karavelov, Liuben 76–7, 78

Karavelov, Petko 90, 93–4, 95, 97, 101, 103, 121, 124, 130
Karlovo 55, 77
Kaulbars, general Aleksandr 92, 103
Kaulbars, Nikolai 101–2
Kavalla 139
Khrushchev, Nikita 191–2, 192–3, 195
Kioseivanov, Georgi 161–4
Kiustendil 26, 39, 74
Kolarov, Vasil 189
Koprivshtitsa 58, 76, 78
Kosovo crisis 243
Kostov, Ivan 235, 236–47, 249, 252, 263
Kostov, Traicho 189–90, 191, 192
Kostov, Vladimir 198, 201
Kotel 35, 48, 55, 58, 75, 114
Kozlodui 203–4, 240, 251
Kremikovtsi 237
Kresna-Razlog rising (1878) 85, 98
Krum, Khan 10, 11, 13
Krushevo 128
Krûstevich, Gavril 73
Kûrdjali 217
kûrdjaliistvo 52–4, 55, 66
Kutchuk Kainardji, treaty of 51, 54, 68
Kyril, Prince 174

Lamsdorff, Count 127
land reform (redistribution) 148–50, 152, 154
League of Nations xv, 154, 164
legal profession 125, 148, 151
Leipzig 54, 161
Leskovats 61, 66
Levski, Vasil 76, 77–8, 209
liberals and Liberal Parties 13, 88, 90–2, 93–4, 96, 103, 108, 117, 121, 124, 127, 129, 135, 156
Libya 226
Lilov, Aleksandûr 214, 219, 230
Livorno 54
local government 88, 90, 148, 152, 157, 159, 161–2
London, convention on terrorism (1934) 158
London, St James's Palace conference 133
London, treaty of (1913) 133
Lovech 66, 71, 76
Ludjev, Dimitûr 219

Lukanov, Andrei 214–16, 226, 227, 230, 233, 256
Lukov, General 171
Lulchev, Kosta 183
Lyapchev, Andrei 154–6

Macedonia 22, 74, 83, 85, 94, 97, 111, 126–9, 126–7, 129, 133, 138, 139–40, 143, 145
    ancient 1, 4
    Bulgarian aspirations towards and policy in 85, 87, 89, 94, 105, 106, 122, 126–7, 132, 132–5, 134, 138, 139, 167, 167–8, 169, 175, 221, 265–6
    and Bulgarian church 71, 72, 73, 74, 89, 94, 106, 107, 108, 126, 128, 129, 132, 135, 168
    Bulgarians in 72
    Greek 169
    Greeks in 106, 126, 133
    mediaeval 10, 11, 13, 20, 22, 24
    and patriarchate 106
    Pirin 135, 190
    Republic of 22, 241, 262, 266
Macedonian language 190, 199, 221, 241
Macedonians in Bulgaria 94–5, 106, 111, 129, 131, 135, 145, 150–1, 153, 154, 155, 156, 158, 160, 164, 199, 221, 265
Magyars 16, 17, 24, 25
Makariopolski, Ilarion 67, 69, 71
Malinov, Aleksandûr 130–1, 135, 143, 157
Mao Tse Tung 192
Marie-Louise, Princess 107
Marinov, minister of war 178
Maritsa 28, 55, 112
Markov, Georgi 198, 201
Marseilles 54
marxism 125, 187
Mediterranean Sea 51, 54
Melnik 127
Midia 134, 138
Mihailov, Ivan 151, 158
Mihailova, Nadezhda 245
mihailovists 151, 153, 154, 155, 158, 160
Mihov, General 174
Milan, Prince of Serbia 99

Military League 152, 153, 156, 158,
    160, 161
Milošević, Slobodan 235
minorities 263
minorities in Bulgaria, Armenian 268
    Greek 85, 96, 108, 113, 126, 129, 167
    Jewish 85
    Muslim 108, 111–13, 205
    see also pomaks
    Roma 199, 244, 250, 252
    Turkish 85, 96, 99, 111–13, 114,
        115, 158, 199, 217, 223, 238,
        248, 268
    Turkish, attempted assimilation of
        204–6, 209, 210–11, 213, 215,
        217, 239, 246
Mladenov, Petûr 210, 212, 213, 214,
    215, 225
Moldavia 60, 69
Moldova, Republic of 54
monarchy 125, 145, 158, 160, 175, 184,
    218, 249
monasteries 39–40, 58, 61, 148, 266
Montenegro 16, 20, 73, 133
Morava 1, 10, 83, 87, 89, 142
Moscow 76, 183
MRF (Movement for Rights and
    Freedoms) 215, 218, 219, 223, 224,
    225, 229, 246, 247, 249
Muraviev, Konstantin 177–8
Mushanov, Nikola 157
Mussolini, Benito 152
Mutkurov, Sava 101

Nabokov, Captain 102, 103
narrow socialists 125, 138, 139, 142
National Alliance 152, 153
National Party 108, 131, 153, 156
NATO 221, 231, 236, 237, 240–1, 249,
    253, 255, 257
    action in Kosovo 240, 244
NEM (New Economic Mechanism)
    202–3, 204
Nesebûr 10
Neuilly-sur-Seine, treaty of (1919) 144,
    152, 164
Nevrokop 190
Nicholas II, Tsar of Russia 110, 111
Nish 66, 75, 76

convention (1923) 151
NMSS (National Movement Simeon II)
    246–9, 249–56, 251, 263
NSM (National Social Movement) 156,
    157, 158, 161

Oborishte 78
Obrenović, Prince Michael 73, 77
Odessa 54, 78
Ohrid 11, 19, 22, 38, 65, 66, 83, 106, 143
Omurtag, Khan 10, 11, 13
Orange Guard 147, 152
Ottoman army 33, 42, 44, 55, 56–7
Ottoman conquest of Balkans 25, 26, 27
Ottoman empire, administration 29–33,
    35, 37, 44, 56, 57, 65, 67–8, 81
    Christians in 51, 58, 71
    decline of 48, 51–3, 126

Paiisi Hilendarski 45–8, 65, 74
Panagiurishte 1, 78
Panev law 219
Panitsa plot 105–6, 107, 108
Paris 58, 198, 210
Paris Commune 78
Paris peace conference (1946-7) 185
Paris, peace treaty of (1947) 186
partisans 181
    in Bulgaria 175, 177
    partisanstvo 119–21, 264
Pašić, Nikola 138
Patriarchate, Bulgarian
    see Bulgarian church, Patriarchate
Patriarchate,
    see Greek church
Pavlov, Ilya 256
People's Bloc 156–8
People's Constitutional Bloc 161, 162
Pernik 115, 147
Persians, ancient 4
Perushtitsa 80
Peshev, Dimitûr 172
Petkov, Nikola 174, 175, 182–3, 186
Petrich 151, 153, 154, 160, 164
Petrov, general Racho 127, 129
Pimen, Metropolitan 219–20
Pirot 74, 83
Pleven 60, 83, 123
Pliska 8, 9, 11, 13, 16

Plovdiv 4, 35, 53, 55, 57, 58, 65, 66, 74,
    76, 78, 80, 98, 100, 102, 115, 161,
    191, 192, 206, 241, 263
Podkrepa (Support) 210, 216
police 105, 107, 119, 124, 147, 151,
    152, 181, 186, 196, 198, 211, 214,
    215, 235, 267
police files 217, 239
pomaks 34–5, 80, 114, 199, 204
Pomorie (Anhialo) 126
Popov, Dimitûr 216–18, 227, 228
Popov, Raphael 72
Popular Front 161
Porto Lagos 135, 137
Prague 60
PRC (People's Republic of China) 193, 211
Preslav 16, 19, 71
Prespa 11
Prilep 60
privatisation 214, 223, 227, 228, 229,
    231, 232, 233, 237–8, 244, 246,
    250, 251–2
proportional representation 130, 135,
    153, 156, 162, 215, 218
Protestant churches 67, 68, 110, 189
Proto-Bulgars 8–9, 11–15
Przemyśl 138
PU (Popular Union) 229, 235
purges 181, 182, 183, 188–90, 190–1,
    192, 196, 198, 219, 265
Pûrvanov, Georgi 250–1, 265

Radical Democratic Party 142
Radical Party 156
Radomir 143
Radoslavov, Vasil 101, 135, 137–43
railways 84, 92–3, 97, 115, 117, 118,
    125, 135, 137, 140
Railways act (1884) 118, 122
railways, BDZh (Bulgarian State
    Railways) 94, 121
Belgrade–Salonika 169
Berlin to Baghdad 122
Oriental Railway Company 121–2,
    130
parallel 121–2, 124
Rusé–Varna 93, 101, 105
Vienna to Constantinople 92, 122
Yambol–Burgas 122

Rakovski, Georgi 75–6, 77
Razgrad 217
Reagan, Ronald 202
Red Army in Bulgaria 154, 177, 180,
    186
refugees 39, 94, 128, 145, 154–5
Regency 174
religious art 25, 26, 39
reparations 144, 147
Rhodope mountains 34, 52, 83
rice 51, 55
Rila monastery 39, 58, 69, 152
Rilski, Neofit 65
Roman empire 4–8, 262
Romania 10, 42, 54, 63, 69, 71, 73, 75,
    110, 139, 144, 157, 165, 177, 213,
    229, 241, 253, 255, 262, 264
Rome 14, 24, 25, 40, 72, 152, 201
Rupel, Fort 139
Rusé 52, 66, 74, 102, 176, 209, 241
Russia 42, 51, 52, 54, 58, 60, 66, 68, 71,
    73, 75, 76, 81, 83, 90, 92–3, 94, 95,
    97–9, 100, 101–2, 103, 108,
    110–11, 119, 180, 243
    and Balkans 126, 127, 128, 132
Russian Provisional Administration in
    Bulgaria 87, 112
Russian revolution (1905) 125
    (1917) 142
Russo-Turkish war (1806-12) 55, 56
    (1828-9) 54
    (1877-8) 81–3, 89

Salonika (Thessaloniki) 15, 24, 52, 63,
    83, 127, 133, 167, 169, 263
    agreements (1938) 164
    armistice (1918) 143
Samokov 60, 66, 71, 74, 114, 142
Samothrace 167
Samuil, Tsar 20
San Stefano, preliminaries of peace 83,
    89, 97, 111, 135, 265
sanctions, Iraq 226
    Libya 226
    Yugoslavia 225, 229, 233, 244, 261
Saxecoburggotski, Simeon
    see Simeon II
SC (supremacists) 126, 128
Schengen area 243

SDP (Social Democratic Party) 125, 145, 147, 153, 174, 175, 179, 183, 212
see also broad socialists
Serbia (Serbs) 16, 22, 25, 27, 42, 48, 52, 55, 62, 71, 73, 75, 76, 77, 83, 88, 104, 114, 137, 138, 169, 264, 266
Serbian church 65, 106, 126, 127, 128
Serbian-Turkish war (1875-6) 78, 80, 83
Serbo-Bulgarian war (1885) 99, 105–6, 113, 115
Seres 66, 83, 139
Shipka pass 83, 127
Shtip 60
Shumen 8, 71, 74, 102, 217
Silistra 52, 74, 102, 133
Simeon II (King of the Bulgarians) 173, 218, 244, 246, 249
Simeon the Great 16
Skopje 22, 66, 83, 106, 127, 132, 168, 241
Slavs 5, 8–9, 11–15
Sliven 55, 57, 78, 80, 114, 142
Slivnitsa, battle of (1885) 99
Slovakia 255
Smyrna (Izmir) 63
Sobolev, general 92, 93
socialism 125, 126
Society for Bulgarian Literature 64
Sofia 4, 10, 37, 39, 40, 66, 71, 74, 78, 83, 87, 89, 92, 94, 100, 101, 110, 111, 113, 115, 127, 129, 132, 135, 152, 154, 174, 213, 215, 227, 228, 234, 235, 237, 240, 244, 263
city council 90, 157
university of 15, 125, 151
Sofiyanski, Stefan 235
Sofronii Vrachanski 62, 67, 96
Sokolski, Josef 72
Sopot 113
spahis 33, 34, 57
St Petersburg ambassadorial conference 133
Stalin, Josef 165, 189, 191, 193
Stamboliiski, Aleksandûr 124–5, 131, 138, 142, 143, 145–53, 154, 159
Stambolov, Stefan 98, 101–10, 115, 117, 119, 121, 265
stambolovist government 1903–7 128–30

Stanimaka 142
Stara Zagora 55, 77, 83, 252
Stefan, Exarch 188
Stoilov, Konstantin 108, 110–11, 117–18, 122–3, 124, 131
Stoyanov, Petûr 234, 235, 244, 251
Straits, the 51
Strandja 128
strikes 125, 130, 147, 151, 161, 177, 186, 191, 192, 215, 217, 218, 228, 229, 235
Struma 133, 135
students 125, 129, 215, 216
Sveta Nedelya cathedral outrage (1925) 154
Svishtov 54, 60, 62, 66, 90–1
Switzerland 233

tariffs 84, 105, 114, 118
taxation 22, 27, 30, 33, 34, 35, 39, 43, 51, 78, 112, 117, 129, 131, 150, 185–6, 229, 267
ecclesiastical 44, 66, 71
tithe 57, 123, 124
Tchataldja lines, Constantinople 133
Thassos 167
Thrace 10, 11, 22, 53, 71, 73, 89, 128, 133, 135, 138, 144, 166, 167, 169, 175
Thracians, ancient 1–4
timar holdings 33, 42
Tito, Josip (Broz) 179, 189, 191
tobacco 54, 161, 191, 192
Toshev, Andrei 160, 161
Totiu, Filip 76
trade 26, 34, 36, 43, 51, 53, 54–5, 58, 65, 114, 117–18, 135, 157, 188, 193, 195, 196, 201, 202, 203, 221, 224, 226, 229, 230, 231, 233, 238, 243, 245, 260, 261, 262
trade unions 125, 145, 153, 155, 159, 172, 181, 188, 210, 214, 216, 217, 223, 263
tripartite pact 167, 176
Truman doctrine 186
Trûstenik 124
Tryavna 66
Tsankov, Aleksandûr 153–4, 156, 157, 158, 161

Tsankov, Dragan 72, 89–90, 91, 93, 94, 104, 119
tsankovists 107
Tsanov 142
Turkey 157, 241, 255
Turkey, second world war 168, 169, 174, 176
Turkish-Serbian war (1875-6) 78, 80, 83
Tûrnovo xvi, 24, 25, 28, 39, 40, 66, 67, 74, 75, 78, 80, 83, 98, 111, 115, 252
Tûrnovo rising (1598) 54

UDF (Union of Democratic Forces) 87, 212–13, 215, 216, 217, 218, 223, 225, 227, 229, 230, 231, 234, 235, 251, 262
Ukraine 10, 54, 176
unemployment 120, 157, 227, 244, 252, 257
Uniatism and Uniate church 72, 73, 74, 195
Union of Bulgaria and Eastern Rumelia (1885) 121, 126
unionists 108, 122
United States of America 63, 65, 142, 264
universities 252
USSR 168, 175, 190
UtDF (United Democratic Forces) 235, 243, 246, 247, 248

vakûf properties 33, 39, 42
Vardar 1, 11, 54, 83, 132
Varna 74, 83, 102, 115, 118, 119, 126, 171, 176, 206, 263
Vasilev, Nikolai 249, 250
Vazov, Ivan 62
Velchev, Boris 198
Velchev, Colonel Damyan 158, 160, 161, 178, 184

Velchev, Milen 249, 252
Velchitrun 1
Veles 71, 74
Venelin, Yuri 48, 62
Venice 17, 54
Videnov, Zhan 219, 229–34, 236, 237
Vidin 25, 28, 52, 54, 55, 66, 71, 74, 75, 114
Vienna 34, 40, 42, 54, 58, 167
Vlachs 71
Vranja 83
Vratsa 1, 48, 66, 74, 78, 80, 197

Wallachia 55, 60, 69
Warsaw pact 220, 241, 245, 265
women 60, 112, 113, 142, 162, 188, 225, 247
World Bank 227, 238
Wrangel, General 152

Yambol 115
Yanina 52, 55
Yeltsin, Boris 231
Young Turks 130, 131, 132
youth 247
Yugoslavia 144, 157, 167, 169
  collapse of 220, 225
Yugov, Anton 192, 193

Zhelev, Zheliu 212, 215, 219, 220, 221–3, 224, 233, 234, 265
Zhivkov, Todor 191–3, 194, 195, 196, 198, 199, 203, 204, 206, 209, 210, 211, 212, 214, 219, 224, 226, 229, 239, 249
Zhivkova, Liudmila 200–1, 267
Zlatev, General Pencho 160
Zveno (zvenari) 156, 158, 159–60, 174, 179, 184

CAMBRIDGE CONCISE HISTORIES

TITLES IN THE SERIES:

A Concise History of Australia 2nd edition
STUART MCINTYRE

A Concise History of Bolivia
HERBERT S. KLEIN

A Concise History of Brazil
BORIS FAUSTO

A Concise History of Britain, 1707–1975
W. A. SPECK

A Concise History of Bulgaria 2nd edition
R. J. CRAMPTON

A Concise History of France 2nd edition
ROGER PRICE

A Concise History of Germany 2nd edition
MARY FULBROOK

A Concise History of Greece
RICHARD CLOGG

A Concise History of Hungary
MIKLÓS MOLNAR

A Concise History of India
BARBARA D. METCALF, THOMAS R. METCALF

A Concise History of Italy
CHRISTOPHER DUGGAN

A Concise History of Mexico
BRIAN HAMNETT

A Concise History of New Zealand
PHILIPPA MEIN SMITH

A Concise History of Poland
JERZY LUKOWSKI AND HUBERT ZAWADZKI

A Concise History of Portugal 2nd edition
DAVID BIRMINGHAM

A Concise History of South Africa
ROBERT ROSS

Printed in the United States
By Bookmasters